HarperEntertainment

An Imprint of HarperCollins*Publishers*

MISSION: COOK!

My Life, My Recipes,
and Making the Impossible Easy

ROBERT IRVINE

WITH BRIAN O'REILLY

MISSION: COOK! Copyright © 2007 by Robert Irvine and Brian O'Reilly. Photographs copyright © 2007 by Tom Briglia/PhotoGRAPHICS. All rights reserved. Printed in the United States of America. No part of this book may be used or reproduced in any manner whatsoever without written permission except in the case of brief quotations embodied in critical articles and reviews. For information address HarperCollins Publishers, 10 East 53rd Street, New York, NY 10022.

HarperCollins books may be purchased for educational, business, or sales promotional use. For information please write: Special Markets Department, HarperCollins Publishers, 10 East 53rd Street, New York, NY 10022.

FIRST EDITION

Designed by Judy Abbate/Abbate Design

Recipes edited and tested by Virginia O'Reilly

Library of Congress Cataloging-in-Publication Data has been applied for.

ISBN: 978-0-06-123789-8

ISBN-10: 0-06-123789-2

07 08 09 10 11 WBC/QW 10 9 8 7 6 5 4 3 2 1

CONTENTS

INTRODUCTION

I HAVE NO IDEA WHERE I AM GOING.

It's not for an immediate lack of direction or information. I am driving to my *immediate* destination in the middle of the night from an appearance at a live cooking event in Morristown, New Jersey. I am driving a sleek new BMW with a technologically advanced GPS system, into which I have fed the coordinates for a hotel in Princeton. In the short term, I think I am probably quite close to that locale. I am hoping to get some food and at least a few hours' rest before the big day tomorrow. Therein lies the mystery.

Tomorrow, I am due to arrive at an undisclosed destination, where I will be cooking for an indeterminate number of people I have never met, in a kitchen I have never seen, with stores of food and ingredients that may or may not be of my choosing. I have no idea how long I will be given to accomplish this task, nor will I have any prior ability to plan ahead in even the smallest detail. And I have willingly . . . no, eagerly, placed myself in this predicament.

There is only one force that could be responsible for devising such an absurd situation with such a markedly high potential for disaster: *television*.

Tomorrow is the day I am shooting the pilot for my first (hopefully successful, hopefully the first of many, fingers crossed) Food Network show. Each episode of the show will feature your humble servant, me, ably assisted (most of the time at least, God and my sadistic producers willing) by my incredible sous-chefs, George and George, in equally absurd and improbable cooking situations, with *no advance warning* or information ahead of the game as to where, how, for whom, and with what we might be cooking at any given time.

Pretty cool, huh?

I am not inherently of an existential bent, but it's hard to avoid a certain level of reflection on one's life when a benchmark for a long-sought and cherished goal such as this has been reached.

As you will see in the succeeding pages, I am a bit of an anomaly in the cooking trade. Although I have a wide-ranging acquaintance with classical technique and world cuisine, I have never been to a formal culinary institute or cooking school. I am equally at home cooking for six people at a time as I am for six thousand, and I discovered that ability within myself whilst I was still in my teens. I have cooked an inordinate proportion of meals in my career on the ocean. I have had the privilege of cooking for royalty, celebrities, politicians, and ambassadors of high rank, diners of every stripe, but unlike, say, Thomas Keller and his most admirable French Laundry, I have never—yet—established a single restaurant kitchen as my home base.

In more than a quarter-century of cooking, I have never settled down, professionally speaking anyway. Not unlike the freelancers of medieval European chivalry or cowboys for hire on the open range in the American West, I have preferred to follow my own path, my own internal compass. I have never liked being constrained within a single system or style of cooking, and I have always looked to the next horizon for opportunity and inspiration.

I am very good at drawing up strategies and attacking problems, but in general, I don't like "plans." Blueprints, manuals, corporate directives, and even recipes essentially leave me cold. I have collected cookbooks from about the age of eleven, and have always enjoyed studying the pictures and figuring my own methods for achieving a dish more than slavishly following every measurement and cooking time listed by the author.

I believe that cooking can be a demonstration of what you have inside of you, whether you are a chef expressing a passion for exquisite culinary detail, a cook dishing up hearty and delicious fare in a diner to fuel your customers for the day ahead, or a mother expressing love and caring for her family at the dinner table. I believe that these feelings are best expressed *in the moment*.

I have created a lot of dishes with which I am quite pleased, that reflect my basic philosophies of how to put a dish together. I try to use fresh and interesting ingredients, to incorporate the element of surprise, ofttimes by combining hot and cold items on the same plate, by pairing unusual textures, by building the dish on the plate in a new and interesting way, all without sacrificing the integrity of the whole. But however well practiced and well calculated a dish might be, I know that I will never make it the exactly the same way twice. I may find a novel ingredient whilst passing a market on the way to the event and throw it into the mix; I may be in a bad mood and thus decide to approach the same old dish in a new and playful way to cheer myself up; it may be rainy, or sunny, or Christmasy—all of these will affect the way I cook on the day. If

I know my audience personally, it changes the plan of attack I might use for an anonymous crowd. If I make a dish tomorrow instead of today, well, that changes everything.

The more open you are to the world and its infinite variety of people and influences, the more they will spill into and around your life. This television opportunity came from totally unexpected sources, and I find myself relishing this next challenge, because, in fact, it suits me. I probably would not have purposely chosen a format in which I will never have any idea what might be coming at me next, but I can already see that it is going to test me and my particular theories about cooking and life in ways that could prove deeply satisfying (if I don't screw up too much). Though I don't believe in recklessness, which carries its own punishments, I do believe that spontaneity is its own reward. One of the biggest rewards is creative satisfaction. The biggest, in my opinion? It makes things a lot more fun.

I also believe in sharing what I have learned; thus this book. There are stories contained herein about how I got to where I am, collaborations and conversations about how to approach and think about the subject of food, and recipes that I think and hope you will enjoy. Make them if they appeal to you, see how they work, and then, please take the liberty of making them your own and using them as a jumping-off point for inspiration. Some of these recipes apply directly to the stories in this book; some of them demonstrate certain qualities that are valuable to the study and discussion of food; some go together thematically, some don't; some are just in there because they're *good* and I thought you might like to give them a try.

A good chef knows how to set the tone for a meal by provoking interest with a taste of things to come that illustrates, ideally, what his cuisine is all about in a single bite or two. The *amuse-gueule*, which literally is an "amusement for the mouth," is a very small chef's tasting, offered upon seating, of a preparation that is exotic, surprising, or special, to prime the palate for what is to come. The amuse-gueule can tell you a lot about the chef and about what he is preparing to set before you. Seems like a good way to start a book, too.

MISSION:
COOK!

1

AMUSE-GUEULE, TIMES TWO

Adventurous tales of two Roberts, from civil war in
South Yemen to the red carpets of Hollywood

FEATURING . . .

"THEY MUST BE FED."

It is this phrase, simple and elegant in its clarity and concision, that comes most prominently to mind when recalling the events of the civil uprising in South Yemen and the details of one of the most unusual and consequential meals that I have ever been called upon to prepare.

I was all of twenty years old, was serving in the Royal Navy, and sailing en route to New Zealand aboard Her Majesty's Yacht *Britannia,* Her Majesty being Elizabeth the Second, Queen of England, and I being Robert Irvine, Royal Yachtsman and a leading cook aboard ship. Our intended mission was to rendezvous with the Queen and her entourage following a planned state visit to that country.

HMY *Britannia,* commissioned by King George VI to replace the royal barge *Victoria and Albert III* in 1948, was, simply put, a floating palace. We sailed the seas of the world in splendor, cleaning and polishing, cleaning and polishing, and, I, of course, cooking. My responsibilities included everything from afternoon tea for the duke of Edinburgh and his estimable wife, to lavish banquets for heads of state and celebrated passengers from every continent, all served at the pleasure of the Windsors, the Royal Family of England. The *Britannia* was richly appointed stem to stern, yet its warm teak decks and paneling, its chintz-covered sofas, deep armchairs, and surprisingly homey appointments, such as the baby grand piano and electric fireplace in the drawing room, the personally favored paintings and family pictures, spoke more of comfort than of regal extravagance. Indeed, Her Majesty was known to have said that she really only felt at home on that splendid vessel. Make no mistake, the Royal Yacht was royally provisioned with the world's finest in china, silverware, linens, and crystal. The food stores on board were always of supreme quality, from the very pinnacle of English beef, the freshest seafood, vegetables, and accompaniments, to every manner of caviar and foie gras, to the tiniest morsel of excellent shortbread for tea. All in all, it was a wonderful place to entertain, sip a gin and tonic, and escape from the weighty responsibilities of the modern monarchy . . . but not today.

I had been summoned to the bridge moments before and informed that we were to be diverted from our present course in a "relief effort." I was to take stock of the provisions we had on board that could be landed ashore quickly and efficiently. No further details were immediately forthcoming, nor did I expect there to be. Life was simpler then; we went where we were sent, and were expected to perform our assigned duties to the best of our abilities and beyond, when and wherever required.

In truth, my superiors hadn't many more details to pass along. The governments of many concerned countries, most prominently Britain and Russia, had been caught unawares by the rapidly spreading civil uprising in South Yemen. At the center of the conflict was a dustup between the besieged current president, Ali Nasser Muhammad, and the disgruntled former president, Abdul Fattah Ismail, who was tenaciously assailing the capital with his band of rebels. Thousands had been killed, the shelling was ongoing, and British civilians stranded in Aden, the capital of South Yemen, had been instructed by BBC announcers in London to assemble in "the northeast sector of the Soviet-embassy compound—repeat—the Soviet-embassy compound, from which you will be taken to the beach for evacuation." Which was exactly where we were headed, apparently to prepare lunch.

In transit to the port of Aden, there was little time to plan or strategize. We rendezvoused with other British naval vessels, including the heavily armed frigate HMS *Jupiter*. The *Jupiter* was not allowed to sail within the twelve-mile territorial limit of South Yemen, but the *Britannia*, which had been originally commissioned as a hospital ship in 1948, was given clearance to enter the port and begin evacuation procedures.

I was informed by the ship's captain that nearly 4,000 evacuees were gathered on the beach, waiting to be spirited away by ships of different nations to the former French colony of Djibouti, 150 miles away. The first load of 350, primarily comprising diplomats and VIPs, was to be transported aboard the *Britannia* as soon as possible.

The remainder needed to be fed. On the beach. Immediately.

With no provisions made for cooking equipment, food stores, or fresh water on the beach, a few decisions had to be made, and quickly, by yours truly. There were undisguised elements of the story of the loaves and fishes in this challenge, and I took some of my cues from the similarities. First priority: to decide on a limited menu that could be produced in large quantities. Second, to keep the preparations simple, but appealing. Third, to provide for the immediate nutritional requirements of those who would partake of the meal. Rice and pulses (beans) would be a marvelous, simple combination of carbohydrates and protein, much like bread and fish had been in Galilee. Lastly, to provide something to buoy the spirit. I knew right away that the menu would include a dessert. And I knew that something sweet to finish would help to provide vitality and energy.

I had taken a cursory inventory of the ship's stores, and soon landed upon a list of ingredients that fit the bill in every regard. My mates and I assembled a small mountain of sacks of rice, dried beans, flour, bags of frozen carrots and broccoli, plastic storage containers of fresh water, powdered milk, coffee, salt, pepper, butter, oil, sugar, sides of salt pork, and a spice mixture that I had dashed together for the beans, primarily composed of paprika, cayenne pepper, white pepper, brown sugar, coriander, cardamom, and cinnamon.

We ransacked the galleys for every last paper plate, plastic bowl, and cup, for plastic "sporks," paper napkins, and sundries. The problem remained of supplying heating equipment and pots big enough to hold food for over three thousand people. Cooking in the galleys and transporting the food to the beach was out of the question. The *Britannia* was to begin evacuation right away, and none of our cooking equipment was portable.

In those moments, it helps to break your problem down to the absolute basics. Need very big pots. Metal. What's big, can hold lots of food, and is made of metal? Wait for it . . . garbage cans. In the storeroom I found a complement of half a dozen fifty-gallon, pristine, aluminum garbage cans that had never been used. We hauled them on deck, then grabbed all of the Sterno and hexiblocks (which is a breakable, paraffin-based fuel) that we could carry, picked up shovels and some folding tables, and hit the beach.

We made our way to shore in a covered barge, which is a goodly sized motor launch, and anchored in the shallows. When we first arrived, we were relatively ignored. I disembarked and tried to get the lay of the land. The terrain seemed hospitable, and we were lucky in that we would be excavating in soft sand instead of hard clay. The sand would also be the perfect medium to hold in the heat from the fires we would have to build. A contingent of marines set up a secure perimeter on the dunes on the landward side, beyond which, only a few miles away, the conflict carried on unabated. The crosswinds were negligible, thankfully, so we hauled our supplies onto dry land. The offshore ships got all of the attention from those gathered on the beach just over a small rise, so I

HMS APOLLO
BFPO Ships

732/8

The Commodore
HMS CENTURION

26 September 1984

VOLUNTEER FOR ROYAL YACHT SERVICE
CK R P IRVINE D194584X

Reference:

A.   CRRN Art 0824.

1.   Application for Royal Yacht Service is forwarded in accordance with the reference.

2.   IRVINE is already a top-quality chef with a culinary skill and flair far beyond his years. He consistently produces excellent results, not only in the work he is directed to do by his superiors, but also in producing new dishes from his own imagination. Recently, in his spare time, he has made a wedding cake for a member of the Ship's Company which when entered in a national competition in Canterbury won first prize. The competition organisers were so impressed with his work that he has been invited to be a judge in forthcoming national competitions. The letter is at enclosure 2. He is always meticulous in his dress, manner and bearing, with a quiet self-confidence in his ability and possessing many of the qualties one would expect to find in the best more senior and experienced man.

3.   In APOLLO, IRVINE has been employed in the Wardroom Galley where he did exceptionally well both in day-to-day cooking for the officers and in presenting lunch and dinner parties for me. During his time in the Ship's Company Galley, although he inevitably found the work less satisfying, he maintained his normal extremely high standard.

4.   Because of the regrettably slow advancement the Navy can offer him I have little doubt that it can only be a matter of time before IRVINE will be attracted to a position commensurate with his abilities and offering higher remuneration by a civilian organisation (he has already been approached by a number of companies and hotels). The Navy would do well to hold his interest for as long as we can by presenting him with the greatest challenge possible in a large retinue. I would not be at all surprised, if, once in the Royal Yacht, he were rapidly employed in preparing Royal Banquets and the like.

5.   IRVINE has been keen to serve in the Royal Yacht since joining the Royal Navy and now that he is eligible to be considered I have no hesitation in most strongly recommending his application.

R N E PAYNE
Commander, Royal Navy

Letter of Recommendation
for the *Britannia*

went to work with my detail, digging pits in the sand, building fires in the bottom of each with Sterno and driftwood, and sinking garbage cans filled with water into each, one by one.

Our work came to a complete standstill for a brief, stirring moment as the *Britannia* pulled away with the first of its human cargo. The Royal Marine Band, which was always stationed aboard, played "Rule, Britannia!" from the foredeck, with all of the ceremonial flourishes, then, "Land of Hope and Glory" as it faded from view. That music was a promise of rescue and return to home, and it is still difficult for me to recall without the hairs standing up on the back of my neck.

I soaked the beans for about twenty minutes instead of the recommended twenty-four hours, then built up the fire and basically cooked the living daylights out of them until they became tender, about two and a half hours later. I skimmed them and added the spice mixture, then divided the rice and cooked it in two of the cans. If you ever find the need to cook rice in a garbage can, bear in mind that it's incredibly heavy and thus difficult to stir, so don't get carried away and try to do it in one big batch.

We needed a colander, so we stretched some cheesecloth across two two-by-fours, managed to drain the rice, then combined the rice and the beans together. I cut strips of the salt pork and steamed them to doneness on top of the rice and bean mixture. In the fourth can, I brought the heat up to a rolling boil for cooking the broccoli and carrots.

Dessert was contrived in the last can, where with the powdered milk, sugar, and rice, I created the biggest bowl of rice pudding known to man.

Over the hill they came, first in smaller groups, then larger, but with great order and dignity. By later reckoning, I found out that we were about to feed more than three thousand of them on our beach that day, all told. They were Russian, British, German, Chinese, French, Jordanian, Filipino, Somali, Egyptian, and Sikh; short and tall, male and female, black, white, and brown, from the elderly to very small children. Some were quiet, some crying, some nervous, others patient and resigned. All of us to one degree or another were afraid, because the explosive sound of shelling and the sight of smoke never ceased in the background. Once we began service, I hardly looked up from ladling food into bowls for hours. It must have been good, because we served every scrap of food we cooked. In the end, the *Britannia* alone rescued 1,082 foreigners before we resumed our voyage to New Zealand and kept our appointment with the Queen.

Everyone who was hungry that day was well fed.

Tastiest Ribs

MAKES ABOUT 4 SERVINGS

I have often thought, if I'd met one of the people who had been stranded that day on the beach in Yemen, and they had a sudden craving for pork, rice, and beans, here's how I might make them today.

This is the most fantastic recipe for cooking pork ribs that I know. Now, I tightly wrap my ribs and cook them in plastic wrap, and people look at me like I'm crazy, but this method does an incredible job of locking in the juices and natural flavor of the ribs. This recipe makes enough rub and sauce for 8 pounds of ribs. For less just halve the recipe or save the extra for another time!

8 pounds pork ribs (baby backs are great; you can also use beef ribs)

FOR THE RUB

¼ cup brown sugar

2 teaspoons salt

⅛ cup paprika

⅛ cup red chili powder

⅛ cup semicoarse black pepper

1 teaspoon garlic powder

1 teaspoon onion powder

FOR THE SAUCE

100 mL Jack Daniel's whiskey (half of a "flask-sized" bottle *or* two "airplane-sized" bottles)

1 tablespoon minced garlic (1 large clove)

½ cup Worcestershire sauce

½ cup apple juice

¼ cup tomato juice

1 tablespoon hot sauce (more if you like it spicy)

1 cup ketchup

1 tablespoon paprika

2 teaspoons black pepper

1 tablespoon onion powder

2 teaspoons salt

¼ cup corn syrup (light or dark)

Wash the ribs to remove any excess liquid and smells, and dry with paper towels.

Combine all the rub ingredients in a large mixing bowl and toss together until well mixed. Season the ribs liberally with the rub, preferably about 2 hours before cooking. Then wrap the entire section of meat in plastic wrap, making sure you cover it well, as the cooking method being used is actually steaming.

Leave the meat at room temperature until you place it in the oven, but for no longer than a couple of hours. (The rub will actually begin to "cure" the meat, acting as a preservative.)

Place the covered ribs into a 200 to 250-degree oven in a baking pan (the bottom part of a broiling pan is great because it is large and heavy duty). Cook for about 2 hours, the slower the better. (Don't have the oven any hotter than 250 degrees because the plastic wrap will melt.)

Whilst the ribs are cooking, begin making the sauce.

To make the sauce, combine the Jack Daniel's and the minced garlic in a large pot and simmer until the Jack Daniel's is reduced by half.

Then add all the other ingredients to the pot and simmer 40 to 50 minutes until all the flavors blend. Set this aside to cool.

When the ribs are cooked, carefully remove the plastic and allow the meat to cool.

When the ribs have cooled, coat with the sauce and cook on the barbecue grill or in a 450-degree oven until beautifully hot and caramelized, which should take about 15 minutes.

These would go great with a fresh coleslaw and a couple of Heinekens.

Finger-licking good!!!

Three Bean Ragout

SERVES 6

For the three bean ragout, the key is in the sauce. I'll bet you a dollar that even if you don't like beans, these beans will change your life forever.

Drain and rinse all liquid off the beans; set aside. Heat the oil in a sauté pan and lightly sauté the onion and garlic until translucent.

Add the red wine and reduce by half. Add the demi-glace and tomato paste, then incorporate the beans. Lower the heat and simmer for 10 minutes. Add the rosemary and chives.

Season with salt and pepper to taste. Serve over rice.

One 16-ounce can dark red kidney beans

One 16-ounce can white kidney beans

One 16-ounce can black beans

3 tablespoons canola oil

1 small red onion, chopped fine

3 garlic cloves, chopped fine

½ cup dry red wine

1½ cups demi-glace (brown sauce)

2 tablespoons tomato paste

2 sprigs of fresh rosemary, stripped from stem and finely chopped plus 1 sprig for garnish

2 tablespoons fresh chives, chopped fine

Salt and freshly ground black pepper

Royal Rice Pudding

SERVES 6 TO 8

5 cups whole milk

¾ cup short-grain white rice (short-grain rice may be difficult to find, so look in the Spanish foods section of your store for medium-grain rice)

⅛ teaspoon salt

¼ cup granulated sugar

1 fresh vanilla bean pod (essence or ¼ cup vanilla extract can be used in the absence of a fresh bean)

¾ cup white raisins (sometimes sold as golden seedless raisins), presoaked in warmed brandy (you can use a 50-mL "airplane-sized" bottle) or warm water

2 egg yolks

1 cup heavy cream

¼ stick unsalted butter

Nutmeg or cinnamon (optional)

EQUIPMENT

Six 6-ounce ramekins *or* eight or nine 4-ounce ramekins or serving dishes

Like everybody else in the world, I have a recipe for rice pudding that has followed me my whole career. It can be served warm or cold and is equally delicious. Please note, you may add cinnamon along the way, or at the very end before service. I leave it out, just because I don't have a taste for it. It is a great rice pudding, with the addition of several special ingredients that make it fit for a king!

A Note on Fresh Vanilla Beans Fresh vanilla beans are sold usually 1 or 2 to a jar in the spice section of the grocery store. They are very expensive, but are the gold standard in vanilla taste. If you decide to use them, split them in half lengthwise and scrape the small vanilla seeds into the pudding, then put the pod into the cooking pot. Remove the pod when you put the pudding into your serving dishes.

In a medium, heavy-bottomed saucepan, put in the milk, rice, and salt. Cook the rice at a low simmer (*do not boil*) until the rice is tender. (In classical French cooking, a "simmer" is *just below* the boiling point, when the bubbles are rising to the surface—but don't break the surface—of the liquid. This is the definition of "simmer" I am using here.) Once you achieve a simmer, the rice should take 20 to 30 minutes to be ready, depending on your cooker.

Remember to *keep stirring* so the rice doesn't stick to the bottom. *Taste the rice to make sure it is tender.*

Once the mixture has cooked, *remove from the heat* and add the sugar, vanilla bean, raisins, and egg yolks. Keep stirring to incorporate all of the flavors, then let the mixture sit for about 10 minutes. The sugar and vanilla will infuse very quickly, giving a flowery aroma.

Add the heavy cream and butter. Just mix them well together in the saucepan.

Spoon into ramekins or individual serving bowls.

Rice pudding can be served warm, at room temperature, or chilled. This particular recipe benefits from sitting overnight in the refrigerator.

You may want to grate fresh nutmeg over the top or sprinkle with cinnamon, as many people do, but I prefer the pudding without.

IN THE YEARS THAT INTERVENED BETWEEN THE INCIDENT AT ADEN AND THE story I am about to relate, I suppose I had gained a measure of notoriety and a good deal of experience, and I was extremely pleased to accept an invitation to create the food for a charity dinner and after party following the 2005 Academy Awards.

In fact, a fellow had approached me the year before to cook for the same affair, the "Children Uniting Nations" Awards Celebration & Viewing Dinner. I was then under contract as executive chef at Caesar's in Atlantic City and was constrained to decline with regret, but this time, a year later, I was on my own and was about the business of establishing myself as what I would describe as an independent culinary operative.

My career to date had been a peripatetic one. Since my stint with the Royal Family, which in itself was characterized by constant travel, I had been executive chef in a number of places, opened and closed many, many restaurants for various employers, on land and sea, in hotels and casinos and on cruise ships. I had literally fed multitudes. I had been given wide latitude to exercise my ideas on food and management and had increased my portfolio of skills to such a degree that I thought I might be able to create a different kind of future for myself. I founded a consulting company, called The Irvine Group, with a business partner, Randall Williams. Mainly, I was looking for my freedom, for the ability to control my own destiny. I saw myself as a sort of an ambassador, an autonomous agent at liberty to pursue my own ideas, to develop products, to advise on and participate in culinary projects, to make live appearances where I could come in contact with audiences who were interested in my food and my ideas, to cook for private individuals, for parties, in restaurants or for large-scale affairs, whilst always reserving the right to come and go as only I saw fit. The Oscars seemed to be a fantastic opportunity for this young enterprise.

The event was to take place on the night of the Academy Awards ceremony at the Factory in West Hollywood, sandwiched between the *Vanity Fair* party and Sir Elton John's *In Style* party. I was certain that there would be lights, cameras, and plenty of action . . . there would be palm trees and crystal blue skies and ocean breezes . . . there would be stars aplenty, glittering in their red carpet finery, some holding golden statuettes, others dazzling onlookers and basking in the flashbulb-illuminated glow of celebrity. And there would be publicity and accolades for the food, which would be spectacular, and its praises would linger on people's lips long after they'd sampled my wares.

Instead, it wasn't long before I felt as though I'd been plunged into the seventh level of culinary hell.

Now, let me state at the outset that the organizers of the event started with every possible good intention, that the charity was well served that night, and that I'm sure they performed wonderful work on behalf of their intended beneficiaries: at-risk youth and children in need. They are humanitarians and deserve full marks for the good work they've done.

They simply had no concept of what it takes financially and logistically to get a truly spectacular dinner and hors d'oeuvres on the table for nearly five thousand people.

Their first thought was to make the food preparation for the party an all-star team event, and names like "Alain" and "Jean-Georges" were bandied about. I thought that was a terrific idea, but warned them that the chefs they were discussing were at the top of the profession. They would need to be handsomely paid, would require first-class travel and accommodations and the finest ingredients and equipment with which to work. "We can do that!" was the incessant reply.

However, soon after having heard repeated promises of private air travel, donated food, and "all expenses paid," and with nothing to show for it, I started to see the writing on the wall. It was clear that the responsibility would fall to me, or the event simply wouldn't happen. I was forced to bring my Rolodex of chefs, vendors, and purveyors into play; my beautiful, unspoiled Rolodex. I began making calls.

There is an implied brotherhood among chefs, especially among those of us who care to venture out regularly into the world beyond our kitchens. I have a very low resistance to appearing before live crowds for charity whenever and wherever I am asked, to cooking for fund-raisers wherein I feel I can do some good for worthy causes and meet new and interesting people, and for participating in fun and exciting events built around the premise of professionals coming together to create and share great food. I love to mingle with my fellow chefs at James Beard Foundation dinners, at theme dinners, at festivals, or at their home restaurants, where we can play and eat and show off our latest and greatest ideas about new dishes. You can make a lot of friends that way.

They came when I called, and agreed to do it all for free: first there was Ming Tsai, master of Asian fusion and a true professional; through Ming, I got in touch with Todd English, sophisticate and brilliant restaurateur. My great good friend, Italian giant Roberto Donna, came; the list further included the brilliant Cesare Lanfranconi; Kirk Avondoglio, fine salmon grower and good friend; German chef Markus Seegert; ¡Pasión!'s Guillermo Pernot; The Four Seasons' Conny Andersson, Marc Fertoukh, Victorio Ivarra, Joe Miller, and Walter Cotta; and Los Angeles's the Jonathan Club's executive chef, Christian Montchâtre.

I also called Rocco DiSpirito. I have known Rocco for a few years and I like him. At that time, he was coming off of a wild ride, largely played out in the public spotlight. He had starred in an ABC series called *The Restaurant*, in which millions saw him portrayed in a highly unusual light, to say the least. The restaurant he had opened in that show, Rocco's on 22nd Street, had closed after a high-profile showdown with his then partner, Jeffrey Chodorow, and he no longer worked at New York's Union Pacific, where he had really made his reputation as a rising star, turning out amazing and innovative flavor combinations. Rocco ultimately answered the call, and his food was delicious but, to paraphrase Carly Simon, he probably thinks this chapter's about him.

With only a couple of weeks to go, the chefs began to submit their dishes for the main event of the evening, an eight-course, sit-down charity dinner for 650 people, for which they paid $10,000 per table. Preliminary to this would be a cocktail and hors d'oeuvres reception *for thousands* and a viewing of the awards ceremony; following would be a lavishly provisioned after party, with live entertainment featuring Chaka Khan and Wyclef Jean. Rocco was still on the fence at that point, with his agent demanding top billing and an appearance fee, neither of which I was in a position to grant.

I gave the rest of the chefs the option of prepping their food from where they were coming, or I offered to source their ingredients and set them up to work in Los Angeles. Todd decided to bring some items in from Las Vegas; Roberto would fly in accompaniments from Washington, D.C. For the most part, it became my job to find everything else. My food budget turned out to be considerably less than I had hoped: it consisted of, basically, nothing. This was all being done in the name of charity, and I had to convince my suppliers from all over the country that they had to give, and "give 'til it hurt."

At this point, let us also be clear about one thing: no chef, myself included, rises to the level of these guys without a big ego and a deep-seated inability to compromise on quality. Translation: they want what they want, when they want it. All week long I had to make sure that their substantial egos were taken care of and that their exacting demands were met, especially since they were coming at my behest, and for charity.

Rocco had finally come on board at that point, and was rather stridently demanding a certain chestnut paste and *purple* sage, which was the only kind he would deign to use. Todd wanted *Maine* lobsters only. He gamely agreed to use a fantastic mid-Atlantic lobster, once I'd managed to get more than six hundred, for *free,* from Pennsylvania. Guillermo needed gold leaf for one of his creations, which I scrounged together at the last minute. I found special flours, oils, pastas, sausages, duck, lamb, and black bass; Serrano ham, Manila clams, black tiger shrimp, enoki mushrooms, Key limes, Manchego and Boursin cheeses, Beluga caviar, foie gras, baby bok choy, Alaskan butterfish, and Hawaiian ahi tuna. For my entrée, I had dry-aged beef tenderloin for 650, donated by Stockyards in Chicago.

The party was to have been set up outdoors under a huge white tent in the parking lot of the Factory. there had been no provisions made for refrigeration or kitchen equipment, so I contacted some associates at a kitchen company and convinced them to donate and install fifteen stoves, a dozen or so industrial refrigeration units, and dishwashing facilities.

Wisps of black smoke began to curl from my cruelly overstressed Rolodex.

It also became clear that I was not to be afforded any real transportation budget to bring in the out-of-towners, so Randall and I somehow managed to cobble together a solution based on the frequent-flier miles of everyone involved. Chefs and cooks began to arrive, though Todd and Ming would not get there until the Sunday of the awards show because of unavoidable scheduling conflicts. Through intermediaries, Rocco was holding out for a first-class plane ticket (which he never got) and also would not arrive until Sunday. Most of the chefs sent or brought one or two sous-chefs to help with prep work. Rocco insisted on, and got, tickets and accommodations for an entourage of seven.

I didn't feel comfortable that anyone knew what they were doing servicewise, so I brought in Kirk's brother Mark, and another friend, Arthur Giordano, to coordinate the troop of experienced waitstaff with the inevitable legion of native unemployed actors and screenwriters.

The food prep was done in Christian Montchâtre's kitchen at the Jonathan Club in downtown L.A. Madhouse would be an apt description. I had to orchestrate food coming in from vendors all over the city and country, as well as space, equipment, and *mise en place* for what felt like a hundred chefs, each holding very sharp knives, each of whom had his own preferred methods for doing pretty much *everything*. Deliveries all had to be routed to the downstairs kitchen through a single elevator. Although I had spent the week scrambling to assemble everyone's specialty items, there is an endless list of items that need to be present in a professional kitchen for cooking to occur, from pots, pans, and plastic wrap, to milk, butter, eggs, flour, plates, and parsley, right down to salt and pepper. We descended on Christian's supplies like a cloud of locusts.

All of the chefs by this time had arrived except for Todd, Ming, and Rocco. Any great kitchen rises and falls on the back of one principle: organization. Escoffier invented the *brigade system*, wherein each position has a station and a defined job. At the beginning of the day, we had chaos, since nobody except Christian and his people knew where anything was and they simply couldn't be everywhere at once. Teams began to assemble and work independently at first, because time was of the essence. They were soon inevitably trespassing into each other's spaces and getting in each other's way. The situation had disaster, murder, and mayhem written all over it, save for the truly awesome professionalism of those involved. The head chefs and I worked together to quickly improvise a brigade system that worked well enough to minimize collisions, to at least head in the general direction of maximizing efficiency, and to keep everyone from working at cross-purposes. The chefs' staff and sous-chefs were incredibly well trained and were not only schooled in the particular cuisines for which they were responsible, but knew how to adapt and think on their feet as well as any cadre of cooks I had ever seen. The crack troops that Ming and Todd sent in were especially impressive.

When it comes down to brass tacks, as we say in Her Majesty's Navy, it's the food that counts, and everybody *got* that and stuck to their guns through all of the difficulty. I give special credit to Roberto Donna for his steely focus and for keeping our spirits high. He is as intense as anyone I have ever cooked with, but the pleasure he takes in his work and in working with people is like a natural force. On Saturday, the day before the event, we found out we had no way to transport all of the prepped food from the Jonathan Club to the venue, so Randall found a local produce company and hired four of their trucks and drivers with a wad of cash out of his pocket, and we formed a convoy from downtown to West Hollywood. Under the big tent at the parking lot at the Factory, each chef had an assigned refrigeration unit with his name affixed to the front. They looked like a long line of stainless-steel stars' dressing rooms. All of the ingredients for the chefs' entrées and hors d'oeuvres for three thousand were somehow miraculously prepared and stored away.

My strategy was to start with a round of hors d'oeuvres and cocktails for about 2,000, serve dinner for the 650 dinner guests, lure the 650 out of the dining area with spectacular desserts and coffees, then clear away the tables and set serving stations for the after-party, where anywhere from 1,500 to

2,000 additional people might be stopping by. Just setting out napkins for almost five thousand people in an evening is a chore. This kind of advanced culinary choreography should not be attempted by the faint of heart.

By the middle of Sunday, my dream team of chefs had all arrived. They assumed their places and plating began. Had you been there, this is what you would have tasted:

Kirk Avondoglio opened with a Mosaic of Salmon, Tuna, and Diver Scallops, with the fresh, salty tang of the raw fish perfectly complemented by the buttery sweetness of the scallops, balanced with slightly bitter wild field greens, lightly dressed with a beautiful extra virgin olive oil.

This was followed by Todd English's Roasted Lobster with Crab-Stuffed Morels, the lobster bursting with his bold, signature flavors, yet marvelously grounded by the earthiness of the crab-stuffed mushrooms, accompanied by Minted Couscous and a pungent Curry Emulsion.

Ming Tsai had the Third Plate, a Miso-Sake Marinated Alaskan Butterfish to die for, its flaky mouthfeel enhanced by the smooth miso-sake mixture, with Vegetarian Soba Noodle Sushi, accompanied by an eye-opening Wasabi Oil and Soy-Lime Syrup.

Markus Seegert created a bracing Braised Red Beet Consommé with freshly grated horseradish, which refreshed every palate at the halfway point of the meal, paired with Sun-Dried Tomato Dumplings that whimsically played the comforting role often filled at banquet by a simple fruit sorbet.

Roberto Donna's Fifth Plate was a Duck Cannelloni, an operatic taste triumph that trumpeted his Piedmont origins, the controlled succulent and savory taste of the duck raised to new heights by an ethereal whiff of Black Truffle Sauce.

Guillermo Pernot's Sixth Plate was a revelation that encapsulated the windswept, grassy plains of his native Argentina: Salvadoran Tomato Tortilla, Huitlacoche, Anaheim Chile Guiso, Roasted Lamb Loin, and Golden Vigoran Slaw with a Salsa Verde. The contrast of the tender lamb played thrillingly off of the crunchy, vinegary slaw and the backdrop of the sparkling Latin flavors.

Rocco DiSpirito presented Seared Black Bass with Blood Orange and Chestnuts, a brilliantly presented dish in its clarity and simplicity; the lightly seared bass lovingly offset by the autumnal colors and flavors of the orange and chestnut.

I reserved the pièce de résistance for myself, a center-cut, twenty-eight-day dry-aged prime beef tenderloin, which is simply the most incredible, beautifully marbled beef I know, seasoned, seared, and finished in clarified butter to lock in the flavorful juices, with an Infant Arugula Salad, a tartly sweet Tomato Confit, and a silky Balsamic Demi-Glace.

And it all went off without a hitch.

All of the chefs had gathered together earlier in a group in our chef's whites and taken a quick bow on the red carpet for photos. Rocco had unfortunately decided to go solo, stylishly dressed in civilian clothes, and he took multiple trips in front of the cameras, squiring some very attractive young ladies. Once noticed, this sudden and prolonged absence from the kitchen did not go over too well back in the tent, and when he finally returned, no one was willing to help him plate his dishes, so that fire had to be put out. Luckily I had drafted a corps of culinary students from the local Art Institute of California, and the kids pitched in with Rocco's chefs to help him get his courses out to the tables.

Following dinner, at the after party we all collaborated on a dramatic array of tasting dishes and small plates. For the next few hours, we became an engine of culinary creation, and some of the most amazing food I have seen collected in one spot was soon circulating about the room. There were salmon, pasta, caviar, and dessert stations, to name only a few, champagne and wine booths from a number of wineries, a Ketel One vodka bar, and a Patrón tequila bar. We served:

APRÈS MENU DE PARTIE

———

Endive leaves topped with curried chicken

*Antipasti di Mare with shrimp, mussels, and clams
and a light lime olive oil*

Bite-sized pear, apple, and Key lime tarts

Assorted sweet crepes with hand-cranked ice creams

*Every manner of and accompaniment to smoked
salmon*

Strawberries marinated with Campari

White chocolate imperial

Serrano ham and Manchego cheese baguette

Fresh mozzarella wrapped in mâche leaves

Crab lollipops with hoisin sauce

Cheese amaretto cookies and foie gras

Carrot and lemongrass vichyssoise

Roasted squash gnocchi

"Shrimp dogs" in brioche buns

Involtini di prosciutto with enoki mushrooms

Seared duck breast salpicón

Ahi tuna poke with pink ginger ice cream

Lamb marquez sliders with hummus

Spicy jerk pork sausage with a fire-roasted pepper relish

There was a vast selection of caviars with crème fraîche and handmade buckwheat blinis, and Cesare served mounds of his Fettuccine Vittoria from a bowl carved out of a huge wheel of Parmesan cheese.

The anticipated cavalcade of stars arrived, and feasted into the night. There were well over a thousand people under the tent and hundreds more waiting to get in. The fire marshal had arrived and was deciding who was to be let in and who would be kept out. I heard that Harrison Ford, Clint Eastwood, and Pierce and Keely Brosnan all made it in, as did Jane Seymour and Babyface and Tracie Edmonds, in addition to Paula Abdul, Governor Gray Davis and his wife, Sharon, and a literal host of VIPs and celebrities. Everywhere I turned there were compliments flying about for the food and the chefs. I was roped into a pretty bad imitation of dancing for a few moments with Paris Hilton. Wesley Snipes, in a moment of irrational exuberance, offered me a job as personal chef. The apex came for me when I was able to shake hands with the winner of the Best Actor Oscar that night, Jamie Foxx. He sampled our creations with one hand and balanced his well-deserved golden statuette in the other.

The evening was a smashing success, and no one was the wiser for all of the chaos, confusion, and sacrifice it took to afford them all the pleasures of the table that evening. Nor should they be.

Looking back, it may have been the hardest thing I've done in my professional life. From mid-January on, there was an incredible amount of press coverage about the event, so the stakes were high. My reputation was on the line, and in my business, you are only as good as your last meal. At times, it felt as if it really might have *been* my last meal. My Rolodex lay in a heap of smoldering ashes. As a logistical nightmare, on a scale of one to ten, the experience was an eleven; but the quality of the food scored just as highly, across the board. It was an eleven, plus. For that week, I had become not only *chef de cuisine* but sous-chef, garde-manger, roundsman, babysitter, expediter, financial manager, travel agent, psychologist, and taxi driver, simply because there was no one else to do it, and I refused to fail at the task: making sure that everyone was fed.

Believe me when I tell you this: everyone who was hungry that night was *extremely* well fed.

Academy Awards Viewing Dinner

One of the biggest challenges of creating any type of menu at home is the organization and timing of food. If you can organize the preparation a couple of days ahead, you will have a successful party and will be able to relax and enjoy yourself whilst the big stars squirm in their seats. To help round out this first chapter, I have put together a beautiful menu for an Academy Awards viewing party at home. I resisted the urge to pun my way through this exercise with Veal Oscar and the like, and instead tried to put together a truly exciting, rich, and elegant series of courses that might satisfy the way a good film does. Best to serve cocktails during the red carpet, dine in elegance with a couple of bottles of fine wine, then enjoy watching the awards with coffee, after-dinner drinks, and dessert whilst your friends sing your praises. They'll like you . . . they'll really like you!

Warm Rock Shrimp and Lobster Flan,

Baby Arugula Salad and Champagne Sabayon

Creole-Style Red Snapper with

Farmhouse Grits and Red Pepper Coulis

Blackened Tenderloin of Beef with Roasted Sweet Corn

and Potato Hash and a Merlot Reduction

Chilled Grand Marnier Soufflé with Macerated Fruits

Real Life Advice for the Home Cook

"Academy Awards Viewing Dinner"

- Familiarize yourself with the menu and read each recipe through from start to finish.
- Picture yourself carrying out each step.
- If you have any questions, do the research *before* you are actually in the throes of cooking.
- Pay attention to, and take advantage of, the suggestions to prepare ahead (i.e., Grand Marnier Soufflé, Crème Fraîche, Red Pepper Coulis, Merlot Reduction, Sweet Corn and Potato Hash), especially if it is the first time you are preparing the recipe.
- Make a detailed shopping list and double-check your cupboard to make sure you have what you need, including equipment.
- Do the shopping in advance (in other words, *not* on the day of the party).
- *Enjoy* the shopping trip as you picture yourself successfully presenting an exquisite dinner party.

Warm Rock Shrimp and Lobster Flan, Baby Arugula Salad, and Champagne Sabayon

SERVES 4 TO 6

The goal in producing a pastry "dough" is a delicate flaky crust, a different goal from the preparation of bread dough. The ingredients of a dough used for pasta and bread benefit from the familiarity of experiencing a good massage together, which gives it the requisite elasticity (defined as "kneading"). However, in the world of pastry dough, familiarity breeds contempt.

Alternatively, you may wish to use prepared pastry. Most stores nowadays carry a wide selection.

Therefore:

1. Pastry should be made as quickly as you can perform the task, with . . .
2. Not too much water (just enough to bind the dough together without being too crumbly to work), with an effort to . . .
3. Try to keep the water and your hands (to the extent that they are used)—and the kitchen for that matter—as cool as possible, to avoid melting the butter too much. (To assist in keeping your hands cool, dip them periodically into a large bowl of ice water and keep a clean dry towel on hand to dry them thoroughly each time before returning to the pastry.) However, the prime directive to remember is . . .
4. **Never overwork your pastry dough.**

There are two definitions of "flan." The first is a tart, usually with some kind of cream filling. The other meaning is "custard." The first definition of flan applies here. What differentiates the flan from, say, a pie is that it is a freestanding tart with vertical sides. The key to making a successful flan (of the tart variety) is the use of a flan pan, a tin with rippled sides whose secret is its removable bottom. One can be obtained at a gourmet cooking store, for less than $20—usually for less than $15—in either a standard or a nonstick variety. You can also use a flan ring, which necessitates its use on a baking tin to serve as the support for the bottom of your pastry crust as it bakes. Whilst you're at the gourmet cooking store, treat yourself to a long spatula with a blade that's not too thick, to help you disengage your "flan" crust from the bottom of the flan tin and to slide it gently to its destination.

A springform pan ring (of the type used to make cheesecakes) can also be used as a makeshift flan ring. Springform pans do not have rippled sides, so you will be fluting the top edge of your crust by hand (for visual appeal) to a height of only 1½ to 2 inches, which is shallower than the 3-inch depth of the typical springform ring.

FOR THE FLAN PASTRY

⅔ cup all-purpose flour (plus some extra to flour the board or cloth when rolling out)

Pinch of salt (defined in some circles as 1/16 teaspoon)

¼ cup softened butter (plus some extra for greasing the baking tin)

3 to 5 tablespoons water (have a glass of ice water standing by)

FOR THE FLAN FILLING

1 red onion, finely diced

2 tomatoes (insides removed), finely diced

½ cup chopped chives

½ cup chopped lobster tail, about ¼ pound

½ cup chopped cooked bacon, about 6 strips if thick sliced or 9 strips if regular sliced

½ cup rock shrimp, chopped (regular shrimp can be substituted), about ¼ pound

3 eggs, beaten

¼ cup (2 ounces) whole milk

½ cup (4 ounces) heavy cream

Salt and pepper

¼ cup fresh chopped chervil (parsley can be substituted, but chervil lends its slightly anise flavor)

¾ cup sharp Cheddar cheese, grated

A pastry cloth and a rolling pin

A food processor with a dough blade, if using for pastry dough

An 8-inch flan pan with a removable bottom (or four 4-inch flan pans with the same feature)

Parchment paper

Ceramic pastry weights (or dried beans can be used)

A long spatula

A salad spinner

A double boiler

An electric mixer

TIME REQUIRED FOR THE FIRST COURSE

Warm Rock Shrimp and Lobster Flan, Baby Arugula Salad, and Champagne Sabayon. Allow about 3 hours or so if you are preparing everything contiguously before mealtime. (This encompasses requisite resting times during which preparation and cooking for the next phase can be accomplished.)

Since my recipe for Warm Rock Shrimp and lobster Flan calls for the final baking to be done after the filling is poured into the crust, you can't use the following idea if you want a freestanding tart. However, in any other recipe where all of the baking of the flan crust occurs before the filling is poured in, an additional idea is to use two 9-inch cake tins. One cake tin is to contain the pastry, and the other one is nested on top of the unbaked crust to hold the pastry down whilst you prebake it. Be forewarned, however, in the use of the "two cake tins" method, you run the risk of a prebaked crust cracking when you try to remove it for a freestanding presentation.

What you don't want to use for a freestanding presentation is a mold with tapered sides, because under the weight of the filling the slanted sides are unlikely to stay intact once you attempt to make the flan freestanding. Of course, you can just make the recipe "pie style" (leaving it a pie dish) if the presentation is not that important to you. In that instance, the salad in the recipe here would be served on the side, rather than as a bed for the flan.

TIME LINE FOR FLAN, SALAD, AND DRESSING

Preparation of pastry dough	*8 minutes*
Rest time for dough overlaps with prep time for flan filling	*30 minutes*
Roll out pastry dough and line pan	*10 minutes*
Chill time for rolled-out dough (30 minutes) overlaps with filling cook time (2 minutes) and cool time (30 minutes)	*32 minutes*
Bake time for pastry crust (30 minutes) overlaps with prep of sabayon (8 minutes) and salad prep (12 minutes)	*30 minutes*
Cool time for crust	*20 minutes*
Flan assembly	*5 minutes*
Bake flan	*35 to 45 minutes*
Rest time for flan	*10 minutes*
Plating/presentation	*5 to 10 minutes*
Total time required	*about 3 hours*

To make the pastry, I offer two methods. In both cases, aerate the flour by sifting it together with the salt into a large bowl.

1. Classical method: Add the butter in pieces and rub it in with your fingertips until you reach a texture similar to that of fine bread crumbs. (Try to keep your hands cool.)

Warm Rock Shrimp and
Lobster Flan

Add ice water slowly, mixing in only enough water as you need to make the dough form.

2. "Modern" classical method (an oxymoron perhaps, but quite satisfactory in its results): Nowadays many people prepare pastry dough in a food processor equipped with a dough blade. To do so, you put the sifted flour and salt into the processor bowl and pulse whilst drizzling the ice water sparingly through the processor tube into the flour mixture until the dough comes together.

In either case, do *not* overwork the pastry dough.

Form the dough into a disk (for ease of handling), place it in a bowl covered with plastic wrap or a clean damp towel, and allow the pastry dough to rest in the refrigerator for 30 minutes.

When the dough is rested, roll it out onto a *lightly* floured surface with a rolling pin, to a thickness of about ⅛ inch, and line a well-buttered 8-inch flan pan. (If you wish, you can also use four 4-inch individual molds instead.) Place back into the refrigerator for about 30 minutes.

Preheat the oven to 375 degrees.

Line the base of the chilled pastry shell with parchment paper. Then fill the shell with ceramic pastry weights (or dried beans) and place on a baking tray in the oven and partially bake ("blind bake") for 25 minutes. Remove the weights, prick the base of the pastry to prevent if from bubbling up, and return it to the oven for a further 5 minutes to dry out the base.

6 ounces baby arugula

2 ripe pears, peeled and
chopped

1 mango, peeled and diced

**FOR THE CHAMPAGNE
SABAYON (DRESSING)**

3 egg yolks

¼ cup sugar

¼ cup champagne or any
sparkling wine

¾ cup heavy cream

¼ cup crème fraîche (French
cultured cream)

⅛ teaspoon freshly ground
black pepper

Remove the pastry shell from the oven and allow to cool. Reduce the oven heat to 325 degrees.

To make the filling, whilst the shell is cooling, heat a little oil in a large sauté pan. Add the onion, tomato, chives, lobster, bacon, and shrimp, and cook until the shrimp turns pink, about 2 minutes. Set aside to cool. (Whilst the shell and filling are cooling, you may want to prepare the champagne sabayon [dressing] if you have not already done so.)

Sprinkle the Cheddar cheese on the base of the cooled pastry shell. Then add the lobster and shrimp mixture once it too has cooled.

Whisk the eggs, milk, and heavy cream together. Season the mixture well with salt and pepper, then add the chopped chervil. Pour over the other ingredients, three-quarters to the top of the shell.

As with any liquid-filled pastry, to avoid a major oven cleanup, set the filled flan pan over a foil-lined cookie sheet to catch drips.

Bake in a 325-degree oven for 35 to 45 minutes, or until when you pierce the flan with a knife in the center, it comes out clean.

Let the baked flan rest for 10 minutes, then, still wearing your oven mitts, push the base of the pan upward from the bottom to release the flan from the sides. You may want to use a spatula to also slide the flan off the base onto your serving plate; however, if it starts to break apart (this is more of a risk with a larger flan than with individual ones), the nearly invisible base of the flan pan enables you to use it for service with little consequence to your presentation.

To make the salad, soak the arugula in a bowl of cold water to remove sand, then repeat with a fresh batch of cold water. Rinse the arugula thoroughly in a colander and drain. To remove excess moisture, spin in a salad spinner or dry with paper towels. Remove the stems of the arugula and when ready to serve, toss with the pears and mango in a bowl.

A Note on Leafy Greens South of Atlantic City (the scene of many of my culinary adventures) is Cape May, New Jersey, at the southernmost tip of the state. Cape May is an entire town that has been proclaimed a National Historic Landmark because of its Victorian architecture. For many years, visitors to its beach have been known to search for what are known as "Cape May Diamonds," sizable pieces of pure quartz that tend to appear in the sand because of the way the currents flow from the ocean into the Delaware Bay. Since the warm sand along these shores of the Atlantic Ocean is soft and white, sifting through it in pursuit of the "diamonds" is part of what makes the activity so delightful. But if encountered in a salad or a soup, the sand will be anything but soft, which brings me to my point.

Arugula, like spinach and many other greens, has a staggering capacity to retain sand in the nooks and crannies of its leaves. (In general, people really don't know too much about arugula, although it is a welcome change to mixed lettuces and has a wonderful peppery taste.) When washing these greens, soak them in a bowl of cold water to let most of the sand sink to the bottom. Agitate the greens by shaking them whilst they are underwater. Repeat the process, making sure that you lift the greens out of the bowl to avoid disturbing the sand that has collected at the bottom of the bowl. Then set the greens on a towel and wash the bowl thoroughly to remove all traces of sand before refilling with subsequent batches of fresh soaking water. When it looks like you've gotten rid all the sand, lift the greens out of the soaking water (leaving the grit undisturbed at the bottom), transfer them to a colander, and rinse them from above with a stream of water from the spigot or handheld kitchen sink hose. The roughage for your Academy Awards viewing dinner should be crunchy—but not gritty.

Also, a salad spinner is remarkably handy to get the greens dry enough to prevent them from making your flan crust soggy.

A Note on Crème Fraîche Also known as French cultured cream, crème fraîche may be found in the dairy or cheese section of an increasing number of stores. You can also prepare your own crème fraîche, but you must allow yourself at least 32 hours in advance (8 hours at room temperature and 24 hours refrigerated), because of the culturing process. If you are positively unable to locate it, and don't have the time to make some, you may substitute ¼ cup heavy cream and an egg. However, I encourage you to use the crème fraîche if at all possible, because it is not too expensive and lends a unique taste that will elevate this dressing to something truly special.

To make the dressing, whisk the egg yolks, sugar, and champagne in a double boiler over simmering water until thick ribbons appear.

Remove from the heat and let stand. Whilst this mixture is standing, whip the heavy cream and crème fraîche together with a beater until nice and thick, about 1 minute on high speed. Fold the two mixtures together, add the pepper, and keep refrigerated until needed.

PRESENTATION

Place a small amount of arugula salad in the center of the plate. Set a wedge of the warm lobster flan on top and drizzle with champagne sabayon.

Creole-Style Red Snapper with Farmhouse Grits and Red Pepper Coulis

SERVES 6

FOR THE RED PEPPER COULIS

3 large red bell peppers, washed, with stems and seeds removed

1 shallot, diced

2 minced garlic cloves

1 cup V-8 vegetable juice

¼ cup balsamic vinegar

Salt and pepper

EQUIPMENT

Oven mitts

A blender

PREPARATION AND COOKING TIME

Approximately 50 minutes

Ideally you can make the red pepper coulis the day before or earlier in the day of the dinner.

Place the peppers in a roasting pan and roast in a preheated 450-degree oven, checking every 15 minutes and turning them with tongs until the skin is fully wrinkled and charred black.

Put the charred peppers into a bowl filled with a couple of inches of ice water. Once they are cooled, you can use your fingers to quickly slip off and discard the skins of the peppers whilst they are in the water. Immediately transfer the still-warm peppers to a plate, then peel away any remnants of the charred skins. You will be left with beautifully cooked red peppers with a wonderful color.

In the blender, combine the peppers with the shallot, garlic, V-8 juice, and balsamic vinegar. Blend these until a smooth consistency is achieved, and season with salt and pepper to taste.

(If the coulis looks too "wet," you could tighten the mix by returning it to a pan and adding cornstarch until it reaches a thicker, smoother consistency.)

If necessary, strain the sauce so there are absolutely no lumps present and set aside.

About 1 hour before the dinner, you can make the grits as follows:

In a large, heavy-bottomed pot, bring the milk and stock to a boil, quickly lower the heat to a simmer, and whisk in the grits. Keep stirring until the mixture becomes smooth; add the cheeses, and allow them to fully blend in with the grits before you taste and season, to account for the saltiness of the cheeses. Cover the pot and set the burner on very low whilst the grits mixture cooks for 20 minutes. Remove from the burner; it will hold its heat for a while and is easy to reheat when you need it.

To make the Creole-style red snapper, preheat the oven to 375 degrees. Wash the fish and pat it dry. Place all of the dried spices and the salt together in a plastic bag, place the fish in the bag, and coat the fish with the spices, pressing firmly to adhere the spices to the fish. Shake the excess spices from the fish.

In a large, nonstick sauté pan, add some grapeseed oil, and when it begins to smoke, place the fish in the pan, skin side up, and cook for a couple of minutes until golden brown. Flip and finish in the oven for a further 2 to 3 minutes, and remove it to rest for 5 to 8 minutes. (Please *don't* overcook the fish. When you touch the flesh and it springs back, it is done! Remember, it will continue to cook after you remove it from the oven.)

PRESENTATION

To plate this dish I would use a large bowl. Begin by placing some of the grits in the middle, then position the fish on top and drizzle the coulis around the fish. Garnish liberally with the scallions.

FOR THE FARMHOUSE GRITS

1 cup whole milk

4 cups chicken stock or vegetable stock

1½ cups stone-ground grits

1 cup grated sharp white Cheddar cheese

½ cup grated Parmigiano-Reggiano cheese

Salt and pepper

¼ cup scallions, chopped on an angle

FOR THE FISH

Six 4-ounce red snapper fillets, boned and not skinned

¼ cup paprika

1 teaspoon cayenne pepper

1 teaspoon sea salt

¼ cup grapeseed oil

Blackened Tenderloin of Beef with Roasted Sweet Corn and Potato Hash and a Merlot Reduction

SERVES 6

This was the main course at the charity Oscars party held by Children Uniting Nations. We will begin with the items that take the longest—like the hash and the sauce—since, as chefs, we prepare in advance. So please remember, so can you!

The hash can be prepared the day before and simply reheated when needed.

Preheat the oven to 375 degrees.

In a large skillet, add ¼ cup oil and get the pan warm (over medium-low heat) on the stovetop. Add the onion, garlic, and corn kernels. Sauté together until the corn feels cooked to the bite, about 5 minutes. Then, set aside.

In a large bowl, toss the diced potatoes with the remaining ¼ cup oil and season them with salt and pepper to taste. *It is important that the potatoes are very dry* (place the potatoes on paper towels to absorb moisture), *and that they get a nice even coating of oil.* Place them onto a large roasting tray.

Top the potatoes with the sautéed corn and onion mixture, and place in the oven to cook. This should take 30 to 45 minutes at 375 degrees (some ovens may need longer than others).

Just before serving, mix in the diced tomatoes and chopped chives, and crumble the goat cheese. *If you have prepared this dish in advance, please reserve the tomatoes and goat cheese until the last minute, after you have reheated the hash.* Adjust the seasoning (using salt and pepper as needed). Keep in a warm place until needed.

The merlot reduction also can be prepared the night before if you want to save time. Some sauces (like this one) actually benefit from sitting overnight; it enhances their depth of flavor.

In a large saucepan, add the oil, and sauté the garlic and shallots over gentle heat until translucent. (If you have any trimmings of meat, you could add them at this time.)

Deglaze the pan with the wine, and add the beef stock and fresh herbs.

Allow this mixture to reduce. It could take 20 to 30 minutes (sometimes longer) at a rolling boil, uncovered. *You want the liquid to evaporate down to about ⅓ of what you started with. By reducing this liquid, you are intensifying the flavor.*

Once you have reduced the liquid to the required volume, remove from the heat, whisk in the whole stick of butter, and allow to rest.

Just before plating, strain the sauce through a chinois (a conical strainer) or some cheesecloth—so you can remove all the vegetables and herbs—giving you a smooth, silky sauce fit for a king!

Now we have the hash and the sauce done; the beef is next!

FOR THE SWEET CORN AND POTATO HASH

½ cup grapeseed oil

1 large red onion, diced

2 freshly chopped garlic cloves

½ pound fresh corn kernels, about 2 ears (Do not use canned corn—it becomes gummy. Frozen fresh corn can be used, however.)

1 pound (about 4 medium) diced potatoes

Salt and pepper to taste

1 tomato (centers removed), diced

3 ounces Boursin cheese or goat cheese

¼ cup chopped fresh chives

FOR THE MERLOT REDUCTION

3 tablespoons grapeseed oil

1 tablespoon (1 to 2 cloves) chopped fresh garlic

2 finely diced shallots, or 1 white onion, finely diced

Any meat trimmings from the beef

½ 750-mL bottle of nice Merlot

½ pint (1 cup) strong beef stock or demi-glace

1 tablespoon chopped fresh thyme

1 tablespoon chopped fresh rosemary

1 stick (½ cup) unsalted butter

FOR THE BLACKENING SEASONING

½ teaspoon dried thyme

½ teaspoon dried oregano

1 tablespoon garlic powder

¼ teaspoon curry powder

1 tablespoon ground fennel seed

1 tablespoon cayenne pepper

½ teaspoon sea salt

1 tablespoon onion powder

FOR THE BEEF

Six 4-ounce beef tenderloins (filets mignon)

⅛ cup grapeseed oil

FOR THE RED CARROT AND ASPARAGUS GARNISH

⅛ cup grapeseed oil

2 tablespoons unsalted butter

12 asparagus stalks

3 red carrots, peeled and cut *lengthwise* into quarters

Six fresh sage leaves

EQUIPMENT

A 3- or 4-inch-diameter circular pastry cutter

Preheat the oven to 375 degrees.

Mix all the seasoning ingredients together; set aside and keep dry until needed.

Take the beef filets and dip just one side of the meat into the seasoning mixture.

In a heavy-bottomed, oven-safe sauté pan, add just enough oil to cover the bottom of the pan and heat on medium high heat to the smoking point. *The pan has to be hot, otherwise you will not be able to blacken the filets.*

Also, start heating a medium saucepan of water to boiling so you can blanch the asparagus and carrots.

When the sauté pan is hot, place the dipped filets coated side down, and cook for 2 to 3 minutes, or until they achieve a blackened look without being burnt (which will taste bitter). It is best to leave the filets undisturbed for the first 2 minutes (in other words . . . no peeking) to allow the seasoning to integrate into the surface of the meat and prevent it from "crusting off."

Turn the filets after the first 2 minutes or so, and when they look "blackened, not burnt," continue the searing process on the other (unseasoned) side of the filets for another 2 to 3 minutes. Using the same pan in which you blackened them, place the steaks into the preheated oven. Cook the filets a further 6 to 8 minutes in the oven (depending on the thickness of the steaks). Remember, the times given in any recipe are relative, because only you know your oven.

Whilst the steaks are cooking in the oven, blanch the asparagus and carrots in the boiling water for 1 to 2 minutes and drain.

In another sauté pan, heat the grapeseed oil for the vegetables and add the butter. Sauté the asparagus and carrots until tender (along with the sage leaves). Discard the sage leaves after cooking.

Remove the steaks from the oven and let rest. (Remember, the meat will continue to cook for another 5 minutes as it rests.

PRESENTATION

Plating is very simple. Take the potato hash (now heated and mixed with the tomatoes and cheese) and, using a 3- to 4-inch-diameter circular pastry cutter as a mold for neat edges, fill the cutter with hash in the center of each plate. Place the filet on top of each of your "circles," and lay the asparagus and carrots (2 lengths of each per plate) flat on the plate, and drizzle with the great aromatic Merlot sauce.

Bon appétit!

Chilled Grand Marnier Soufflé with Macerated Fruits

SERVES 6

This is best when allowed to set overnight.

FOR THE SOUFFLÉ

6 egg yolks

½ cup light corn syrup

1 cup sugar

¼ cup vanilla yogurt

1½ cups heavy cream

¼ cup Grand Marnier (you can purchase the 50-mL "airplane-sized" bottle)

⅛ cup freshly squeezed lemon juice (about ½ of a fresh lemon)

¼ cup cocoa powder (for dusting)

FOR THE MACERATED FRUITS

¼ cup blueberries

¼ cup sliced raspberries (slicing the raspberries initiates the maceration process by causing the berries to release their natural juices)

2 tablespoons mint

½ cup raspberry sauce (ice cream topping from a jar, optional, for a sweeter taste)

EQUIPMENT

A double boiler

A sugar thermometer (candy thermometer)

Six 4-ounce soufflé dishes

Parchment paper

An electric mixer

PREPARATION AND COOKING TIME

About 30 minutes to prepare and cook the soufflé

At least 4 hours or overnight to allow the soufflé to set in the freezer

With this method of soufflé making, there is no water-bath cooking as with soufflés that are unmolded, nor is there any fear of a hot soufflé falling! Also, it can be done as early as 2 days ahead.

Begin by lightly greasing six 4-ounce soufflé dishes with a little butter. Then, using parchment paper, cut 6 strips, each about 10 inches long by 2¼ inches wide. Place one of these into each soufflé dish, bringing the ends of each paper strip together to form a circle that "lines" the edge of each dish and protrudes at least ¾ inch above its rim. The butter will help hold these edge-liners in place. The idea is that you will be able to fill the dish with soufflé mix to a level *above the lip* of the container (the way we visualize soufflés), so that when the soufflé is set, the paper is removed for a beautiful presentation.

Combine the egg yolks, corn syrup, and ¼ cup of the sugar into a bowl, and stir over a double boiler. (Do not allow any water to splash into this bowl.)

Insert the sugar thermometer into the mix and watch it until it reaches 170 degrees. Whisk in the yogurt and remove from the heat quickly, stirring the entire time.

Transfer the mix to a large bowl that fits on the electric mixer, and whip it until it gets very thick and cool, about 5 minutes. Set aside.

Wash your mixer blades, rinse in cool water, and dry them.

In another mixer bowl, combine the heavy cream with the remaining ¾ cup sugar and the Grand Marnier, and whip with the mixer on high speed until soft peaks form. Gently fold the cooled egg mixture and lemon juice into the whipped cream slowly.

Spoon the mixture into the soufflé dishes that you have already prepared, and place in the freezer until set (at least 4 hours or overnight), similarly to hard ice cream.

To prepare the fruit, mix all the ingredients together.

PRESENTATION

To present this dish, remove from the freezer about 15 minutes before service and slide the parchment paper away whilst the soufflé is still frozen. (A butter knife can be used to smooth the vertical edge if the soufflé becomes too mussed during the removal of the parchment paper.) Top with the berry mixture and sprinkle with cocoa powder using a sieve.

A PHILOSOPHY OF CUISINE, OR WHAT I THINK ABOUT FOOD

THERE ARE THEMES THAT RUN THROUGH THESE TWO STORIES THAT HAVE meaning not only to me, because they recur over and over again in virtually every meal I have prepared, but, I think, to anybody who is interested in cooking and in cooking well.

I will start with the simple premise that food is one of the most important things in the world.

Eating is a requirement that is common to every living being on the planet, whether you are a huge Hollywood star, the Queen of England, or an evacuee stranded on a beach in South Yemen. Think of how quickly those people on that beach might have fallen into despair or disputation had they not been given a warm, sustaining meal. And how telling is it that the first stop after attaining the greatest honor that one's profession can offer, the Academy Award, is a party at which to share a drink and a bite to eat with your friends and admirers?

Food has the ability not only to nourish the body but also to inspire the soul! It can be as simple as a slice of warm bread from the oven covered in fresh creamery butter, or as sublime as a whisper of caviar on a dollop of toro tuna tartare. Getting it can be as easy as plucking a blackberry off a bush, or as difficult as delicately hand-extracting saffron threads from the heart of a crocus that does not even exist in nature and must be painstakingly cultivated by man.

The consumption of food goes far beyond mere nourishment. Sure, in the beginning, man got hungry, woman got hungry, saw berries on a bush or apples on a tree, as far back as the Garden of Eden, and ate them. The simple answer to the question "Why do we eat?" is "We eat to live." The truth behind that answer is that most of us live to eat.

The most meaningful moments of our lives, great and small, are often planned around lunches, dinners, quick bites, and sumptuous banquets. Weddings, baptisms, funerals, retirements, award ceremonies, testimonials—all are inevitably accompanied by food. Practically every romance starts with an invitation to lunch, dinner, or coffee. If you want to understand a country or a people, take a look at how they dine with one another. The great Jackie Mason once said, "When a Gentile says 'let's get coffee,' he wants a drink. When a Jew says 'coffee,' he means 'cake'!" The immortal Brillat-Savarin famously said, "Show me what you eat and I'll show you what you are."

Food has the power to bring us together with our friends, families, loved ones, and business associates, even across cultures and nationalities. What gesture is more universally acknowledged and gratefully accepted than that of sharing a meal with another human being? How much conflict might be avoided in the world if everybody simply had enough good food to eat? Where there is plenty, there is peace.

Provençal Vegetable Soup

SERVES 6 TO 8

A Note on Pistou "Pistou" sounds like, but is different from, "peace too." (Although some peace would be nice, too.) It is a basil-garlic condiment.

To make the pistou, put the garlic, basil, and Parmesan cheese in a food processor and process until smooth, scraping down the sides once. With the machine running, slowly add the olive oil through the feed tube. Or, alternatively, pound the garlic, basil, and cheese using a mortar and pestle and stir in the oil.

To make the soup, if using dried navy beans, place them in a saucepan and cover with water. Boil vigorously for 10 minutes and drain. Place the parboiled navy beans (or fresh fava beans, if using) in a saucepan with the herbes de Provence and one of the garlic cloves. Add water to cover by 1 inch. Bring to a boil, reduce the heat, and simmer over medium-low heat until tender, about 10 minutes for fresh beans and about 1 hour for dried beans. Set aside in the cooking liquid.

Heat the olive oil in a large saucepan and add the onion and leeks. Cook for 5 minutes, stirring occasionally, until the onion just softens. Add the celery, carrots, and the other garlic clove and cook, covered, for 10 minutes, stirring.

Add the potatoes, green beans, and water, then season lightly with salt and pepper. Bring to a boil, skimming any foam that rises to the surface, then reduce the heat, cover, and simmer gently for 10 minutes.

Add the zucchini, tomatoes, and peas, together with the reserved beans and their cooking liquid, and simmer for 25 to 30 minutes, or until all the vegetables are tender. Add the spinach and simmer for 5 minutes. Season the soup

FOR THE PISTOU

1 or 2 garlic cloves, finely chopped

½ cup (packed) basil leaves

4 tablespoons grated Parmesan cheese

4 tablespoons extra virgin olive oil

FOR THE SOUP

1½ cups fresh fava beans, shelled, or ¾ cup dried navy beans, soaked overnight

½ cup dried herbes de Provence

2 garlic cloves, finely chopped

1 tablespoon olive oil

1 onion, finely chopped

2 small leeks or 1 large leek, finely sliced

1 celery stalk, finely sliced

2 carrots, finely diced

2 small potatoes, finely diced

4 ounces green beans

5 cups water

Salt and freshly ground black pepper

2 small zucchini, finely chopped

3 medium tomatoes, peeled, seeded, and finely chopped

1 cup shelled garden peas, fresh or frozen

with salt and freshly ground black pepper to taste. Ladle into serving bowls and swirl a spoonful of pistou into each bowl. Garnish with basil and serve with a little grated Parmesan cheese.

A handful of spinach leaves, cut into thin ribbons

Sprigs of fresh basil to garnish

Freshly grated Parmesan cheese

A Note on Herbes de Provence Herbes de Provence are dried herbs that typically grow wild in the south of France and traditionally include lavender, thyme, sage, rosemary, and sometimes basil.

FOOD INSPIRES PASSION, AND I'M NOT JUST TALKING ABOUT APHRODISI-acs, though there exists plenty of material on that subject. Why else would food inspire so much variety, experimentation, excitement, literature, film, television, creation, conversation, and obsession? My experience at the Academy Awards illustrates this point on a number of levels. Think of all the thought, creativity, and expertise that went into the making of the food for that event. Think of the knowledge and experience that each chef brought to the design and creation of his dishes, and of their collective dedication to flawless ingredients impeccably prepared and served. The passion was reciprocated by the diners. Who among us wouldn't want to partake of some or all of the items on that menu? That kind of passion draws people in, attracts them, no matter what station in life they may occupy.

My passion for food has taken me literally all over the world, from England to the Americas, the Far East, and beyond. It has opened doors for me through which few have passed. I have cooked for once and future kings and queens, prime ministers, and presidents, for shipmates, fellow travelers, and fellow cooks. Food can transport you even if you never leave your kitchen. Isn't the taste of lasagne Bolognese, shrimp étouffée, *phad nor mai*, or tarte tatin the next best thing to being in Emilia-Romagna, New Orleans, Phuket, or Marseilles?

Food provides *pleasure*. I would say to you that eating is and always has been one of the greatest sources of pleasure for the human animal. If you find yourself in the presence of a very small child (and if someone else hasn't already beaten you to it), take a tiny spoon and give him his very first taste of vanilla ice cream. Look at that face. Case closed. Giving pleasure to someone by presenting him/her with a beautiful meal, whether it's something new, bold, and exciting or an old, comfortable favorite, is about the best instant karma I know.

Windsor Angel Food Cake

SERVES 6

With a nod to the Royal Family as well as to the exquisite maple syrups of Vermont, I present this very special angel food cake. A tiny wisp of this icing on the end of your finger can serve the same function as a tiny spoonful of vanilla ice cream for little angels.

Heat the oven to 375 degrees. Sift ¼ cup of the granulated sugar together with the sifted cake flour 3 times to aerate the mixture. Gently set aside for the moment.

In a mixer fitted with a whisk attachment, or using a hand mixer, whip the egg whites until foamy. Add the cream of tartar and salt and continue whipping until soft peaks form. With the mixer running, gradually add the remaining 1 cup granulated sugar and continue whipping until the egg whites are stiff, about 30 seconds more.

Fold the sifted sugar and cake flour mixture into the beaten egg whites. Then fold in the vanilla and maple syrup.

Spoon the batter into an ungreased 9- or 10-inch tube pan or 6 miniature ones. Smooth the top with the back of the spoon. Bake until light golden brown, 30 to 35 minutes. Cool by hanging the cake (in the pan) upside down around the neck of a bottle until it cools to room temperature. Run a long, sharp knife blade around the cake to loosen it, then knock the cake out onto a plate. The outside crumb of the cake will remain in the pan, exposing the white cake underneath.

To make the icing, stir the syrup and confectioners' sugar together until smooth, adding more maple syrup if necessary. Pour over the top of the cake and spread with a spatula, letting the glaze trickle down the sides. Let set for at least 30 minutes, or until the icing is hard, before serving. Slice with a serrated knife, using a sawing motion.

A Note on Baking Ingredients Cake flour is different from all-purpose flour. It is ground from specific grains to a specific fineness by people who know all about baking. Using such a flour for cakes will increase your chances of successfully producing the quality of cake we know as angel food.

Cream of tartar, as a substance that causes leavening, must be fresh.

A Note on Using the Real Thing: Pure Vanilla and Pure Maple Syrup Nowadays grocery stores are more apt to carry imitation vanilla extract made with artificially produced flavoring. The pancake syrup in supermarkets is often made of corn syrup and natural and artificial flavors.

Vanilla beans are obtained from vanilla orchids, which grow in Central America, Madagascar, and wild on the islands of Oceania. Vanilla beans must be cured and then tightly closed up so they will "sweat." It's an expensive process, but the result is so good.

Pure maple syrup is made from the sap of North American sugar maple trees and it takes 30 to 50 gallons of the sap to produce 1 gallon of the syrup. So it, too, is precious. And there is nothing quite like it.

You deserve to use the real thing for your Windsor Angel Food Cake.

FOR THE CAKE

1¼ cups granulated sugar (¼ cup plus 1 cup measured separately)

1⅛ cups sifted cake flour

1½ cups egg whites from about 12 eggs, at room temperature

1¼ teaspoons cream of tartar

½ teaspoon salt

1 teaspoon pure vanilla extract

3 tablespoons pure maple syrup

FOR THE ICING

½ cup pure maple syrup; more as needed

1½ cups confectioners' sugar

EQUIPMENT

A mixer

One 9- or 10-inch tube pan or 6 miniature ones

A bottle on which to hang the cake upside down. (An unopened bottle of wine works great for this because its weight is heavy enough to hold the cake in its pan, and the neck of the bottle is narrow enough to fit the tube on the cake pan. Besides, it gives you a good excuse to go out and get a bottle of wine for dinner.)

THE ATTRIBUTES YOU DEVELOP AS A GOOD COOK WILL SERVE YOU IN THE rest of your life. Every meal is a new beginning, and requires a different level of planning, organization, judgment, and skill. The French have a term that many cooks are familiar with, *mise en place*, which is a fancy way of saying: make sure you have a place for everything and that everything is in its place before you begin.

Cooking demands discipline, focus, attention to detail, and determination. Though I believe that they might occur to me if I were in their immediate presence, the names of the brave men who assisted in the cooking and distribution of the meal, and of the Marine Guard who stood sentinel on the beach that day twenty years ago at the Port of Aden, largely escape my recollection. Yet I remember most every element, texture, measurement, and technical preparation of the food, point for point. I think this might be true of many of the men and women in my profession, primarily because we are an obsessively detail-oriented lot, and as a matter of tradecraft and daily practice, narrowly and almost pathologically focused on the task at hand. Sherlock Holmes, another Englishman with a highly specialized profession, once made the point to Dr. Watson that he tried to forget most of the information he ran across in daily life that didn't pertain directly to his work, and I heartily agree. Aside from matters that attend directly to my family (I'm still pretty good at birthdays, anniversaries, and holidays), I try not to concentrate on matters that don't relate to my trade, such as politics, sport, entertainment, and stamp collecting. I'd be a lousy *Jeopardy!* contestant, but I am a *good* cook.

It is an awesome responsibility to be the cook. Ask anyone who has cooked for their children. When someone allows you to cook for them, they entrust you with their time, their fellowship, their pleasure, their good health, literally with their experience on the planet whilst they are eating what you have prepared. When they are eating your food, they are in your hands. That is why it is so difficult for me to imagine not finishing the task in both Yemen and Hollywood, because in both cases, those people were counting on me for their next meal. Some of them had just donated enormous sums of money to charity and wanted to feel as good as possible about themselves. Some had just reached the pinnacle of their career and were in the midst of an evening that they would remember for the rest of their lives; what a shame it would have been to have served them food that was forgettable. Some of them were just trying to survive until the next ship came to take them away to home and safety. They needed a hot meal to give them hope, to give them a connection to a better place and time. When you are the cook, people are counting on you to do your best. For just about everyone, the most important meal is the one sitting in front of them.

Crisp Sea Bass with Stuffed Leeks

SERVES 6

This dish might scare you at first, but the way in which you set yourself up—your mise en place—will make you feel like a seasoned professional.

If you are looking for oohs! and aahs! for a presentation, mimic the architecture of Stonehenge when you assemble this dish. (See the accompanying photograph.)

The leeks, which are about as floppy as wet noodles after steaming, become quite sturdy when they are piped full of the mashed potatoes. (And you thought Play-Doh was fun . . .) Just for the record, I come upon this influence honestly because I grew up around the corner from Stonehenge. If you think I'm kidding, look at a map to see where my hometown of Salisbury is!

3 tablespoons olive oil

2 white onions, sliced

2 leeks, white part only, sliced

2 shallots, sliced

1 red onion, sliced

2 cups white wine

3 cups vegetable stock

1 cup vegetable demi-glace
(use only enough to create a
smooth silky sauce as
described)

Salt and pepper

4 medium to large potatoes,
peeled and cut into uniform
chunks for boiling

6 leeks, white part only (2½ to
3 inches), thoroughly washed
(see Note on page 43)

½ bunch chives, finely
chopped

1 tablespoon unsalted butter

Salt and freshly ground black
pepper

In order to easily peel the cipollini onions (as listed in the ingredients for the sea bass), blanch them for 2 minutes in boiling water. Slip off the skins and remove the roots, then set aside.

For the leek and onion sauce, heat a medium sauté pan over medium heat, and in it combine the olive oil, white onions, leeks, shallots, and red onion, and sauté until translucent. (During this time you should preheat the oven at 375 degrees for the cipollini onions.) Deglaze the pan with the wine and reduce until the liquid is almost all gone. Add the stock, bring to a boil, reduce the heat, and maintain at a simmer until reduced by three-quarters. (Whilst the stock is reducing, start steaming the leeks and boiling the potatoes as described below, and place the cipollini onions with a little oil poured over them to begin roasting at 375 degrees for about 20 minutes.)

When the reduction is reduced by three-quarters (to about ¾ cup), strain through a fine-mesh sieve and set aside.

To finish this sauce, slowly whisk in the demi-glace *using only enough as you need* to create a silky sauce that coats the back of a spoon. Season with salt and pepper to taste.

To make the stuffed leeks, boil the potatoes until soft enough to mash, and steam the leeks until tender. Then mash the potatoes, whipping in the chopped chives, butter, salt, and freshly ground pepper to taste with a beater. (Whip the potatoes until they are smooth enough to flow through the pastry bag.)

Transfer the potato mixture to a pastry bag fitted with a 1-inch round tip. To remove the center part of the leeks, you will slip out the inner layers by pushing from the bottom end of each leek. (The steamed leeks will be delicate after they are steamed. In order to avoid tearing them, use the pointed end of a chopstick to gently slide out the inner layers, pushing from the bottom end upward. Leave only one or two layers to create a hollowed-out leek.) Pipe the potato mixture into each leek and set aside, keeping warm. (Check on your cipollini onions in the oven. When they are tender, remove them and set aside.)

To cook the fish, in a medium sauté pan, heat the oil over medium heat. Season the sea bass, place skin side down in the pan, and sear on both sides (2 minutes each side), then cook to desired doneness. (The fish is done when the flesh springs back upon being touched.) Remove from the heat and set aside, keeping warm.

PRESENTATION

Just before serving, rewarm the leek-and-onion reduction and add the demi-glace as described above. To serve, place a piece of sea bass on a plate, place a stuffed leek next to it, and top with a cipollini onion. Spoon some sauce around the dish and garnish with garlic chives, sliced raw leeks, and basil.

> *A Note on Cleaning Leeks* No vegetable seems to retain sand as much as a leek does. To banish the grit, you must rinse, soak, rinse, soak, and rinse and soak until you are sure no sand remains. Leeks are unwieldy because of their size, so you must persevere and keep at it until you are satisfied that you've gotten all the grit. Once you've tasted your Stuffed Leeks, you will be glad you went to all the trouble.

FOR THE SEA BASS

4 tablespoons olive oil

Six 5-ounce pieces sea bass

Salt and freshly ground black pepper

6 cipollini onions

Budding garlic chives

Thin slices of green leeks

Minced basil sprigs

EQUIPMENT

An electric mixer/beater

A pastry bag fitted with a 1-inch round tip

A chopstick

FOOD HAS POWER. BASIC CHEMISTRY TELLS US THAT FOOD COMBINES with other elements in our bodies and converts to usable energy. We use that energy to work, to think, to heal. It drives our memories and emotions, and we are also genetically programmed to use quite a bit of that energy in the search for more food. Food activates the mind and stirs the imagination, and the resulting sensations are penetrating and physiological.

Close your eyes and try to conjure up a memory of the last best meal you've had. I find myself thinking, at this moment, of a beautiful pork tenderloin that I rolled lightly in sea salt, fresh rosemary, and smoked paprika, pan-seared to a golden brown and finished in the oven, then sliced down and paired with a lovely lump crabmeat risotto to create a kind of "poor man's surf-and-turf." Just reading about this, and thinking about the succulent, juicy, slightly spicy pork playing off of the sweetness and al dente texture of the crab risotto, I can feel an immediate, physical response.

When I am hungry, I don't just jump up and grab something and shove it in my mouth. I take the time to sit quietly and think about all of the foods that I could eat, imagine how each might feel on my tongue, savor the images, decide on something delicious, then seek it out. I revel in the creative process, fully experience the peeling, slicing, baking, braising, frying, the *cooking* of it all. I sample the flavors, devour the aromas, listen to the music, the crunch, the snap, the crackle, the sizzle of it all. Then, and only then, do I feel ready to eat it. Food, at its best, is irresistible.

Cooking takes commitment, and I believe that *flavor* is at the heart of the matter. Cooking well means commitment to flavor. Dedicate yourself to finding and using the freshest ingredients, and to learning what foods are *supposed* to taste like. Compare a vine-ripened tomato's smell and texture and taste to one that's been genetically manipulated for size and an ability to be transported long distances without squishing. You will instantly know what I mean. Cook with whole, unprocessed foods whenever possible. Whether through trial and error, through absorbing techniques and recipes from more experienced cooks, or by studying books like this one, find out what works. Try growing your own herbs, even if only in a small window garden with a few select items. Experiment with new flavor combinations. Be bold. Just for instance, try drizzling a fine, aged balsamic vinegar over a cool, freshly picked and sliced peach with a little ground black pepper. It might change the way you think about fruit forever. Follow these practices over even a short period of time, and the difference to your dishes, your senses, and your health will be more dramatic than you can imagine.

And, please, *taste*. Taste everything, every step along the way as you cook. Try new things when you eat out and remember what they tasted like when you try to re-create them on your own. Cooking is a talent that can be developed and nurtured through practice and observation. The partaking of good food, especially when you are eating alone, can be meditative. Use your time alone with food to think about it, and understand it. Once you know what is good, when you can satisfy yourself, chances are others will be satisfied, too. That fine old fellow Will Shakespeare wrote, " 'Tis an ill cook who cannot lick his own fingers."

Horseradish-Crusted Salmon with Braised Endive and a Beet Reduction

SERVES 6

FOR THE SALMON

1 cup panko bread crumbs

2 teaspoons finely chopped herbs (a combination of rosemary, tarragon, and chives)

1 cup freshly grated horse-radish

2 tablespoons wasabi paste

¼ cup olive oil

2 tablespoons unsalted butter

Salt and freshly ground black pepper

Six 8-ounce portions salmon

FOR THE BRAISED ENDIVE

6 heads of Belgian endive

¼ cup olive oil

1 tablespoon sugar

Salt and freshly ground black pepper

1 tablespoon unsalted butter

¼ cup chicken stock

This is a good recipe to help you start thinking about variety. It has heat, succulence, sweetness of different kinds, a combination of textures all on one plate.

Preheat the oven to 350 degrees. Prepare the horseradish crust by mixing together the bread crumbs, herbs, horseradish, wasabi, 1 tablespoon of the olive oil, and the butter. Season to taste with salt and pepper. Set aside.

To make the braised endive, cut the endive in half and trim the core. Lightly sear the cut sides of the endive in olive oil over medium heat in an oven-safe nonstick pan. Sprinkle in the sugar, salt, pepper, and butter—cover and place in the oven, and continue to cook until soft—15 to 20 minutes. Use oven mitts to return the pan to the stovetop (the handle will be hot) and add the chicken stock. (Leave the oven on for the salmon.) Reduce the cooking liquid to a syrup and, if needed, season with salt and pepper.

To make the beet reduction, sauté the carrots, onions, and celery in the olive oil until brown. Add the thyme halfway through the process. Add the port and red wine, and reduce to a syrup. Then add the beet juice and reduce to a syrup. Strain and set aside.

Have a baking sheet ready. Season the salmon with salt and pepper. Heat the remaining 2 tablespoons olive oil in a pan and sear both sides of the salmon over high heat. Transfer the salmon to the baking sheet and press a horseradish crust into the surface of each piece. Bake the salmon until done, 5 to 7 minutes, but do not overcook. The fish is done when it springs back upon being lightly prodded. (Because of "carryover" cooking, the fish will continue to cook even after it is removed from the oven.)

Toss the raw endive and frisée with the lemon juice, olive oil, and salt and pepper. Reheat the beet reduction, remove from the heat, and whisk in the butter. Season with salt and pepper.

PRESENTATION

Place 2 halves of a braised endive on each plate and top with the cooked salmon. Drizzle the beet reduction around the salmon. Top the cooked salmon with the greens and serve.

> *A Note on Mirepoix* In French cooking, a mirepoix is used as the basis of flavor in many dishes. Classically, it is celery, carrots, and onions sautéed in butter to bring out their sweetness. In the beet reduction, we are cooking it in olive oil instead.

FOR THE BEET REDUCTION

1 cup mixed diced carrots, onions, and celery

2 tablespoons olive oil

3 thyme sprigs

½ cup port

1 cup red wine

1 cup strained red beet juice

1 stick (8 tablespoons) unsalted butter

Salt and freshly ground black pepper

FOR THE GREENS

3 small endive leaves

2 heads frisée lettuce, washed and roughly chopped

Juice of 1 lemon

2 teaspoons olive oil

Salt and freshly ground black pepper

LET YOUR CREATIVITY BE YOUR GUIDE. AS A PROFESSIONAL, I HAVE A PERsonal conceit that I never do the same dish twice. However, in thinking about it, I realize that no one ever cooks the same dish twice.

Even if you have made the same dish a thousand times, even if you follow your favorite recipe down to the minutest detail, you will never cook with the same carrot, the same onion, the same sprigs of thyme, the same splash of wine, the same cut of beef or fish, even the same spoonful of sugar or honey or flour. An experienced gardener will tell you that no crop of herbs, fruits, or vegetables is the same as the one from the year before. Variations in climate, rain, soil amendments, the weather on the day you harvest the crop, as well as the time of year you harvest, all have an impact. If the ingredients are different, how can the meal be the same? Be mindful of the ingredients in front of you; make sure they are fresh and beautiful, be attentive to their quality, be expressive in the way you prepare and combine their flavors. *Be the food.*

Let the food in front of you speak to you and inspire you. Really *look* at your family and friends when they are eating your food. Examine your own palate and thoughts and feelings when you eat. Most of all, *enjoy* your food. Do your best to make sure that whatever you make is a pleasure to eat. There are few higher callings.

SUNDAY ROASTS AND
THE WHITE RABBIT

Charming stories of Sunday dinner and a meeting with
a surprising culinary character whilst out at sea

FEATURING . . .

Robert Irvine in the Sea Cadets, tallest in back row, third from right

FOOD IS A PRISM THROUGH WHICH I VIEW THE WORLD, AND THE WORLD reflects its light back into my cuisine. When I travel, when I meet new people, when I take on a new position or challenge, when I read a book or hear a song, when I speak to other chefs and taste their food and see their approaches, when I eat something new and am impressed or depressed about it, these experiences influence, however profoundly or subtly, the very next dish I make.

Like many a cook before me, my earliest influences and attitudes about food came at my mother's knee. I grew up in working-class Salisbury, in Wiltshire, England, with my mom and dad, older brother, Gary, and younger sisters,

Colleen and Jackie, in a town that boasts the tallest cathedral spire in the country and is just a stone's throw from Stonehenge. I always thought my mother was the most beautiful woman in the world, with her long, dark hair and olive skin, like Sophia Loren. My dad, a former professional soccer player, had brown wavy hair and the hallmark leanness and keenness of a former athlete, and he was always the very expression of the staunch and steadfast Belfast Irishman. He earned his living as a painter, of houses and rooms, and my mother worked in a wallpaper shop, so between the two of them, they had us pretty "well covered."

You could say that I grew up before the Revolution. In the England of the late sixties and early seventies, there was no Food TV, no celebrity chef culture, no fascination with cookbooks or kitchen experimentation, and no gourmet food stores, and regular folks seldom ventured out of the house for dinner. This fact is easily borne out by the general and worldwide sneering opinion of the phrase "English cuisine," which has persisted up until just the last few years.

My mother, Patricia, was a typical English cook. That meant that in the span of a week, we usually ate lots of tinned and processed foods, our mains were inevitably indifferently cooked, and starches were plentiful but invariably bland unless smothered with salt or butter or English mustard. Fat was welcome; bright green color on a plate was not. Desserts were sweet puddings. I often subsisted from day to day, once I stood tall enough to reach the icebox, on boxes of cereal drowned in gallons of milk. Fresh was an adjective seldom applied to ingredients in our house. Special attention was reserved for anything that resembled or was reputed to be a vegetable. These were boiled mercilessly until pulverized, and with extreme prejudice.

But my mother was a born roaster.

Whether she chose to roast a chicken, a joint of beef, a goose, or a whole turkey, it was always *delicious*. The aromas would permeate and anoint the household as anticipation built toward the climax of its presentation at the table. The skin was crispy and perfect, the flesh tender and succulent, juicy, and bursting with flavor.

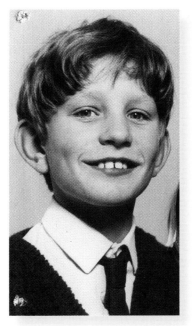

Robert as a young boy

Therein lay the redemption of the typical British cook.

I remember participating in the preparation of Sunday dinner at about age ten. Our kitchen at that time was simple, neatly tiled, small but comfy and functional. In fact, the ancient Aga range was the source of most of the heat in the house, which was not all that unusual in our neighborhood then. I can remember often scrambling out of my room in winter through utterly chilly hallways to the crispy, comforting warmth provided by that oven. My mother would dry the washing on a line by the range, and it was her practice to heat water on the stovetop for the children's baths when we were all small enough to be scrubbed in a big tin washtub on the kitchen floor.

I would help my mother "prep," often with my sisters, dressing the roast the night before. Mom would rise early Sunday morning and put it in the oven. The scents would make their way through the house, greeting me when I rolled out of my bed. My father, Patrick, would nearly always leave to play a round of golf. I would busy myself tending to the grass in the garden, or playing soccer with my friends.

The man of the house would arrive back at home at exactly 2:30, and dinner would be on the table. Mom would usually serve three or four different kinds of potatoes with dinner. My dad has an Irishman's fascination with every kind of potato imaginable. My mother's roasted potatoes were delectable and memorable. She would parboil them first, then roast them to a faultless golden brown, salty and crunchy on the outside, moist and soft on the inside. Sides would include mashed carrots or peas, Brussels sprouts, turnips, or parsnips, cooked to death. You had to eat them to get to your dessert, and the price was well worth paying. Treacle custard, spotted dick, or steamed pudding might be on the menu, all excellent.

Mom plated each of our dinners and served us individually. Our plates were piled high and we feasted. Those meals remain some of the most satisfying in my memory. I was a kid who ate as much good food as I could get my hands on, but I always left room for dessert. On that score, I usually managed to grab my father's dessert as well. The man simply overestimated his capacity for potatoes and ran out of room.

A PERFECT SUNDAY DINNER AT THE IRVINES'

THE SUNDAY DINNER IN ENGLAND IS MORE THAN JUST FOOD; IT'S A TIME when families sit and dine together. It's the end of the week, and the whole dinner turns into a ceremony. It is the weekly celebration of an Englishman's house as his castle. Sunday dinner means as much to an Englishman as does Mass to a Catholic.

A great Sunday lunch might consist of an appetizer, like shrimp cocktail, followed by roast beef and yorkshire pudding, and normally finish with a dessert like a banana bread and butter pudding.

Here is one way to create a fabulous "English-style" Sunday dinner.

Sunday Roast Beef

SERVES 6

FOR THE ROAST

6 pounds sirloin roast (top round or bottom round will do as well; make sure the meat has some fat on it, which will help with self-basting)

2 tablespoons flour

2 tablespoons stone-ground mustard

¼ cup canola oil or grapeseed oil

Sea salt or kosher salt

Freshly ground black pepper

2 carrots, washed but not peeled, roughly chopped

2 medium onions, peeled and roughly chopped

2 celery stalks, washed and roughly chopped

4 bay leaves

FOR THE YORKSHIRE PUDDING

1 cup all-purpose flour

¼ teaspoon salt

2 medium eggs

1 pint whole milk

Canola oil

Freshly ground black pepper

The first thing you need to do is preheat the oven to 425 degrees.

Wash the beef to remove any unwanted smells, and pat it dry with paper towels.

Mix the flour, mustard, and oil together, and coat the beef with the mixture. Season with salt and pepper pretty heavily, which helps the flavor when cooking.

In a roasting pan, place the chopped carrots, onions, celery, and bay leaves, then sit the beef on top of the chopped vegetables.

Place the pan in the preheated oven and cook for the first 20 minutes at 425 degrees, then reduce the temperature to 325 degrees until the roast is cooked. (A good rule of thumb is to cook the meat for 10 to 15 minutes per pound. When using a meat thermometer—which every cook should have—the internal temperature should be 115 degrees.)

When the roast is cooked to your liking, remove it from the roasting pan and let it rest for 20 to 30 minutes under tented aluminum foil prior to carving. Make sure you reserve the juices for the gravy later, and remove the bay leaf.

Once the roast is in, it's time to make the Yorkshire pudding:

To make the Yorkshire pudding, sift the flour and salt into a bowl, add the eggs, and then slowly incorporate the milk, being careful to add the milk slowly, as each batch of flour is different and some flour may absorb more milk than others. (You want the mixture to be smooth, but not runny.) Whisk into a smooth batter and let rest for 30 minutes in the refrigerator.

Take a muffin tin and place some oil in each mold (about ¼ inch in each); place the tin in the oven for 2 to 3 minutes until the oil smokes. Add the batter into each mold (two-thirds to three-quarters full) and return to the 325-degree oven to cook for 15 to 20 minutes until they have risen and are golden brown. You want them to be hard when you remove them from the oven.

The Sunday roast is often accompanied by roasted or mashed potatoes and any number of side dishes. The following are a couple of my favorites.

Sunday Roast Dinner *(clockwise from lower left)*: Hassleback Potatoes, Carrots and Rutabaga, Roast Beef, and Yorkshire Pudding, served with mashed potatoes and Brussels sprouts

Margate Shrimp Cocktail

SERVES 6

1 cup mayonnaise

½ cup tomato ketchup

Juice of 1 lemon

1 pound small cooked shrimp (larger shrimp can be used, if you prefer)

Salt and pepper

⅛ cup brandy (optional)

1 head iceberg lettuce, finely shredded

1 red onion, finely diced

2 large tomatoes (insides removed), diced

2 hard-boiled eggs, chopped

2 tablespoons chopped chives or parsley, for garnish

Cayenne pepper

With most shrimp cocktails, one suffers a letdown when all the shrimp is eaten. Not so with this one. By the time the shrimp is gone, the dressing has had a chance to trickle down into the serving glass to infuse the remaining ingredients with its flavor, now enhanced with a fresh seafood essence by having coated the shrimp. This is a savory treat from top to bottom.

Mix together the mayonnaise, ketchup, and lemon juice. Add the shrimp and adjust the seasoning with salt and pepper as needed (be careful with the salt; there's already some in the ketchup and mayonnaise). If you choose, add the brandy at this time. Set aside in the refrigerator.

Using a stemmed wineglass, place enough lettuce in the glass to fill it halfway, then add the red onion, tomatoes, and chopped eggs.

Take the prepared shrimp mixture and cover the lettuce in the glass; sprinkle with chopped parsley or chives and cayenne.

Serve with a crisp white wine, a Pinot Grigio or something not too sweet.

Hassleback Herbed Roasted Potatoes

SERVES 6

> Since my father is Irish, my mother would always make extra potatoes because he loved them. This recipe can be halved, if you want.

2 pounds medium potatoes (your choice of type)

1½ tablespoons flour

Salt and freshly ground black pepper

⅓ cup grapeseed oil

¼ cup very finely chopped herbs (sage, parsley, or tarragon)

PHASE 1: BOILING

Peel the potatoes and rinse to remove any traces of dirt.

Cut the potatoes into uniform pieces. (It will reduce the cooking time if they are all of a similar size.)

With a sharp knife and beginning on one end, cut about two-thirds through the potato. Repeat the same incision from one end of the potato to the other, spacing the cuts uniformly. (The idea is to create the look of a fan, which is why you don't cut all the way through the potato.)

Place the potatoes in a large saucepan and cover with water. Add a pinch of salt and cook until just tender. (Do not overcook. The potatoes should remain a little hard, as they will continue to cook during roasting.)

PHASE 2: ROASTING

Preheat the oven to 400 degrees.

Drain the potatoes and place them on an absorbent towel to remove excess water. Mix the flour and salt and pepper to taste in a bowl, and carefully toss with the already blanched potatoes.

Spread the oil onto a baking sheet and roll the floured potatoes in the oil, coating them evenly.

Bake until golden brown, 30 to 40 minutes.

To finish, scoop the potatoes with a slotted spoon onto absorbent paper towels to drain off any excess oil. Then immediately sprinkle with the fresh herb mixture and transfer to your favorite serving bowl.

Serve these magnificent potatoes with your great Sunday roast.

Potato Pie

SERVES 6

4 large Idaho potatoes

1 small onion, sliced

1 garlic clove, chopped

2 tablespoons chopped
fresh parsley

Fine sea salt and freshly
ground black pepper

1 package (17.25 ounces) of
puff pastry

¼ cup all-purpose flour, for
dusting work surface

1 egg yolk, beaten with 1
tablespoon water to make an
egg wash

1½ cups heavy cream or
crème fraîche

EQUIPMENT

An 11-inch metallic pie dish

If your dad is Irish and as obsessed as mine with this tuber, you may need more ways to serve potatoes as a backup plan. This cannot miss; it's potatoes and cream sauce in a puff-pastry crust. There's something of the barony about it.

To prepare the potatoes, peel the potatoes and slice them into ⅛-inch rounds, preferably on a mandoline. Put them in a large bowl and add the onion, garlic, and parsley. Season generously with salt and pepper to taste and set aside.

Preheat the oven to 375 degrees.

Shape 1 sheet of the puff pastry to an 11-inch metallic pie dish. Add the potatoes. Cut around the perimeter of the pie dish, removing the excess pastry but leaving about 1 inch of dough hanging over the side. Discard the scrap pastry and fold the portion hanging over the side back over so that it encloses the potatoes. Brush the upward-facing dough with egg wash. Place another sheet of puff pastry on top of the pie dish and cut it so it conforms to the top of the pie dish. Brush the top with egg wash.

Put the dish on a baking sheet on the oven's center rack and bake until cooked through (a sharp, thin-bladed knife inserted in the center will come out hot), 45 to 50 minutes. Remove the dish from the oven and cut around the perimeter of the top, removing the pastry from the top. Set the pastry cover aside. Pour the cream into the pie and jiggle the potatoes with a spoon to let the cream seep into the deepest part of the pie. Season with salt and pepper to taste, return the cover, and let the cream infuse for 15 to 20 minutes, covered with a clean, dry cloth.

To serve, present the pie in its dish in the center of the table.

Carrots and Rutabaga

SERVES 6

My mother does a lovely job on this mash and it is to this day one of my favorite dishes.

Boil the carrots and rutabaga together until just soft. Drain and add the butter. Smash both together using either a potato masher or a food processor until the mixture looks like a puree. Season with lots of pepper and a little salt to taste. That's it! (They're not all this easy.)

1 pound carrots, chopped

1 pound rutabaga, peeled and chopped

¼ stick (2 tablespoons) unsalted butter

Salt and pepper

Parmesan Peas

SERVES 6

1 pound fresh-frozen English
green peas

¼ cup canola oil

2 large shallots, diced

1 cup heavy cream

½ cup grated Parmesan
cheese

¼ cup chopped fresh mint
(optional)

In a large saucepan, cook the frozen peas in water until they are tender without losing their bright green color, 3 to 5 minutes. Strain and rinse the peas under cold water, and set them aside.

In a large sauté pan, add the oil and shallots on medium heat and cook the shallots until they are transparent and tender, about 5 minutes. Add the cooked peas and warm through, then add the heavy cream and Parmesan cheese, and continue to cook until all of the cheese has been incorporated. Adjust the seasoning just before serving and, if you like, sprinkle with chopped fresh mint.

Banana Bread and Butter Pudding

SERVES 6

Thanks to my dad's potato gluttony, I usually got extra of this dessert as a kid, if I was quick enough to grab his serving before my siblings did!

⅔ cup unsalted butter, softened

1 fresh vanilla pod

2 cups heavy cream

12 slices white bread (you can also use leftover coffee cake as a substitute)

2 to 3 bananas, sliced

⅔ cup raisins

6 eggs

4 tablespoons sugar

Using a little of the softened butter, grease an ovenproof baking dish.

Slit the vanilla pod lengthways in the middle and remove all of the seeds by scraping the inside of the pod with a paring knife. Put the seeds and the pod itself into a saucepan with the heavy cream and bring to a boil, then set aside for about 20 minutes to allow the vanilla to infuse.

Take the remainder of the softened butter and spread it on each slice of bread on both sides. Cut each slice of bread diagonally, so that you are now left with two triangles for each single slice.

Preheat the oven to 350 degrees.

In layers, first arrange some of the buttered bread in the ovenproof dish and top with slices of banana and a sprinkle of raisins for each layer, reserving 1 tablespoon for the top. Continue to layer the bread and bananas until you have used them all.

Whisk together the eggs and the sugar in a bowl, then pour the warmed vanilla cream over the eggs, whisking constantly (because you don't want scrambled eggs!).

Then pour the mixture through a sieve over the bread and top with the remaining raisins. Place the ovenproof dish in a larger, deep roasting pan. Pour hot water into the roasting pan until the water comes halfway up the outside of the ovenproof dish.

Cook for 35 to 40 minutes, or until the blade of a knife inserted into the center of the pudding comes out clean.

Serve topped with a scoop of any type of ice cream you like!

LEFTOVERS

conflict, just in the beginning, but a happy ending, and I think it's one of the most interesting and romantic stories I know.

You would never know it if you met them today, but when I was very much younger, my parents actually legally divorced. I don't know what the issues were, and have never asked even as an adult, because I believe that they wish to keep it private. I was just a little scrapper, about six, when my mother gently pulled me aside and gave me the talk so many kids have heard: "Your daddy has to go away for a while; Mummy and Daddy can't live together right now . . ." I can't claim to have really understood what was going on, but out of the house Dad went. Dinners were still served at the same time, at the end of his working day, as if he'd be coming in the door any minute, but his chair remained stubbornly unfilled. Too many potatoes remained in the serving dishes, depressingly uneaten. It was surely an empty feeling.

My dad owned a maroon Vauxhall Victor at the time. It was a spacious mode of automotive transport, especially for England in the day, broad in the beam with a sweeping panoramic windscreen. This one was well worn and had been through the mill a time or two; it reminded me of a Dalmatian, it had so

The four Irvine children: Robert, Colleen, Gary, and Jackie

many different colors of purple speckled all over it. Well, week one after his leave-taking, didn't I wake up in the morning and immediately notice my dad sitting in his Vauxhall across the street from the house, like a cop on a stakeout? Every day, on our way to and from school, he was stationed there to make sure all was as it should be, and to let us know he was still on the job. He was sticking to the letter of the divorce agreement, I suppose, by staying out of the house, but he pursued his one-man conspiracy with cool determination. Looking back, I think my mom must have known what he was about and was tacitly approving, since she graciously let him get away with it for so long.

In spirit, it made a huge difference, especially to me, to know that he was never far from me. I looked for that car everywhere I went, and to this day I remember the license number: BYA177J. I didn't know where he was staying, but if I ever really needed to talk to him, about school or whatever, I would make my way down the pub and perch beside him where he sat at his Saturday post at the Plough, quietly sipping and chatting, and waiting it all out, seemingly.

About six weeks past the divorce, with, I promise you, no explanation whatsoever, my dad moved back into our house, and as far as I have ever been able to tell, life went on as before, ranging from the normal, tiny, reassuring domestic squabbles to the blissfully happy union of a well-married couple.

And every Sunday since then, after dinner during the washing up, my father asks my mother to marry him again and she always says no.

They have been together in total for close on to fifty years. They are supremely well matched, and I know that the ties that bind are many and run deep, but I have to think that the attraction of a good English Sunday dinner must at least have something to do with it.

Here's a classic use for leftovers from your Sunday dinner, called bubble and squeak. It is an "Olde English Favourite." Some say that its name comes from the sound your tummy makes after you've eaten it; I believe that it was named because of the noises it makes in the pan when you cook it. This dish is traditionally made with leftovers from the big Sunday meal, filled out with inexpensive green cabbage. The main ingredients are potato and cabbage, but I have added carrots, peas, Brussels sprouts, even breakfast sausage. If I want to serve it along with leftover meat, be it beef, chicken, ham, or turkey, I always serve it on the side, so that the bubble and squeak is hot and the meat is cold. This is a *great* summer dish. Be sure there is a proper, stiff-necked English mustard on the table at all times, along with a jarred chutney or a Branston pickle, and don't forget to open a nice, cold beer.

Bubble and Squeak

SERVES 4 TO 6

MADE WITH LEFTOVERS

1 tablespoon cooking oil, for the pan

Leftover boiled or mashed potatoes

Boiled cabbage

Boiled carrots

Roasted Brussels sprouts

1 small onion, red or white, diced

Salt and pepper

1 tablespoon Tabasco sauce or 1 finely diced jalapeno pepper for heat (optional)

MADE FROM SCRATCH

6 medium Idaho potatoes (or any potato you prefer), peeled

1 small head white cabbage, cut into wedges

¼ cup vegetable oil

1 pound sausage (English bangers, or any breakfast sausage you prefer), chopped

2 carrots, diced

2 red onions, diced

Salt and freshly ground black pepper

1 tablespoon Tabasco sauce or 1 fresh, finely diced jalapeño for heat (optional)

¼ cup chopped chives

METHOD FOR LEFTOVERS

Add the oil to a cast-iron skillet or a shallow frying pan and heat until it begins smoking. In a large mixing bowl, combine all of the other ingredients and stir until you have a nice, lumpy mixture. Season lightly with salt and pepper to taste. You can add the Tabasco sauce or jalapeño for heat.

Place the mixture in the hot skillet and cook for 5 to 10 minutes, making sure to stir so that all of the ingredients are warmed. To serve, dollop onto the plate with a big wooden spoon.

METHOD FROM SCRATCH

One hour before serving, boil the potatoes and cabbage until tender, about 25 minutes, then drain off the excess liquid and set them aside.

In a sauté pan, heat the oil until hot (but not smoking). Cook the sausage for about 20 minutes, lower the heat to medium, and then add the carrots and onions, cooking until the vegetables are tender, about 10 minutes.

At this point, add the potatoes and cabbage to the pan with the other ingredients, and continue to cook for 5 to 10 minutes more. Season with salt and pepper to taste. At this point, if you choose, you can add Tabasco or jalapeño.

The mixture should be getting a golden brown as you turn it, which is what you want for both flavor and texture. Finish the dish by adding chopped chives as a garnish.

THE BIG, WHITE RABBIT

WHEN I BEGAN TO SEE AND TASTE MORE OF THE WORLD OUTSIDE OF MY home and little town, I realized that there was a world of food to be explored. At first, I suppose I was just hungry and always pleased to find something to eat outside my everyday experience that actually tasted good. As I look back, though, I can see that in the important choices in my life, many of which changed me forever, I often used food as the springboard. It occurs to me that there is a question to be answered in this musing, as to whether we are drawn to the people and things in our lives that change us, or whether we draw them to us by concentrating on them. I'll have to chew that one over for a while and get back to it later.

I'm not sure why to this day, but my wanderings began at an early age and often led to open waters. When I was about eleven years old and near the beginning of my stint as a Sea Cadet, I had the opportunity to sail aboard the SS *Uganda*, an old-fashioned, classical cruise ship that had been converted from the tourism service to a floating "School to Work" program. It was a place where kids from all over the British Isles could meet, see another side of life outside of their comfortable home waters, and keep up with their school lessons at the same time. It was to be my first time on an extended trip away from home, sleeping and sailing on a real ship on the swelling seas, and it felt like an adventure waiting to happen before I even stepped out my front door.

It was on the *Uganda* that I had an epiphany, and met a sort of big, white rabbit that led me down a hole, or into a kitchen, into a world that I have been exploring ever since. The "big, white rabbit" was a chef named Robert Roper.

Robert Roper was a burly man who paraded past us in chef's whites wearing the big, poofy white chef's hat that made you an immediate target of laughter for preteenaged boys. Now, it may come as a shock to you, but at certain times in my youth, I could come off as a bit of an obnoxious show-off, though in my own defense and opinion, a talented one. I focused on the chef like a laser beam, and had a pretty fair imitation of him worked up in about two seconds. I did the voice, the scowl, and the classic "sneak up behind him and walk like him 'til he turns around and chases you" routine. For about fifteen minutes, I had him on the run. Then the tables suddenly turned. He stalked up behind me and slapped a big metal spoon down on the table in front of me, good and hard and loud. "If you think it's so easy, *big mouth*, and you can do better, then come and show me," he snarled. After the initial shock and affront of being called "big mouth" in front of my adoring fans, I followed him into the kitchen, and that ended up being "it" for me. Looking back, I think I was behaving in much the same fashion as a schoolboy with a crush on a pretty girl. I jumped about, made fun, demanded in no uncertain terms to be noticed, no matter what, until the man had no choice but to confront me. Secretly, unbeknownst even to me, I wanted to meet him and find out what he was up to back there.

At 6:30 the next morning, I reported to Third Chef Roper in the galley of the *Uganda*. He provided me with my first chef's jacket, pants, apron, and hat, and gave me my first task in the kitchen: preparing meat platters for lunch. I set to it with enthusiasm, not only because I was excited and intrigued to be behind the scenes but because it seemed I'd also neatly negotiated my way out of my school chores for the time remaining in the voyage, in exchange for "work study" in the kitchen.

This was everything I'd dreamed life on board a ship would be. Rather than being trapped in classes all day long, I rolled out of my bunk every morning with a *purpose*: to feed my shipmates. In my mind, I couldn't imagine how the chefs had ever gotten the job done without me.

Bob let me travel from station to station and learn. Under his watchful eye, I chopped onions and peeled potatoes, prepared cold cuts for lunch platters, learned how to roll out the dough for rolls and biscuits. I hauled food in and out of the walk-in refrigerators, wiped down the counters, swabbed the floors, and even learned how to make a couple of basic sauces. It was glorious. I was quickly adopted by the kitchen crew, an imposing collection of galley cooks, of pirates and old sea salts with fantastic stories to tell on breaks. The best part of my day was listening to them lie and laugh about times long past whilst I took pulls on one of their cans of cold Victoria Bitter.

After two weeks of hard, sweaty, satisfying work, I returned home on the train. Stuffed in my traveling bag among the dirty laundry were treasures. I had managed to get my hands on duty-free cigarettes for my mom and spirits for Dad, but most importantly, Bob Roper had sent me home with my chef's jacket and kit and my own set of kitchen knives. His parting words were plain and simple: "Enjoy 'em." My mom naturally inquired if I'd had a good time, and the stories came out of me in a rush. I produced my new clothes and ran up to my room to put them on, so she could get the full effect. I appeared in the front hallway just as Dad was coming in the door.

"What's all this, then?"

He had a quizzical look on his face, happy to see me home but clearly wondering what the getup was all about. It's a look that all good fathers acquire, that lasts from the birth of their children to their entrance into the pearly gates: a mixture of curiosity, fatigue, and pleasure, with a touch of "This isn't going to cost me too much, is it?"

I answered proudly, "I got it on the boat, Dad. I'm gonna be a cook!"

His reaction was the same as if I'd been standing there in scuba gear and announced that I was going to be a frogman, or in crown and scepter and announced I was going to be the king of Spain. He took it in stride, as do most parents of eleven-year-olds when they hear about a new career direction.

He has supported me, though, all this time, eating my early experiments and taking me from a young age to see friends who owned restaurants. I remember being allowed to watch a real brigade system in action for the first time in the kitchen at Crane's, a little family place on Crane Street, when my father told his friend, "My son wants to be a chef." He also worked to keep me on the straight and narrow as much as possible. There's still a part of me that is convinced that he would have been more pleased had I followed in his footsteps and tried for professional soccer, but I think the "cooking thing" has worked out better than either one of us could have imagined.

After my stint on the *Uganda*, I had food on my mind a lot, and was constantly on the lookout for information and new experiences. I started to collect cookbooks from secondhand shops. I started experimenting by creating dishes at home for the family, which they gamely sampled whenever offered. I often traveled down the road to our Australian neighbors', John and Wendy Waddington, who owned a favorite local pub called the George and Dragon. They let me work in the kitchen from time to time, and I mastered the art of toad-in-the-hole, fish and chips, and steak and kidney pie.

By the same token, my scholastic performance was underwhelming, to put it kindly, except in home economics, a subject that I pretty much took to on a dare and to meet girls. There was a thirty-to-one ratio of female to male in the class, me being the one, and the class turned out to be another early indicator of my life's work. I found it easy to complete the assigned cooking tasks, and spent the rest of my time helping out the young ladies with theirs; a good time was had by all. The rest of my marks were substandard, due to a lack of motivation and a general irritation with just about everything that had to do with my schooling.

I was always a highly competitive kid, and the fact that I was unsuccessful and unfocused in class fueled my frustration. My sisters were good students, and my brother, Gary, was exceptional academically. I liked sports, and I was good at soccer, swimming, and rugby. At school, I was cheeky to my instructors, I played truant, and it was only when a man named David Bodfish, an adviser and mentor at my school, figured out that I was bored and unchallenged and helped to put me right that I started to get on track, at least in terms of my outlook. He was the one teacher who would prefer actually to set me down and talk rather than to chastise me. It was through David that I learned that everyone in authority wasn't necessarily out to get me. I will always be grateful for his influence.

On weekends, as a kid, it seemed as if my dad, a former military man himself, was always taking the family to some sort of naval installation for tours and souvenirs, usually in Poole or Hamworthy in Dorset. These were always fun outings, with lots of fresh air and neat things to see. My father often had a drink and darts with a friend and retired chief in the Navy named Harold Steadman, who introduced me to the Sea Cadets. The Sea Cadets were an English combination of the Boy Scouts and the Navy ROTC. I was soon going to meetings every Monday and Thursday, learning basic seamanship, rowing, running cross-country, performing color guard drills, and having a bash with guys my own age. We would often go away from home on weekends to camp and sail. We would board the HMS *Salisbury,* voyage out and back, and do our level best to act like the world's greatest sailors. At every chance, I still gravitated toward the kitchen, toward the chefs. I would sail by day and cook by night, and I knew I could always cop a free beer back with the cooks.

Soon, joining the Royal Navy just seemed like a natural progression. My dad was ex-Army, so that might have been his preference for me, but all in all, the military seemed like a good option, since nuclear physics was probably not in the cards for me, given my grades at school.

My father accompanied me down to the recruitment office when I was fifteen and we had a chat with the officer in charge. He liked my background in the Sea Cadets, and we all agreed that the Navy seemed like a good bet for yours truly, so I took the test. The test wasn't much different from most of the tests I hated taking at school, with some posers that basically called for common sense thrown in for good measure. Unlike in the adverts for the military today, there was no questioning about a career track, as in "Would you like to go in for submarine captain or test pilot?" anything like that. I certainly was never offered the chance to tell them about my hobbies, interests, or ambitions. They did, however, want to get an idea of what I might be good at, so they could best decide how they could put me to work.

A couple of days later, my results came back. The Navy was clearly not impressed, and had a fate in store for me that they reserved for those recruits whose aptitude scores fell as monumentally short of rocket science as mine had. I had done well enough to get in, was proclaimed physically fit, but my scores in math and English were as far below the mark as I had managed to keep them at school, with my resolute determination to ignore instruction and to never study.

Based on my testing, their recommendation for the best way for me to spend my time in the Navy was stated in a single word: "Cook."

Ironically, it's one of the few words in the English language that is both a job description and a call to action. You are now a cook, my son . . . so cook. And so it went. Once I was in the service, I was required to bring up my scores in those "school" subjects. I took remedial classes while I trained, and I bloody well studied this time around. My attitude having now been severely readjusted, and having finally recognized that those grades could and would have a real impact on my life, I applied myself academically and aced them all.

And that's when I really started to cook.

I certainly benefit from the cumulative influence of my personal biases and of knowledge gained from having spent most of my life in professional kitchens. You learn to speak the language of food with an accent, and just like the accent of your birth and rearing, it is an accumulation of your thoughts, your upbringing, what you hear, what you see, what you select or neglect to say, that is apparent to the outside world. With some chefs, you can see where they are coming from before you ever meet them, just by looking at what they choose to put on a plate and how they decide to do it.

The style in which you choose to cook is unique to you—it is your culinary fingerprint—and you should learn to celebrate it. If you do, others will enthusiastically join you. Art, music, nature, vacations, relationships, weather, all these things influence our attitudes and moods and, therefore, our cooking. Paul Bocuse compared cooking to music, in that the finished dish and the performance depend on an element of improvisation, which are never part of the recipe or score. When this goes right, the results are magical.

Here are a few "classic" dishes that I have chosen to do in my own singular style because of some of the influences in my life. Once you've made them your own, you will probably do them a little differently, too.

Cooking is an expression of what's inside of you. It's the magic that matters.

French Onion Soup

SERVES 6 TO 8

1 tablespoon butter

2 tablespoons olive oil

4 large onions (about 1½ pounds), thinly sliced

2 to 4 garlic cloves, finely chopped

1 teaspoon sugar

½ teaspoon dried thyme

½ cup dry white wine

2 tablespoons flour

8 cups chicken or beef broth

2 tablespoons brandy (optional)

Salt and freshly ground black pepper

6 to 8 thick slices French bread, toasted

1 garlic clove

12 to 16 ounces Swiss cheese, grated

EQUIPMENT

6 individual ovenproof crocks

In a large, heavy saucepan, heat the butter and oil over medium-high heat. Add the onions and cook for 10 to 12 minutes until they are softened and beginning to brown. Add the garlic, sugar, and thyme, and continue cooking over medium heat for 30 to 35 minutes until the onions are well browned, stirring frequently. Add the flour as a thickener. Pour in the white wine to deglaze the pan. Add the broth, brandy, if you desire, and salt and pepper to taste. Bring to a gentle boil, reduce the heat, and then simmer for 25 minutes.

Turn on the broiler in the oven. Smash the garlic clove and rub on the inside of each of the oven-safe crocks. Spoon the soup into the crocks. Lay a slice of toasted bread on the surface of each bowl of soup, then sprinkle 2 ounces of grated cheese on top of each slice. Melt and brown the cheese under the broiler. Serve immediately.

Maryland Crab Cakes with Mango Salsa

MAKES 4 CRAB CAKES

Attention crab cake aficionados! You can make your own, and they will be as good or better than those you've eaten in your search for the perfect crab cake. The finish on this mango salsa is a treat for your taste buds.

In a mixing bowl, combine all the salsa ingredients and let the salsa sit in the refrigerator to chill.

Preheat the oven to 325 degrees.

In a bowl, mix together all the crab cake ingredients except the crabmeat and bread crumbs, then add the crabmeat and the crumbs. Try not to break down the lump crabmeat; leave it in chunks. Form the crab mixture into 3½- to 4-ounce cakes. Place a sauté pan on the stove to get hot and pour 2 to 3 ounces canola oil in the pan. Place the crab cakes into the pan; brown on both sides, turning carefully. Transfer the crab cakes to a cookie sheet and place in the preheated oven. Bake for 8 to 10 minutes.

PRESENTATION

Place a crab cake in the center of each plate. Top with a lemon wedge. The mango salsa should be spooned to one side of the plate, with two strands of whole chives on the other side.

FOR THE MANGO SALSA

1 mango, diced small

2 teaspoons diced red onion

2 teaspoons diced red bell pepper

2 teaspoons diced green bell pepper

1 teaspoon chopped chives (save 8 strands or so for plating)

Juice of 1 lemon

1½ teaspoon honey

1 teaspoon rice wine vinegar

Salt and pepper to taste

FOR THE CRAB CAKES

2 teaspoons whole-grain Dijon mustard

2 teaspoons Old Bay seasoning

2 teaspoons chopped fresh parsley

2 teaspoons chopped fresh chives

2 egg yolks

Juice of 1 lemon

1 cup mayonnaise

Salt and pepper

1 pound jumbo lump crabmeat

1 cup fresh bread crumbs (no crust)

Canola oil, for browning

4 lemon wedges

Lemon Meringue Pie

SERVES 6

To make the crust, sift the flour and salt into a bowl. Add the shortening and cut in with a pastry blender until the mixture resembles coarse crumbs. With a fork, spoon in just enough ice water to bind the dough. Gather the dough into a ball.

On a lightly floured surface, roll out the dough about ⅛ inch thick. Transfer to a 9-inch pie pan and trim the edge to leave a ½-inch overhang.

Fold the overhang under and crimp the edge. Refrigerate the pie shell for at least 20 minutes.

Preheat the oven to 400 degrees.

Prick the dough all over with a fork to prevent bubbling up of the empty crust. Line with crumpled wax paper and fill with pie weights or dried beans (referred to as "blind baking"). Bake for 12 minutes. Remove the paper and weights or beans, and continue baking until golden, 6 to 8 minutes more, to dry out the base.

To make the pie filling, in a saucepan, combine the lemon zest and juice, 1 cup of the cold water, ½ cup sugar, and the butter. Bring the mixture to a boil over low heat.

Meanwhile, in a mixing bowl, dissolve the cornstarch in the remaining 1 tablespoon cold water. Add the 3 egg yolks and combine.

Add the egg yolk mixture to the lemon mixture on the stove and return to a boil, whisking continuously until the mixture thickens (you don't want scrambled eggs), about 5 minutes.

Cover the surface of the lemon filling with wax paper to prevent a skin from forming and let cool.

To make the meringue, using an electric mixer, beat the 3 egg whites with the salt and cream of tartar until they hold stiff peaks. Add the remaining 6 tablespoons sugar and beat until glossy.

Spoon the lemon mixture into the pie shell and spread it level. Spoon the meringue on top, smoothing it up to the edge of the crust to seal. Bake until golden, 12 to 15 minutes.

A Note on an Effective Modern Convenience Many competent home cooks prepare pastry dough in a food processor equipped with a dough blade with excellent results. To do so, put the sifted flour, salt, and shortening into the processor bowl and pulse while drizzling the ice water sparingly through the processor tube into the flour mixture until the dough comes together. This method has the advantage of reducing your likelihood of overworking the dough.

FOR THE PIECRUST

1 cup flour

½ teaspoon salt

⅓ cup (5⅓ tablespoons) cold shortening, cut into pieces

2 tablespoons ice water (have a glass of ice water handy)

FOR THE PIE FILLING

Grated zest and juice of 1 large lemon

1 cup plus 1 tablespoon cold water

½ cup plus 6 tablespoons sugar

2 tablespoons unsalted butter

3 tablespoons cornstarch

3 eggs, separated

⅛ teaspoon salt

⅛ teaspoon cream of tartar

Shrimp Bisque

SERVES 6 TO 8

1½ pounds small or medium cooked shrimp, in the shell

1½ tablespoons vegetable oil

2 onions, halved and sliced

1 large carrot, sliced

2 celery stalks, sliced

8 cups water

A few drops of lemon juice

2 tablespoons tomato paste

Bouquet garni

4 tablespoons butter

⅓ cup flour

3 to 4 tablespoons brandy

Salt and white pepper

⅔ cup heavy cream

This is a great soup based on a classic thickening method that you can play with in any number of ways. If you happen to be cooking in the military, you can easily adjust it to serve six to eight hundred.

Remove the heads from the shrimp and peel away the shells, reserving the heads and shells for the stock.

Heat the oil in a large saucepan, and cook the peeled shrimp just until they begin to turn pink, then remove them to a utility platter and chill in the refrigerator. Add the shrimp heads and shells to the same pan, and cook over high heat, stirring frequently, until they start to brown. Reduce the heat to medium, add the onions, carrot, and celery, and fry gently, stirring occasionally, for about 5 minutes until the onions start to soften.

Add the water, lemon juice, tomato paste, and bouquet garni. Bring the broth to a boil, then reduce the heat, cover, and simmer gently for 25 minutes. Strain the broth through a sieve.

Melt the butter in a heavy saucepan over medium heat. Stir in the flour to make a roux, and cook until just golden, stirring occasionally. Add the brandy and gradually pour in about half of the shrimp broth, whisking vigorously until smooth, then whisk in the remaining liquid. Season with salt, if necessary, and white pepper. Reduce the heat, cover, and simmer for 5 minutes, stirring frequently.

Strain the soup into a clean saucepan and add the cream. Then stir in most of the shrimp (reserving a few for garnish) and cook over medium heat, stirring frequently, until hot. Serve at once, garnished with the reserved shrimp and a little extra lemon juice on the surface of the soup.

A Note on the Bouquet Garni A bouquet garni is . . . well . . . a bouquet! Really you can put any herbs that complement your recipe into a bouquet garni. But classically it is a small bunch of parsley (or parsley stems), about 8 sprigs of fresh thyme, and a bay leaf wrapped in, or tied together with, a thoroughly washed leek leaf and/or celery "strings." Of course it can be tied with clean cotton string as well, which provides a means of anchoring it to the handle of the pot. (Be sure the string is clear of any flame.) The purpose of the bouquet garni is to keep the herbs out of the way when you have to skim the surface of a pot of soup, or to make it easy to remove the herbs when you are finished with them.

Many people also think of the bouquet garni as being wrapped in cheese-cloth (or contained in one of those small drawstring bags available in stores). However, technically, at that point it becomes a *sachet d'épices*.

3

A COURSE IN PLEASURE

Delicious days with Mum and Dad and the
Tale of the Prince and the Wok

Robert uses a turkey as an artist uses his canvas

WHEN I WAS A CHILD, I USED TO ACCOMPANY MY MOTHER TO TESCO, our local chain food market, to shop for groceries, and it was always a neat experience. When a Brit tells you he's about to "nip down the shops," he's probably heading for a Tesco. Marvelous stores for the British working family, home of the Oxo cube, frozen mince pies, Bird's custard, Crosse & Blackwell's Branston Pickle, Weetabix cereals, and Yorkshire pudding mix in a box. I got to pick out foods I liked, and we inevitably stopped at Wimpy's to grab a Wimpy Burger on the way home. (In fact, not that long ago, I was on the Isle of Malta, and was invited to be one of the very first customers of the first Wimpy's on that island. Having that burger again was like meeting a long-lost friend.) Nowadays, I "shop" with some of the finest purveyors in the business, and when I want a really good snack I go and see my friend Michel Richard at Citronelle in Washington, D.C., and maybe have a Monte Cristo on his freshly baked marble rye (he is possibly the best baker in the world—and he *will* object to the word "possibly") with razor-thin slices of ham and turkey, Manchego cheese, and caramelized shallots. But those early pleasurable impressions never leave you.

Once I had entered the Navy at fifteen, I considered myself an adult, and I expanded my horizons in terms of continuing culinary self-education. As I was being schooled in the basics of cooking in the Navy, I was also able to wander farther afield in my search for inspiration. It wasn't long before I made my way to London and Harrods' Food Hall.

Harrods is unlike any store on the planet. Its founding predates the reign of Queen Victoria, and it takes up about a million square feet in a sedentary neighborhood in Knightsbridge. Its Latin motto is *Omnia Omnibus Ubique*—"All Things, for All People, Everywhere"—and it is filled wall to wall with every imaginable item of any possible interest to any shopper, anywhere. If you ever have the pleasure of visiting it, you will agree that it lives up to its billing as the number one department store in the world.

For a young chef, wandering the legendary Food Hall at Harrods is like walking inside a virtual food encyclopedia. Its vaulted ceilings tower over a staggering collection of foodstuffs, and I used to stalk through those aisles endlessly. I have to admit to being a bit overwhelmed at first, but then I began to understand the organization of the place and know my way around and soon felt right at home. The counter displays are phenomenal. I saw breads in shapes and sizes I'd never imagined, from French baguettes and *épées* to multicolored braided loaves of sourdough, pumpernickel, and rye to brioches and focaccias layered with caramelized onions, roasted peppers, dates, or figs. I saw and sampled the cheeses of the world: Camembert, Brie, Gruyère, Edam and Gouda, Sage Darby, Parmigiano-Reggiano, Port Salut, and every variation on the theme of Cheddar imaginable, including one infused with claret that reminded me of red-veined marble.

I loved the charcuterie displays: terrines and pâtés; salamis, sausages, and *boudins* of every description; hams from America, Spain, and Italy as well as the English countryside. I saw my first prosciutto here. The seafood counters featured a large display of fish—fresh, smoked, and cured—lobsters, langoustines, and clams, and so many oysters that I imagined that they must have had bucketsful of pearls piled up in the basement. Harrods has its own butcher shop, stacked with beautiful cuts of beef, pork, veal, and poultry, and they gladly break down fresh rabbits, duck, grouse, or pheasant to order. There are miles of salads, pickles, and chutneys, nuts from every corner of the Earth, coffee beans, every kind of tea, every kind of ice cream, and every kind of everything else from Christmas puddings to caviar. Harrods Food Hall has its own *patisserie* and its own chocolate confectioners, and both are madly creative.

My special fascination was the wedding cakes display. They laid out models of cakes built out of Styrofoam that showcased the most inventive designs I have ever seen, and I could watch master craftsmen actually bringing these designs to life in the bakery. I still have a book on the art of cake decorating from Harrods that I page through to this day.

There are moments in your life when taste, variety, presentation, tradition, and atmosphere all come together to create perfect pleasure at the table, which thought brings immediately to mind the time that I decided to take my mother to high tea at Harrods.

Please bear in mind, everything is bigger, cleaner, and nicer at Harrods. Mother and I made our way in from Salisbury to Knightsbridge, and strolled through floor after magnificent floor together on our way to the food levels. From the standpoint of consumer goods, for an afternoon I was able to lay the world at my mother's feet. We window-shopped past the latest fashions from Milan and Paris, fine linens and woolens, exquisite glass and crystal, jewelry and cosmetics, magnificent furniture pieces, the most modern appliances, and the most amazing antiques and paintings. My mom's eyes were wide as saucers. We weren't at Tesco anymore.

Then we stopped in for tea. If the way to an English man's soul is through Sunday dinner, the way to an English woman's is through tea. Every available surface of the tearoom was layered with crystal, white linen, china, and silver. The servers wore clean white gloves, and the service itself was even crisper and cleaner. Multitiered silver trays bore all of the traditional dainties and more. We feasted on delicate sandwiches filled with smoked Scottish salmon, egg mayonnaise with watercress, cucumber with cream cheese, creamy chicken salad with onion marmalade, and ham with just a whisper of mustard. The pastries were beautiful: Viennese swirls, miniature napoleons, colorful fruit tarts, and cookies dotted with fruit jellies. The crumpets were pillowy, the scones were hot out of the oven, filled with raisins and apples and paired with clotted cream from Devonshire, creamery butter, and every manner of preserves. We had stepped off of the busy streets of London into a timeless space measured out in sweet sips of warming, milky tea and bite after bite of pure pleasure, and we made an everlasting memory.

I maintain that there are very few hard-and-fast rules in the culinary world, but one of the few to which I subscribe is that you must seek and find pleasure in the making and eating of food. Now, I don't want to tell you how to live your life, but I cannot stress the following more strongly:

TAKE YOUR MOTHER TO AFTERNOON TEA.

Mince Pies

When you want to sit down with your mom (or dad, for that matter) and have a lovely cup of tea, serve these mince pies in any season.

To make the pie filling, mix the nuts, dried and candied fruit, suet, citrus zest and juice, brown sugar, apples, and spices in a bowl. Stir in the brandy. Cover and leave in a cool place for 2 days.

To make the crust, sift the flour and confectioners' sugar into a bowl. Cut in the butter until the mixture resembles coarse crumbs.

Add the orange zest. Stir in just enough orange juice to bind. Gather into a ball, wrap in wax paper, and refrigerate for at least 20 minutes.

To assemble the "pies," preheat the oven to 425 degrees. Grease 3 or 4 muffin pans, depending on the number of muffins each will hold. Beat together the cream cheese and granulated sugar. Roll out the piecrust dough ¼ inch thick. (You will be cutting out 72 rounds in total, for top and bottom crusts.) With a fluted pastry cutter, stamp out three dozen (36) 3-inch rounds. Transfer these rounds to the muffin pans. Fill halfway with mincemeat. Top with a teaspoonful of the cream cheese mixture.

To make the top crusts, roll out the pastry trimmings and stamp out three dozen (36) more 3-inch rounds with a fluted cutter. Brush the edges of the pies with milk, then set the rounds on top. Cut a small steam vent in the top of each pie.

Brush lightly with milk. Bake until golden, 15 to 20 minutes. Let cool for 10 minutes before unmolding. Dust with confectioners' sugar.

Cook's Tip The mincemeat mixture may be packed into sterilized jars and sealed. It will keep refrigerated for several months. (The citric acid "cures" the mixture and the brandy and spices act as preservatives.) Add a few tablespoonfuls to give apple pies a lift, or make small mincemeat-filled parcels using phyllo pastry.

A Note on Pastry Made in the Food Processor Many home cooks have excellent results with pastry dough they make in a food processor equipped with a dough blade. To do this, put the sifted flour and salt into the processor bowl along with the butter (or shortening) and pulse until the mixture looks like bread crumbs. Then sparingly drizzle the ice water (or orange juice in the case of the Mince Pies recipe) through the processor tube into the flour mixture whilst you "pulse" the food processor until the dough just comes together.

FOR THE PIE FILLING

1 cup blanched almonds, finely chopped

1 cup dried apricots, finely chopped

1 cup raisins

1 cup currants

1 cup candied cherries, chopped

1 cup candied citrus peel, chopped

1 cup finely chopped beef suet

Grated zest and juice of 2 lemons

Grated zest and juice of 1 orange

1 cup dark brown sugar, firmly packed

4 tart cooking apples, peeled, cored, and chopped

2 teaspoons ground cinnamon

1 teaspoon grated nutmeg

½ teaspoon ground cloves

1 cup brandy

8 ounces cream cheese

2 tablespoons granulated sugar

Confectioners' sugar, for dusting

FOR THE CRUST

3 cups all-purpose flour

1¼ cups confectioners' sugar

1½ cups (3 sticks) cold unsalted butter, cut into pieces

Grated zest and juice of 1 orange

Milk, for glazing

A PRINCE OF A FELLOW

CIRCA 1980 I WAS STATIONED AT THE ROYAL NAVAL AIR STATION AT CUL-
drose, at the southern tip of Cornwall. I had completed my fundamental
culinary training with flying colors. I was only sixteen, but brimming with
confidence. I had sailed through cookery school with the highest grades
and served aboard the naval base HMS *Pembroke*, running a watch of fifteen men, serving an average of two thousand lunches a day. I had a hand
in changing and modifying all of the recipes we used and was given reasonably free rein in the kind of experimentation that has fueled my entire
career.

Did I occasionally demonstrate the kind of youthful high spirits that are
generally frowned upon by military disciplinarians? Sure, but my exploits never
ran far past drinking a few extra beers, staying out late with the fellows, and
chasing after exemplary members of the local feminine population. But when
I was working, I worked hard and focused on the food. As I look back, though
I still wasn't much more than a kid, I had a mix of competence that bordered
on real skill combined with a self-assurance that sometimes crossed the border
into cockiness.

The former landed me a coveted spot at the Royal School of Cookery and
found me assigned to a special detail that aided in the construction of the cake
for the royal wedding of Charles, Prince of Wales, and Lady Diana Spencer. It
was an imposing pastry, a titanic English fruitcake of all things, housed in a
cooled airplane hangar; an octagonal, eight-tiered, 350-pound cake with elaborate side panels that depicted the histories of the royal lineages of both the
Windsors and the Spencers . . . in icing.

The latter tendency, characterized by my big mouth and a depressingly regular habit of telling my superiors what I really thought of their ideas, all too
frequently had me consigned to said hangar painstakingly inspecting, culling,
and cleaning billions of individual bits of dried fruits for inclusion in the mat-
rimonial confection, often for days upon end. This was "KP" of the highest
order for Queen and country. I'm happy to say, though, that I also participated
in the design and execution of the beautifully crafted side panels, with time off
for good behavior.

Still in all, my service was well received and I was now at Culdrose, stationed as cook in the officers' wardroom, and things were going along swim-
mingly. I was momentarily popular with my superiors, the officers seemed to

like the food I was serving up, and the sun simply rose and set on my little corner of the British Empire.

Then came the dawn of the T-Fal electric wok, and my life changed forever.

The chief cook of the officers' mess was a bit of a gadget freak, and the discovery of a new toy of this magnitude pleased him no end. He was disinclined to suffer the learning curve, however, and cheerily passed that duty along to me. I was handed the wok, power cord, manual, and recipe book, and given a commission to "play with it and see what it can do."

I attacked my assignment with relish. Most of my training to that time had been basic British Naval Cooking 101, or had been founded in general European principles. But just by gleaning the essentials of Asian wok cooking from the recipe book, I could begin to see the possibilities in flash-frying meats and fresh vegetables with exciting new ingredients.

I prepped all morning, cooking up a batch of rice; selecting and julienning carrots, onions, peppers, broccoli; thin-slicing breasts of chicken; peeling shrimp; picking out greens I was going to experiment with; zesting and squeezing oranges and lemons for their juices and essential citrus oils; rummaging for spices like ground ginger, cardamom, and cumin. Armed with sesame oil and soy sauce at the ready, I was well prepared a full half hour before luncheon service, proudly standing by to initiate my new Far Eastern campaign.

The door swung open, and an officer I had never met before came in, accompanied by a retinue of about six men. He was dressed in a flight suit, and seemed like an amiable chap, which was not always the preferred demeanor of officers at a Royal Naval Air Station. I greeted him formally, as befitted his rank, but soon found myself just talking with him, mainly about his day and mine. He mentioned that he was on the base to update his helicopter certification, and was learning to fly the Wessex Mark III helicopter. He was more fascinated, seemingly, by the preparations I had made for lunch, and asked me if I wouldn't mind showing him what it was all about.

I was more than ready for my maiden voyage on the good ship *T-Fal*, and went to work. I don't remember precisely what I grabbed and tossed about in the wok that day, but it looked and smelled great. The garlic and ginger were properly singed and infused with sesame and soy; the vegetables were crisp and flavorful, the meat, succulent. I proudly whipped it onto a plate and offered it to that kindly gentleman, when I noticed the chief waving his arms madly from across the wardroom. I waved back, playing the innocent, then proceeded to cook something up for the rest of his party.

Before I was able to finish serving the rest, the gentleman was back for seconds. I threw together a completely new combination, which seemed to please him even more.

"What is this called?" he asked politely.

"I don't know, sir," I said, "but it looks pretty good."

"It is. Thank you very much." They all finished eating and left, happily well fed. Finally, the chief, rather nervously I thought, made his way over to my nouveau Asian station.

"Did he like it?" he asked.

"Yeah, he loved it."

"Thank God almighty. Irvine, do you have any idea who that was?"

"No, sir."

"Does the name *Prince Charles* ring a bell?!"

Now, in my own defense, there are probably lots of young people in England and America and the world at large who are so busy with living their lives that they might not know who the ruling politicians or future monarchs of the day are at a glance. I was slightly taken aback for a moment; this certainly had been a brush with greatness that I would have to write home to the folks about. I was definitely impressed that he had liked my food. In fact, he liked it so much that he came back every single day of his training, thirty-eight days in a row, and asked me to make him the same exact lunch. We parted friends, or at least cordial acquaintances, and life carried on.

Eight weeks later, I got a call from the supply officer, Lt. Commander Portius, ordering me to report to his office in my full, number one dress uniform. This did not make me happy. My relationship with my superiors ran the gamut from delight in my accomplishments in the kitchen, to genuine, heartfelt comradeship-in-arms, to, well, crankiness with some of my less than desirable behavior. I had been out late the night before and my head hurt. There is every chance that I might have—accidentally, mind you—violated the base curfew for younger enlisted men whilst enjoying a drink or two, or nine, with some of the older, more worldly of my base mates the night before I was asked to report. A stern reprimand could easily have been in order, though I'd never been asked to dress up for one before.

Portius took one look at me and sent me off to the base commander. If the command chain of the air station had formed a conspiracy to scare God's own religion out of me that day, they had succeeded. I began to compose the letter in my head:

Dear Mum and Dad,

Have been unceremoniously drummed out of the service for Lord knows what.

Will be returning home soon in disgrace to live in my old room.

Your loving son, Robert

The commander was civil, and also seemed more concerned with inspecting my uniform than in mercifully doling out my final punishment. Sadist. He crooked a finger at me, and I followed him out of the building, where we packed into a car and drove the short distance to Naval Air Command and the office of the full ranking *admiral*.

"The admiral. Very funny . . . well played," I thought, in my despair.

Then, unexpectedly, I began to relax. Unless perhaps he'd won me in a card game, it seemed unlikely that a full ranking admiral would be getting involved in my dismissal and punishment, if such were to be my fate, even if they had decided to shoot me before kicking me out of the Navy.

True to form, the admiral was by far the politest of all, and informed me that I would be taking a little trip in a helicopter to London.

"Yes, sir!" said I, thinking to myself that a trip in a helicopter was the only possible next logical step in my day, and off we went.

We sped off in his car, took the helicopter to London—lovely flight—set off in another car, and cruised down the road to Buckingham Palace.

Buckingham Palace. Sure, why not? Where else? Nipped into the old palace, marched down the hall, kept the old legs moving, left, right, left, bang in to see the Prince of Wales.

"How are you, chef?" he said, without a trace of irony.

He reached out and greeted me as he had each of the thirty-eight days. I instinctively flexed my wok-flipping hand, controlled myself, and managed to reach back and return his proffered handshake. We had a ripping good chat, about my family, my life in his Navy, whether I was well fixed financially, on and on, and he capped it all off by asking if I would like to come work for him in the family business. Being a loyal subject of the Crown, I'm sure I said yes, or the legally binding equivalent. I would love to be able to tell you intimate details of the experience, what the carpeting was like, what knickknacks were on the prince's desk and so on, but I was sixteen, just slightly hungover, and had not only been plucked from obscurity but had been practically plucked straight out of my bed, overdressed, overstressed, hurled through space and quick-marched into a castle to be offered a job by the future emperor of my country. I am incredibly pleased that I remembered my own name. My lingering first impression of the palace from that day was that it was extremely large and seemed very clean.

Wonderful time, Your Majesty, best to your mother, thanks for the tea, back to the base. Two days later, I was off on a quick plane ride to rendezvous with the Royal Yacht *Britannia*, from which point I embarked on my first trip on board, to Brindisi, Italy.

This was among the great turning points of my life so far. And I am convinced that it was largely due to the fact that I was able to provide a *pleasurable* eating experience for a true gentleman, look after him at his lunchtime, and do it in such a way that he could take to heart.

Here are a few recipes that I would recommend for their qualities of providing pleasure at the table. I hope they change your life for the better.

Beef with Bamboo Shoots

SERVES 6

I think I would be remiss if I didn't put at least one recipe for a good stir-fry into this chapter.

Cut the beef across the grain into thin slices. Place the beef in a bowl and add the marinade ingredients one at a time, mixing in well and adding the cornstarch last. Marinate the beef for 25 minutes (or longer if you wish). Bring 2 cups salted water to a boil in a medium saucepan and add the rice to cook for about 20 minutes, or until tender.

Whilst the beef is marinating, whisk together the sauce ingredients and set aside. Rinse the bamboo shoots in warm water to remove any tinny taste and drain. Clean the green onions and slice them on the diagonal into thirds.

Heat the wok over medium-high to high heat. Add 3 tablespoons of the oil. When the oil is hot, add the minced ginger. Stir-fry until aromatic, about 30 seconds. Add the beef and stir-fry at high heat until cooked. Stir-fry in two batches if necessary so as not to overcrowd the wok. Remove the beef from the wok and set aside on a utility platter.

Clean out the wok and add the remaining 2 tablespoons oil. When the oil is hot, add the green onions and bamboo shoots, and stir-fry. Add a bit of soy sauce or brown sugar if desired. Make a well in the wok by pushing the bamboo shoots up the side. Give the sauce a quick restir and add to the middle of the wok, stirring to thicken. Add the cooked beef back into the wok. Turn the cooked rice onto a serving platter and spoon the stir-fry mixture on top of it. Serve and enjoy!

1 pound flank steak

One 8-ounce can bamboo shoots

2 teaspoons minced ginger

2 green onions (scallions), sliced on the diagonal into thirds

5 tablespoons oil for stir-frying, or as needed

1 cup rice

FOR THE MARINADE

1 tablespoon light soy sauce

2 teaspoons Chinese rice wine or dry sherry

2 teaspoons brown sugar

Pepper to taste

2 teaspoons vegetable oil

1 teaspoon cornstarch, dissolved in 4 teaspoons water

FOR THE SAUCE

2 tablespoons oyster sauce

1 tablespoon dark or thick soy sauce (available at Asian markets)

¼ cup water, or as needed

1 tablespoon cornstarch

EQUIPMENT

A wok

A utility platter

Rösti Potatoes with Goat Cheese and Wilted Arugula or Spinach

SERVES 4 TO 6

This is a classic recipe that I love and use whenever the opportunity presents itself. I changed the original recipe from the standard years ago after a wonderful trip to Paris. I had the pleasure of dining out with a couple of friends in a little bistro in the downtown area, and one of the dishes I had that night was the old favorite rösti potatoes with cured salmon. After dinner I had a thought about this dish and how I could make it more exciting and tastier. Knowing that I was hosting a cocktail party that evening in HMS Hunter for the British attaché and some foreign dignitaries, I added a little variation to the dish to add another dimension to it. Once I cut it into little triangles and put a little caviar on top, it was an instant hit! You should try it.

1 pound (3 to 4 medium) Yukon gold potatoes

¼ stick (2 tablespoons) unsalted butter

Salt and pepper

¼ cup canola oil

¼ cup crumbled goat cheese

½ cup baby arugula or spinach

1 ounce caviar (optional)

EQUIPMENT

A box grater

A heavy sauté pan with ovenproof handles, or a cast iron skillet (if finishing in oven)

To prepare the potatoes, simply peel them and grate them on the large side of a box grater into a large bowl. (Do this just before you are ready to use them, otherwise the potatoes will turn black.)

On low heat, melt the butter in a heavy sauté pan or cast-iron skillet. (If finishing this dish in the oven, be sure to use a pan that can go directly into the oven—no plastic handles. Otherwise, plan on finishing the dish on the stovetop.) When the butter has melted, pour it into the bowl over the grated potatoes, season with salt and pepper to taste, and toss together.

Add a little canola oil to the sauté pan or skillet, enough to cover the bottom of the pan. Heat the pan over medium heat, and add half the potato mixture. Press the potato down and form a cake that's about ¼ inch thick, and cook for 8 to 12 minutes without burning the bottom. Add the goat cheese and arugula or spinach on top of the potatoes in the pan, and then cover with the remaining half of the grated raw potatoes. You will form a cake that's about ½ inch in thickness.

Once this is done, the bottom of the potato should be browned nicely and ready to be turned. Take a large plate and, lifting the pan off the heat, turn the plate upside down over the top of the pan and in one motion, flip it over and slide the "potato cake" back into the pan so both sides will be golden brown.

At this point you can finish in the oven at 375 degrees for 6 to 8 minutes, or continue to finish on the range. Top with caviar if you like.

A Note on Caviar Caviar will probably always be considered a luxury. But . . . you can enjoy it without breaking the piggy bank. Caviar is fish eggs (the roe) of sturgeon. There are levels of quality—based on the type and location of the sturgeon, and the size, color, and texture of the eggs said sturgeon produce. The highest (most expensive) to lowest (least expensive)—presumably in terms of quality—are: beluga, osetra, sevruga, and American sturgeon. I say "presumably" because each type has its own unique profile and is not necessarily to be written off because it is not considered "the best" or most rare.

Chocolate and Oatmeal Cookies

MAKES 2 DOZEN COOKIES

1 cup unsalted softened butter

1 cup granulated sugar

1 cup brown sugar

2 eggs

1 teaspoon pure vanilla extract

2½ cups oatmeal

2 cups all-purpose flour

½ teaspoon salt

1 teaspoon baking soda

1 teaspoon baking powder

¾ cup semisweet chocolate chips

¼ cup chocolate mini-chips

1½ cups chopped nuts (walnuts or almonds), optional

These cookies are my personal favorites, and it's nothing for me to eat about a dozen with a piping hot cup of English Breakfast tea, any time of the day!

Preheat the oven to 375 degrees.

Cream the butter and both sugars together. Add the eggs and vanilla.

In a blender, blend the oatmeal until it resembles a powder and put it into a mixing bowl. (If you like chunkier cookies, don't blend as much.)

Into the mixing bowl containing the oatmeal, sift together the flour, salt, baking soda, and baking powder, and mix. Then add the chocolate chips and nuts. (If you don't like nuts, just omit them.)

Roll the dough into golf ball–size spheres and place them 2 inches apart on a lightly greased cookie sheet. Bake until done, approximately 6 minutes.

Maryland Corn Crab Chowder

SERVES 6

On a cold day when the winds are blowing in off the Chesapeake, or when any old cold wind is blowing, you can sip this soup from a crock or a cup and mentally slip into it like a warm bath.

In a saucepot, melt the butter. Add the corn, onions, and celery, and sauté until the vegetables are translucent.

Stir in the flour to make a roux. (It will thicken the soup.) Add the clam broth and bring to a simmer, then add the potatoes and cook until done (but do not overcook them or they will turn mushy).

Add the heavy cream, Old Bay seasoning, Worcestershire sauce, and fresh thyme. Let simmer for ½ hour more. Stir in the crabmeat and warm until it is heated through. Serve with or without sherry.

> *A Note on the Sherry* Our home test cook enjoyed adding the bottle of Osborne Fino Pale Dry Sherry to the liquor cabinet after selecting it as a condiment for the Maryland Corn Crab Chowder.

2 sticks (1 cup) butter

1½ cups corn

2 onions, diced

½ bunch celery, medium diced

1 cup flour

1 quart clam broth

3 large potatoes, peeled and medium diced

1 cup heavy cream

3 teaspoons Old Bay seasoning

3 teaspoons Worcestershire sauce

2 teaspoons chopped fresh thyme

One 16-ounce container/can (jumbo lump) crabmeat

Sherry (your choice), as a condiment

Fried Green Tomatoes and Goat Cheese, Topped with Greens and Lemon Oil

SERVES 6

FOR THE TOMATOES

¼ cup all-purpose flour

Salt and freshly ground black pepper

1 teaspoon Old Bay seasoning

2 large eggs, beaten

⅔ cup plain dried bread crumbs

½ cup freshly grated Parmesan cheese

1 pound green tomatoes, sliced ½ inch thick

½ cup olive oil

12 ounces goat cheese

FOR THE MIXED GREENS

2 cups mixed greens (lolla rossa, frisée, baby arugula)

Juice of 2 lemons

2 ounces extra virgin olive oil

Salt and pepper

FOR THE LEMON OIL

1 large lemon

⅓ cup canola oil or grapeseed oil

To make the tomatoes, set up your breading station. In a medium bowl, season the flour with salt, pepper, and Old Bay seasoning. Put the beaten eggs into a second bowl. Toss the bread crumbs with the Parmesan cheese in a third bowl. Dredge the tomatoes in the flour mixture, then coat them in the egg, letting any excess drip back into the bowl. Coat in the bread crumb mixture, pressing to help them adhere.

In a large, nonstick skillet, heat the olive oil, add the breaded tomatoes in a single layer, and cook them over moderately high heat, turning once until deeply golden and crisp: 5 to 7 minutes. Transfer the tomato slices to a paper towel to drain.

Soak the greens in a bowl of cool water and agitate them with your hand to shake the sand out. The sand will fall to the bottom of the bowl. Lift out the greens and briefly set aside whilst you thoroughly rinse out the bowl and refill it with fresh water to repeat the process. You will have to do this a number of times to ensure that all the sand has been removed (particularly with arugula). Do the final rinse in a colander, then spin the greens in a salad spinner and pat dry with a towel. Cut the greens into manageable sizes. In a mixing bowl, toss them with the lemon juice, oil, and salt and pepper to taste.

Remove the zest of the lemon in 1-inch wide strips with a vegetable peeler.

Heat the oil in a heavy pot over moderate heat. Place the zest in the oil and cook until golden brown, 3 to 5 minutes. Remove from the heat and discard the zest. Place the oil in a mason jar and let cool.

PRESENTATION

Lay the hot tomatoes, 3 slices each, on round plates. Place one slice at 2 o'clock, another at 6 o'clock, and the last one at 10 o'clock. Cut a 2-ounce cylinder of goat cheese and place in the middle of the tomatoes. Divide the greens, place on top of the goat cheese, then drizzle the lemon oil on top, and serve immediately. (See the photograph for an alternative presentation.)

I HAD A LOT OF FREEDOM TO MOVE ABOUT WHEN I WAS A KID. TIMES WERE different then (though it doesn't seem *that* long ago), and our parents trusted that, for the most part, we were highly unlikely to get lost or kidnapped once they'd showed us the ropes and taught us to navigate from point A to point B and home again.

I have previously established in our tale a certain predilection for truant behavior, a freewheeling nature, and a taste for beer that developed early on. When I was about twelve, I had a good neighborhood pal, Nick Weston. We liked to have a good time and go parading about whenever possible, and as we crisscrossed the vicinity looking for fun, we soon chanced on a place on Fisherton Street called the Fisherton Arms.

I was always tall for my age, and Nick and I made it our practice to at least try to get served a pint if ever the opportunity presented itself. At the good old Fisherton Arms, two pints of lager were immediately forthcoming. It was a sort of biker bar, not a dangerous one by any means, more of a funny British one. There were lots of folks in leathers, older and younger, and some friendly biker ladies, who were actually all very polite and liberal-minded about two young lads throwing back a few in their midst. Drinking practices in Britain were always much easier and more open than in the States, so we weren't really even that out of place. We grabbed a couple of billiard cues and made a great night of it.

Soon, it became our regular hangout. We would set off from our houses with towels and trunks in hand for swimming practice in the evening and make straight for the Fisherton Arms. We would spend our allowance knocking back a few beers, then grab a bag of fish and chips on the way home to mask the drink, and wet our towels under the hose tap outside the house to simulate recent immersion in water. It was the perfect plan.

One Saturday afternoon, Nick and I were shooting pool and drinking our usual. We were bantering casually with one of the biker chicks; golden bits of sunshine filtered through the windows as the sun was lowering in the sky, and all was right with the world. I sauntered . . . yes, sauntered up to the bar for another round.

As the glasses were filling I glanced at a friendly-faced fellow to my left.

"Hi, Dad." I swallowed.

He smiled. My dad was a pretty successful pro soccer player and a bit of a local legend for it. There are ninety-six pubs in Salisbury, and my father knows at least somebody in every single one of them. This is why I make my living today as a cook and not as a chess grandmaster. Outflanking me was child's play for a guy like him.

"What are you doing?" he asked.

Sadly, I had nothing left but the truth.

"Havin' a beer."

"Well. If you're going to have a drink, you drink with me."

Now, my dad can be a very genial fellow, and there are few men in Wiltshire who can resist his invitation to a friendly drink. I was pulled in easily, happy to find myself potentially, miraculously, walking away from this unpunished, happy to be having a beer with my dad—in short, happy to be alive. I pulled up a stool and we had a drink.

Many drinks. Somewhere in the course of the next couple of hours, Nick melted away into the night. I foggily remember hearing the phrase, more than once, that has led to the downfall of many a drinking man: "Come on. Let's have *just one more*."

With great care and gentleness, my dad drank me under the table, then delivered me home to my mother's warm embrace.

I remember her saying something like, "Oh, Patrick. What did you do to him?"

He replied something about how I would be fine in the morning and about a "lesson" having been learned. I distinctly heard a satisfied chuckle. I nodded off and they put me to bed.

I promise you, that hangover lasted for a full three days. My head felt like a bingo tumbler filled with hot broken glass. My father, bless him, was always responsible for keeping me on the straight and narrow, and I never even looked at a beer again until I was well into my service in the Navy.

Thus endeth the lesson.

Years later, I decided to pay him back.

By this time, I was in the employ of the Royals, still in the Navy, and had taken a leave to be home for my father's birthday. I brought home a good friend of mine, a fellow cook and sailor whom I'd met in cookery school, named Kenny. He was and is a pretty cocky Scotsman. I am fairly sure he thinks he is a better cook than I am to this day, but we have remained good friends. He's actually such a friendly guy, I let him marry my sister Colleen.

Kenny and I hatched a plan to put together the surprise party of all surprise parties for my dad. It was going to be big and the food was going to be great, not only because our brains were full of food and we were going to be trying to outdo and show off for each other but because Kenny was going to be showing off for my sister whilst trying to get my dad to like him (which he does, *now*, since we're all one big happy family!).

Invitations went out and family members started to trickle into town, from as far as Manchester. We stashed them at local pubs and guesthouses, and in the houses of neighbors who would be coming to the party. I had concocted a brilliant cover story, somewhat based on my recent exploits aboard the *Britannia*. I told my parents that Kenny and I were responsible for putting on an affair for Lord Pembroke, whose ancestral estate, called Wilton House, just happened to be down the road in Salisbury and that we would have to do all of the preparations in our home kitchen. Wilton House is a huge, rambling stone manor house that goes on forever, can probably be seen from outer space, and is familiar to everyone in the neighborhood as a national monument. I was hoping that they would just assume, "Oh, Bob's cooking for Lord Pembroke . . . must be a friend of the Queen's . . ." and leave it at that, and it worked.

Kenny and I shopped for days and we invaded my mother's kitchen on the morning of my father's birthday. All of the kids got together and told the folks that we were sending them out for an early dinner to the Red Lion, a warm and hospitable local inn that dates back to the thirteenth century, for a nice birthday dinner. They made themselves scarce most of the day whilst we cooked.

We tried our level best to go all out. We poached whole salmon to serve *chaud-froid* with some nice white cream sauces. We made deviled crab cakes, prosciutto with melon, and cold boiled shrimp with a peppery aïoli. For salads, we had wilted spinach and bacon with a mustard vinaigrette, Caesar salad, a watercress and apple salad with a sherry-based dressing, a vinegary potato salad with haricots verts, and a cold roasted vegetable salad with leek, parsnips, and squash. We made chicken fricassée with white wine, mushrooms, and onions; boeuf Bourguignon, the classic beef and red wine stew, paired with roasted potatoes and buttered peas; and baked cod with oven-roasted tomatoes, shallots, and courgettes. We served up cold ham and roast duck with mango chutney. Just for fun we whipped up a couple of smoking curries, a salmon mousse, and jellied eel in aspic. Among the desserts were apple and caramel tarts and a flashy variety of pastries and cakes.

We had asked my mother to call ahead before they came home on the premise that we would have time to clean up, so she wouldn't have to walk into a disaster area. Colleen fielded the calls and deflected her hour after hour, pleased, I think, to be in on the plot with Kenny. Guests began to sneak in and we packed them, cheek by jowl, all onto the second floor. We ran platters out to a big party tent that we'd had set up across the road, and after hours of work, it was lights out and we were ready to go.

Finally, the old Vauxhall pulled up in the drive, and we casually walked outside to greet my parents. We begged off staying around on the pretext that we had to deliver all of the food down the road for His Lordship's event the next day. We were as pompous about it as we could possibly manage. My dad fired off a couple of grumpy asides about being kept out so "bloody late," and they headed into the house through the back, as was their custom.

Kenny and I darted inside the front ahead of them and hid. I heard the familiar sound of my dad dumping his keys on the kitchen counter, the light being clicked on, and he walked into the front parlor. We had set up an elaborate bar in the corner of the room, stocked to the nines with whiskeys, gin, spirits of every kind, jugs of wine, bottles of beer, and soft drinks. He passed it by, and somehow it didn't twig in his head that anything was going on.

Somewhere, someone let out a giggle and there was a cry of "Surprise!" My mom came into the room, and down the stairs they tumbled: Auntie Barbara, Uncle Wesley, kids and cousins and neighbors from the road, Aunt Ellie, Uncle Paul, friends from the pub and from his work. Good old Bob Roper even showed up and helped out with the serving. I went over to Dad, and his first reaction was to gruffly call me a rude name and give me a manly punch in the arm; but then he hugged me and I saw that he had tears in his eyes, and that night we shared a few drinks in true love and friendship and toasted his birthday well into the night.

I think I paid him back pretty well.

These next three dishes—the lamb salad, the short ribs, and the apple tart—are all elegant, creative, and incredibly flavorful ways to feed a lot of people, if you've a mind to.

Seared Lamb Loin with Roasted Beets, Feta Cheese, and Orange Mint Salad

SERVES 6

4 pounds trimmed lamb loin

2 tablespoons extra virgin olive oil

Salt and freshly ground black pepper

FOR THE BEET SALAD

4 tablespoons red wine vinegar

4 tablespoons grapeseed oil

6 cooked beets, peeled and diced

1 orange, segmented

1 small red onion, diced

2 tablespoons chopped fresh mint

Salt and freshly ground black pepper

4 ounces cubed feta cheese

Preheat the oven to 350 degrees. Rub the lamb loin with some of the olive oil, then sprinkle with salt and pepper. Heat a skillet over high heat and add the rest of the oil. Sear the lamb on all sides until golden brown. Place the lamb loin in the oven and roast until medium rare. Since the lamb will continue to cook for 5 to 8 minutes after you have removed it from the oven—carryover cooking—the meat thermometer will continue to rise in that period of time. So, the idea is to pull the lamb out at an internal temperature of 120 degrees, so it ultimately ends up where you want it for medium rare, which is an internal temperature of 125 degrees. Chill the lamb in the refrigerator.

Mix the vinegar and oil. Add the beets, orange, red onion, and mint, and mix well. Season with salt and pepper to taste. Fold in the feta cheese. Chill.

PRESENTATION

Slice the chilled lamb and divide among 6 plates. Spoon the beet salad over the lamb. Drizzle extra dressing from the beet salad over the lamb.

Short Ribs Braised with Mushrooms, Pearl Onions, and Bacon

SERVES 4

2 tablespoons neutral oil, such as canola oil or grapeseed oil

4 tablespoons unsalted butter

4 pounds short ribs

Salt and freshly ground black pepper

1 large onion, roughly chopped

1 large carrot, roughly chopped

1 large celery stalk, roughly chopped

4 large garlic cloves, peeled and smashed

One 750-mL bottle of fruity but sturdy red wine, such as Côtes-du-Rhône or Zinfandel

3 thyme branches

4 sprigs of parsley

1 bay leaf

4 ounces slab bacon, cut into strips 1 inch long and ¼ inch thick

8 ounces pearl onions, peeled

1 teaspoon sugar

1 tablespoon extra virgin olive oil

8 ounces small mushrooms, trimmed

About 2 tablespoons minced chives

> *This dish is easily prepared in advance and reheated when needed.*

PREPARATION AND COOKING TIME (ESTIMATES)

Ingredients prep	*30 minutes*
Browning	*20 minutes*
Sauté vegetables	*10 minutes*
Meat cooking time (braising) overlaps with preparation of bacon	*10 minutes*
Pearl onions	*15 minutes*
Mushrooms	*10 minutes*
Plating and sauce prep	*10 minutes*
Total time	*4 hours 10 minutes*

Put a tablespoon each of the oil and butter in a deep, heavy skillet with oven-safe handles, and turn the heat to medium high. A minute later, brown the ribs well on all sides, seasoning well with salt and pepper as they cook. This will take about 20 minutes for 4 pounds of beef. Work in batches if necessary to avoid crowding. Remove the ribs to a utility platter, pour out and discard the fat, and wipe out the pan.

Preheat the oven to 350 degrees. Put the remaining canola oil and another tablespoon of butter in the same pan, turn the heat to medium, and add the chopped onion, carrot, celery, garlic, a large pinch of salt (⅛ teaspoon), and pepper to taste. Cook, stirring, until the onions are soft, about 10 minutes.

Add the red wine, thyme, parsley sprigs, and bay leaf to the skillet, and bring to a boil; return the ribs to the pan, cover, and put in the oven. Cook until the meat is very tender and falling from the bone, about 3 hours; turn the meat once or twice an hour.

Whilst the meat is cooking, put the bacon in a small skillet and cook over medium heat, stirring occasionally, until crisp, about 10 minutes. Drain on paper towels.

Put the pearl onions in a separate small saucepan with another tablespoon of the butter, enough water to cover the onions, a pinch of salt, and the sugar, and cook over high heat until most of the water evaporates. Reduce the heat to medium and cook until a nice glaze forms. Continue to cook, stirring occasionally, until the onions brown a little. Set aside.

Start a skillet on medium heat and put in the olive oil. Add the mushrooms with a little salt and cook, stirring occasionally, until they give up their juices and brown a little, about 10 minutes. Set aside.

When the ribs are done, arrange them on a serving platter. Whilst they are resting, take another large pan and into it strain the vegetables and liquid, pressing hard on the vegetables to extract all of their juices. (Then discard the vegetable and herb pulp.) Bring the juices to a boil and stir in the remaining 1 tablespoon butter; whisk until slightly thickened. Adjust the seasoning as necessary, then stir in the bacon, pearl onions, and mushrooms; cook for another minute or two. Surround the ribs with the onions, mushrooms, and sauce. Serve, garnished liberally with chives.

A Note on Cooking with Wine This is said all the time, but bears repeating: always cook with a wine you wouldn't mind drinking. (Our home test cook prepared Short Ribs Braised with Mushrooms, Pearl Onions, and Bacon using Georges Du Boeuf 2004 Côtes-du-Rhône, and was very pleased with the results.)

Upside-Down Apple Tart

SERVES 8 TO 10

½ pound puff pastry or shortcrust pastry

10 to 12 large Golden Delicious apples

Lemon juice

½ cup butter, cut into pieces

½ cup superfine sugar

½ teaspoon ground cinnamon

Crème fraîche or whipped cream, to serve

On a lightly floured surface, roll out the pastry into an 11-inch circle that is less than ¼ inch thick. Transfer to a lightly floured baking sheet and chill.

Peel the apples, cut them in quarters lengthwise, and core. Sprinkle the apples generously with lemon juice.

In a 10-inch tarte tatin pan (see Note), cook the butter, sugar, and cinnamon over medium heat until the butter has melted and the sugar dissolved, stirring occasionally. Continue cooking for 6 to 8 minutes until the mixture turns a medium caramel color, then remove the pan from the heat and arrange the apple halves, standing on their edges, in the pan, fitting them in tightly, since they shrink during cooking.

Return the apple-filled pan to the heat and bring to a simmer over medium heat for 20 to 25 minutes until the apples are tender and caramel colored. Remove the pan from the heat and cool slightly.

Preheat the oven to 450 degrees. Place the pastry on top of the apple-filled pan and tuck the edges of the pastry inside the edge of the pan around the apples. Pierce the pastry in two or three places, then bake for 25 to 30 minutes until the pastry is golden and the filling is bubbling. Let the tart cool in the pan for 10 to 15 minutes.

To serve, run a sharp knife around edge of the pan to loosen the pastry. Cover with a serving plate and, holding them tightly, carefully invert the pan and plate together. (Do this carefully, preferably over the sink, in case any caramel drips.) Lift off the pan and loosen any apples that stick with a spatula. Serve the tart warm with cream.

A Note on the Tarte Tatin Pan The tarte tatin pan is actually designed and named for the "upside-down" dessert that originated in France. It is a stovetop-to-oven vessel with handles on the sides, which facilitate the smooth rotation of the tart onto the serving plate. Some of these pans are made of porcelain over cast iron, some are entirely made of metal or of heatproof glass or glasslike material. You can actually use any stovetop-to-oven pan that is 10 inches in diameter and 2 inches deep, which will be easy enough to handle when flipping.

IF YOU STOP AND TAKE A GOOD LOOK AT THE GOURMET ITEMS ON YOUR plate next time you're eating in a fancy restaurant, you might easily ask yourself, "Who ever figured out that this was something good to eat?" Oysters immediately come to mind. How about the early Japanese fisherman (and probable sushi chef ancestor) who captured a sea urchin or an octopus in his net and decided he just had to find out how they tasted? Who was the guy who decided that fermented, moldy milk had the potential to become cheese and not garbage? Was it a French gardener who ate the first escargot? I mean, come on, how hungry do you have to be?

What adventuresome diner first had the patience to eat his way through an entire artichoke, leaf by leaf? I have heard eating an artichoke compared to licking thirty or forty postage stamps. Yet we know that when it's mated with a nice lemon yogurt dressing or a little crème fraîche, or when the hearts are marinated with a fine olive oil and fresh herbs, an artichoke is a wonder to behold.

So, experimentation obviously came into play in early culinary exploration. You watch a bird or an animal eat a plant (or each other), and maybe you give it a try. If your fellow tribesman tries some and dies, you give it a pass next time around. Pretty soon, you've got it narrowed down to what's good to eat and what's not.

But it doesn't stop there. Ingredients are combined, and recipes are born, because human beings are driven by something else. Why not just stick with berries and apples and the occasional haunch of wild goat?

The answer is *pleasure*.

That good old culinary quote machine, Brillat-Savarin, said, "The discovery of a new dish does more for human happiness than the discovery of a new star," and I heartily agree. There are over nine thousand taste buds on the human tongue, and every one of them is looking for a good time.

The discovery of pleasure through food can be a satisfying and lifelong pursuit, because the variety of dishes and ingredients are as infinite as words in the English language. Each dish is like a new sentence, each meal is a paragraph, and we all progress through chapters of eating in our lives, from the simple, beloved, and memorable meals we eat as a child to the wider-ranging explorations that transport us out of the safe strictures of the commonplace. We choose different themes as we go; some of us eat for health, some of us overindulge, happily or unhappily, comically or tragically; some, like Craig Claiborne or M.F.K. Fisher, find a level of refinement in their choices to rival the greatest prose; some seek adventure, some comfort, others, romance; some celebrate family and friends with every meal, some choose to dine alone. Some write poetry, some short stories, some novels, but in many ways, the way we eat and think about food forms a large part of the narrative of our lives.

4

THE ALTAR OF FLAVOR

Making breakfast for Her Majesty, the Queen,
and musings on the essential meaning of good taste

FEATURING . . .

In my time with the royals, I spent quite a lot of my free hours exploring new techniques, seeking out instruction with master chefs, and having new culinary and dining experiences to broaden the range of my skills and palate. But my time in direct service to Her Majesty, the Queen, and her family gave me a different level of appreciation for the importance of the notion that, in many ways, the truest test of skill for a chef is to coax out and put on display the maximum amount of flavor from the *simplest* ingredients and preparations.

The most surprising thing you have to know about the Royal Family is that for all of their vast estates and holdings, all of their fame and responsibilities, all of their charms, intrigues, and eccentricities, at their core I believe they are a typical English family. Because of the intense scrutiny they receive from subjects and press, the constant examination under which they live their lives, even in their own homes, where they are perpetually, if respectfully, under the watchful gaze of servants, staff, and courtiers, they are essentially a typical English family in a very *concentrated* form. If the eligible son of a respectable English mother decides to marry the pretty daughter of friends of the family in the local chapel, you can be sure that a splendid time will be had by all the locals at the ceremony. If the same happens in the Royal English family, Western civilization as we know it stops and watches until the vows have been spoken.

It wouldn't take a huge leap of imagination in your mind's eye to see Her Majesty, sans crown and scepter, padding into a warm kitchen in a typical English cottage home, in housecoat and slippers, and greeting her affable husband, who patiently waits for his breakfast to arrive whilst he examines the football scores in his paper. She affectionately pats her aged mother, at the other side of the table, who is stationed behind her empty cup in anticipation of her usual breakfast tea. The Queen puts the kettle on. A gentle tap on the back door precedes the entrance of her eldest son, who has stopped by on his way to work because he has a few papers for Mum to sign, just boring family business. He is a likable chap, slightly awkward, but a well-respected citizen in their little community. She worries about him. She knows he works hard and is responsible, but she also knows that in his heart he has always longed for the simple country life. She hopes he can find happiness in marriage someday. She fishes the bacon out of the icebox and puts the pan on the stove. She asks her son to stay for a bite, but duty calls; he's late to the office and must be off.

Then, out of nowhere, imagine that *I* appear to take over cooking breakfast for everybody whilst she is suddenly freed to relax and watch the BBC morning news on the telly!

That is a pretty good analogy for the routine of cooking for the Royal Family. They don't spend their idle time scanning newly published cookbooks looking for exciting recipes that they can send down to the galleys to spice up Wednesday dinner. They like what they like and they generally like it to be simple and consistent.

A regular breakfast for Her Majesty, whether at one of the palaces or on the Royal Yacht, would be fried eggs and bacon served with tea and chilled freshly squeezed orange juice. There are at all times, of course, an array of breakfast items that can be ordered, such as poached eggs and chipolatas (small English breakfast sausages), fish cakes, kippers, sautéed kidneys, smoked haddock; the list goes on and on. If you are ever fortunate enough to be invited to breakfast at Buckingham Palace, please feel free to order up as much as you'd like, but Her Majesty will most likely be contented with fried eggs and bacon, her tea, and chilled freshly squeezed orange juice.

At one of the palaces, there would probably be a snack around elevensy, which would consist of hot tea and good tinned biscuits (*cookies*, in the colonies). Each day, the Queen selects the afternoon and evening meals from menu books, leather-bound in either red or black, inscribed on the cover with the words "Menu Royal." They are beautifully bound volumes, and you wouldn't be surprised if a trumpet sounded when you opened the cover. Inside are written suggestions from the chef for the day's menu, invariably fashioned to please the royal palate. She marks her selections in pencil, making additional notes if she wants something that isn't on that particular day's carte du jour, then the book is returned back to the kitchens and we go to work. These books also contain any special or unusual dishes that might have been prepared for visiting dignitaries or heads of state if they have dined privately with the Queen. The esteemed visitor's name is duly placed thereby. Once filled, these volumes are stored and cataloged in the Royal Library as part of the official record of the reign of Elizabeth II. These books stretch back into the history of the monarchy. There are a lot of fried eggs in these books.

Depending on the day of the week and travel schedules, lunches usually consisted of four dishes, and were generally catered for up to eight people, depending on which family members were about and what invited guests were expected. A typical lunch would feature smoked salmon, a roast veal or beef with two vegetables, a dessert, and cheeses. There are few if any English homes that haven't put on a lunch of "meat and two veg," sweets for after, and "a bit of cheese would be lovely." No tacos, no dim sum, no spaghetti alla puttanesca, no egg rolls, no cheese steaks, no turkey wraps, no big Greek salad with extra dressing on the side, no pizza, no gyros, and no knishes. I think I can say with little fear of contradiction that if you went down to the diner with Her Majesty, the Queen of England, she might try the fried chicken, but she will not be ordering the chili.

The menus for the Royal Family, on every occasion, were written in French, which was very elegant, but a thinly veiled disguise for some simple, homey dishes.

MENU ROYAL

Cottage Pie *de Boeuf braisé*

(In reality, cottage pie with ground beef, veggies, and mash)

Navarin d'Agneau aux Légumes

(A savory lamb stew)

Côtelettes d'Agneau

(Tasty grilled lamb chops)

Rumpsteak *Grillé Béarnaise*

(A nice grilled steak with a béarnaise sauce)

You could have all of these dishes down the pub, although I have to admit we used to do a very nice job on them. You'll also note that there is a bit of a nod to understandability for the English eye on these menus. Cottage pie could be translated as *pâte en croûte de petite maison*, but that might be pretentious and nobody would order it.

On the *Britannia* and at Windsor or Buckingham palaces, we always tried to show off the best of English food: salmon, hare, grouse, turkey roasts, partridge, venison, potatoes, sprouts, chutneys, pear tarts, and the like. This is where I learned a fundamental truth about cooking that every chef and cook should know. If you shop well, you can cook well. That simply means that the better your ingredients, the better your flavors. It is very nice when your venison and beef is culled from the royal herds at Balmoral Estate, when your honey for biscuits comes from one of the 450 hives on the estate, when your salmon is freshly caught from the River Dee in Scotland, which borders your employers' property. Often is the time when the Royal Game Warden would deliver freshly shot grouse, pheasant, or quail to our kitchens, which we would butcher, hang, and dress for that evening's dinner.

The flavors available to you from these kinds of ingredients are pristine. You have to care for them, cherish them and, for the most part, stay out of their way. This need is accentuated when the taste buds of your employers are finely attuned to the simple perfection of these flavors, since they have been served them virtually from birth.

Traveling with the Royal Family is much the same routine. On a number of different levels, the rule when you are traveling in a personal retinue is: take care of your principal. I often traveled with the Prince and Princess of Wales, Charles and Diana. I had to be trained not only in protocol and etiquette but also in evasive driving and small arms. The president of the United States travels with literally hundreds of people when he moves and is accompanied by a huge security force. The Royals usually moved with small parties, often just me, a small advance team, and a couple of butlers. In crowds, the principal is the star and your job is to be as invisible and as available to them as possible. On the food side, my job was to make sure that the menus wherever we stayed were what they wanted and were appropriate to the occasion. That often meant consulting with the chefs on site and supervising their preparations. We spanned the globe, from Australia and New Zealand to America to the Far East, from Boston to Brindisi to Bahrain, and were as likely to be cooking for the sultan of Oman as Elton John. Outside of England or the Royal Yacht, I seldom did a lot of "hands-on" cooking.

A big part of our accepted practice for high-profile public affairs at home was to dig into the family archives, the Menus Royal, not unlike the way you might dig out a worn scrap with Grandma's potato salad or that Swedish meatballs recipe Great Granddad liked so much on it. These affairs might take four days to prep and cook, and might feature a VIP gathering of two hundred dining personally with Charles and Diana, and an additional thousand dining otherwise. We might pull a recipe for *Mayonnaise de Homard,* or lobster salad, from the coronation banquet of His Majesty, George VI, from May 1937, and a *Filet de Boeuf Mascotte,* a whole roasted tenderloin of beef with artichoke, whole peeled truffles, and parsley, from the coronation day feast of Her Majesty, Elizabeth II, from June 1953. She'll like that. A *Salade d'Asperges à la Vinaigrette,* or roast asparagus with dressing, from the tables of Albert and

Victoria might go nicely, and didn't we whip up a *Parfait à la Meringue au Citron*, a frozen lemon and orange soufflé, when the president of Finland came over that time?

I was generally consulted for state affairs and remember particularly helping to make some of the menu decisions for a birthday dinner for President Reagan, which was celebrated on the yacht in the port of San Diego, but for the most part, the Queen herself always made the final decisions about the bill of fare. The Master of the Household, who is essentially the head of all "below stairs" operations for the family, provided me with the itinerary, and menus were often determined four or five weeks in advance. I worked the galleys with another cook named Jan Yoeman, the big guy, and given my basic nature, I would persistently look at him and say, "Why don't we try it this way? Why are we doing it like that?" to which his reply was always, "Because she likes it that way." In our business, the customer is always right.

There's something very "regal," yet homey about Beef Wellington, so in honor of Her Royal Majesty, may I present . . .

Beef Wellington with Bordelaise Sauce

SERVES 6 TO 8

This dish can be done using either a whole beef tenderloin or individual 5- or 6-ounce filets. The choice is yours.

Preheat THE OVEN TO 425 DEGREES.

In a large roasting pan, arrange the whole filet, brush with melted butter, and season with salt and pepper to taste.

Roast in the oven for about 30 minutes until a meat thermometer reads an internal temperature of 115 degrees. *Note*: If you are using individual filets, season the filets, and in a large sauté pan, sear on both sides until golden brown and remove from the pan to cool. Then follow the rest of the steps.

Remove from the oven and let the filet rest for 30 to 40 minutes, or until the meat is cold. The meat has to be cold—otherwise, the pastry will become soft and unworkable.

Leave the oven on, as you will need it again shortly.

Using a large skillet or sauté pan, add the 1 stick butter and cook the onion until translucent. Add the mushrooms, thyme, pâté, and red wine, and cook until all the liquid has evaporated and the mixture is almost dry. (The mixture will resemble a coarse pâté.) When you reach this point, you can adjust the seasoning with salt and pepper, and set aside to cool.

On a lightly floured surface, roll out the puff pastry into two rectangles, approximately 16 by 14 inches (depending on the size of the filet).

Place one pastry rectangle on a greased cookie sheet. Place the filet on the pastry, and top with the mushroom mixture. Brush the pastry with a little water, and then cover the filet on top with the other piece of pastry, completely enclosing the filet. Press the edges of both pieces of pastry together, making sure they seal, and trim off any excess.

In a small cup, beat the egg yolks together with a little salt, and brush the finished filet liberally. Repeat this a couple of times more, allowing to dry between coats.

Bake the Wellington for a further 10 minutes at 425 degrees, then reduce the heat to 375 degrees and bake for a further 20 minutes, or until it is golden brown and done to your liking.

Transfer from the oven and let the Wellington rest for at least 10 minutes (so all the flavor returns to the meat).

Whilst the meat is resting, you can make the Bordelaise sauce. The following is a variation on my basic recipe, which I favor for this dish.

FOR THE BEEF

1 whole filet (beef tenderloin, about 5 pounds) or six 5-ounce filets (see Note at left)

6 ounces (1¾ sticks or 10 tablespoons) unsalted butter, melted

Salt and pepper

4 ounces (1 stick) unsalted butter

1 onion, minced

2 ounces sliced mushrooms

1 teaspoon chopped fresh thyme

½ pound goose liver pâté or duck liver pâté

2 tablespoons red wine

1 large package of frozen puff pastry (1 to 1½ pounds)

2 egg yolks

Sauce Bordelaise (Bordeaux Sauce)

3 ounces (6 tablespoons)
unsalted butter

1 onion, finely diced

3 tablespoons all-purpose
flour

¾ cup beef bouillon or
consommé

½ cup red wine

1 tablespoon chopped
fresh thyme

2 tablespoons chopped
fresh parsley

Melt the butter in a saucepan, and sauté the onion until tender. Add the flour and cook until the flour has browned slightly, 3 to 4 minutes.

Slowly stir in the beef bouillon or consommé a little at a time, stirring continuously. Once all the bouillon is in, add the red wine and simmer over a low heat to allow the flour to cook out (10 to 15 minutes).

Just before you are about to serve, add the thyme and parsley, and adjust the seasoning with salt and pepper.

PRESENTATION

Whether you decided to cook individual Wellingtons or a whole one, the presentation is amazing. You can serve the whole one on a platter with baby carrots and Brussels sprouts, or simply place the individual Wellingtons on plates and garnish with the vegetable of your choice. Enjoy!

On the royal yacht especially, there were strict guidelines for behavior, and many of them were based on the principle that you were to be seen and not heard, or heard and not seen. Eye contact with the Royals in passing was not encouraged. You learned a different rhythm and a different level of expectations based on which members of the Royal Family might be on board at any given time. In living around them for extended periods of time, I found that their example was both instructive and fascinating, because for all of the pomp and circumstance that surrounds them, the honoraria and privilege, they are born to a life of service. Distance was established and strictly kept to, but outside of this discipline there were still allowances made for warmth and spontaneity, and it was possible to be reminded that they were just people from time to time.

It is customary to make a Christmas pudding for whomever is in residence on the ship at Yuletide, and it is their concomitant duty to christen the pudding before the meal. On one such occasion the Prince and Princess of Wales were in residence and they joined us in the galley for the ceremony. We all gathered around the copper. Prince Charles held a galvanized bucket with an egg, and Princess Diana held one that contained spirits. He dumped in his egg (not unlike throwing out the first pitch in a baseball game), which slid into the copper but then took off like a ski jumper straight onto Diana's tangerine dress. No damage was done—we cleaned it up in a second—and she teased him about it playfully. He repeated his charge, successfully this time, and she added her spirits. We poured in the rest of the mixture, and they took turns stirring the thick, glistening pudding. As the pudding came together and began to stiffen, Diana poked it and innocently remarked, "Oh, it's getting hard." I didn't have the courage to look him in the eye, but I would be willing to bet that even the Prince of Wales had a tough time keeping a straight face after that one. After more stirring, a couple of swigs of punch, and a bit of general merriment, the princess soon discovered that somehow the backing to her earring had fallen off—and into the pudding. My team and I, experienced food divers all, donned plastic gloves and soon recovered it. She accepted it back, rinsed and washed, most gratefully. A short while and a couple of "Happy Christmases!" later, they were gone, and we'd shared their company not so much as a couple of the crowned heads of Europe, but as a lovely English couple who'd slipped back in the kitchen to visit with the cooks and grab a cup of cheer.

Years later, I had left the Navy and was working as an executive chef in Jamaica. In the interim, Diana had left the Royal Family as well, and we were all anticipating her arrival on the island for an affair for the opening of a battered women's shelter, one of the many charitable interests to which she lent her name and time. It was in August of 1997, and of course, she never arrived. Let me tell you, that was a sad day.

Flavor is an endless subject, and in my philosophy, it is at the very heart of cooking and eating. As a chef, my goal is to strive to keep the flavors of the food I make bold and distinctive, and to combine them in ways that are both exciting and surprising. My job is to make flavors jump off the plate. If I do my job right, you will be talking about the food during dinner, on the way home, the next day at the office, and at Christmas, telling your grandchildren about it and and possibly even remembering it on your deathbed. I take it very seriously.

Flavor is one of the great equalizers in human experience. There is no special dispensation given to the manner in which a king or queen may enjoy their dinner over the pleasure experienced by the simplest of their subjects. They may have access to more expensive ingredients and more proficient preparers, but true enjoyment is in the taste buds of the beholder. The basic preparations have been executed a trillion times over in the history of the planet, but every time a meal is cooked, there is a chance for something new to occur. The immediate ingredients in your kitchen can always be freshly caught or picked and have never been cooked or eaten before. Consider the obsession winemakers need to cultivate over the climate's effect on the grapes used for their wine. No two harvests are the same—ever. The art of flavor lies in understanding and mastering the techniques that can enhance or augment the flavors of the food you are preparing, and perhaps more important, knowing when to keep it simple and get out of the way. You might take a rich and flavorful ingredient like goose liver, combine it and manipulate it in dozens of very technical ways to create a marvelous pâté; yet when faced with a beautifully marbled center-cut prime filet of beef, two words may suffice: salt and pepper. Combine with heat and serve. Both can be excellent choices made by a master of flavor.

Humans are true culinary adventurers. Why do we seem to have an inbred desire for variety when it comes to the foods we eat? I'm sure there's an evolutionary advantage. We are omnivores, which means we can eat both meats and vegetables, and the more different kinds of foods that we can safely and healthily ingest and digest, the wider the universe of foods that are available for our survival. That's the scientific answer.

We are not just engines powered by evolutionary forces. We are the thinking animal, we have imagination and creativity, the ability to attain civilization and spirituality, and we have a craving for mental excitement. We are explorers and organizers, and that is why our culture of food is so rich and diverse. Cooks and chefs have literally spent centuries trying to figure out how to best serve the human need to eat and to eat well.

Everyone knows that no matter how delicious something tastes, even chocolate chip cookie dough straight out of the package, it's not long before you have had too much of a good thing. A constant diet of even the most succulent tastes becomes quickly dreary. In eighteenth-century England, compassionate legislators in Parliament actually had to pass a law forbidding the serving of lobster to prisoners more than three days a week.

What is flavor? What tastes good? If you ask a dozen people, I am sure you will get more than a dozen different answers in return.

I have always been instinctively inquisitive about flavor profiles, how different foods can be combined to change and enhance their flavors, to become more together than the sum of their parts. I can remember one of my earliest experiences in cooking for a lot of people, at a YMCA camp in the summer of my twelfth year. The kind lady who was doing the cooking for the campers allowed me to join her behind the camp stoves, steam tables, and boiling coppers to help prepare breakfasts and lunches. Oven-roasted tomatoes were on the menu, which I regarded as being tasty but a bit boring. I decided, on my own recognizance, to dress each with a drizzle of HP (House of Parliament) steak sauce and a tiny mound of bread crumbs. Done in the oven, it formed a nice, crumbly, but crispy sort of a crust with a savory sweet bite from the steak sauce to combine with the tartness of the tomato. It must have been a success, because my creation was added to the breakfast and lunch menus for the remainder of the week, by popular demand of the campers. I now have many more creative and startling combinations to my credit, but from an early age I realized that chefs are constantly looking for ways to push the edge of the envelope.

Ever since that early experiment with broiled tomatoes, my mind is always searching for a new way to enjoy them. I love to experiment with roasting tomatoes because the combination of sweetness and tang are so unique. Here is a pairing of which I am particularly proud.

Oven-Roasted Tomatoes, Asparagus, and Hearts of Palm, Tossed with a Sherry Mustard Vinaigrette

SERVES 6

Slow-roasted for 6 to 8 hours and worth every second.

Ingredients prep	*20 minutes*
Slow-roast tomatoes	*6 to 8 hours*
Cooking time for other ingredients and assembly	*15 minutes*
Total time	*6½ to 8½ hours*

Preheat the oven to 200 degrees (a low temperature because you will be slow-roasting).

Prepare the vinaigrette by combining the vinegar, garlic, and mustard in a bowl and mixing well. Pour in the oil in a slow stream whilst whisking constantly. Add the parsley, salt and pepper to taste, and lime juice.

Line a baking sheet with aluminum foil. Slice the tomatoes in half lengthwise and remove the stem end and core. Scoop out and discard the seeds, leaving as much pulp as possible. Place the tomatoes, cut side up, on the baking sheet. Combine the garlic and oil, and spoon over the tomatoes, then season with salt and pepper. Slow-roast for 6 to 8 hours. Remove from the oven to let cool. Cut the tomatoes in 1-inch pieces or halves.

Preheat the oven to 350 degrees. Toss the asparagus with the oil, salt, and pepper. Place in a preheated 350-degree oven for 6 to 8 minutes. Remove from the oven and let cool. Cut into 2-inch pieces.

Cut the hearts of palm on an angle ½ inch wide.

Combine all the vegetables in a large mixing bowl and coat with the vinaigrette.

PRESENTATION

Transfer to your favorite serving bowl and serve family style.

FOR THE VINAIGRETTE

2 ounces (¼ cup) sherry vinegar

1 garlic clove

1 tablespoon whole-grain mustard

4 ounces (½ cup) canola oil

1 teaspoon fresh chopped parsley

Salt and pepper

Juice of 1 lime

FOR THE TOMATOES

2 fresh vine-ripened tomatoes

2 fresh yellow tomatoes

2 garlic cloves, minced

3 tablespoons extra virgin olive oil

Kosher salt and freshly ground black pepper

FOR THE ASPARAGUS

1 bunch asparagus

2 tablespoons extra virgin olive oil

Salt and freshly ground black pepper

FOR THE HEARTS OF PALM

1 can hearts of palm

THERE ARE ONLY A FEW ESSENTIAL FLAVORS BUT, LIKE THE LETTERS IN the alphabet or musical notes, they can produce an infinitude of combinations to excite the palate.

"Sweet" encompasses carbohydrates like bread, potatoes, and rice; milk, cream, and butter; meat and fish, and, obviously, sugar. We have gone a bit over the top with it in recent years. Start scanning your food labels for fructose and corn sugars and you will see what I mean. But in real cooking, you must have an awareness of the sweet taste, when to add or subtract it, from where you can coax it and enhance it, whether you wish to feature it, sublimate it, or effectively conceal it in the background. Caramelization of meats and vegetables is one of the most fundamental operations you can perform to add flavor.

"Sour" would include lemon, vinegar, yogurt, and cheese, among others. Perception of the sour taste is the "acid detector," and is a guide to finding and using that element in your cooking. Acids can act as a preservative, but more prominently as a sharpener of flavors.

"Salty" is rather self-explanatory, but it's a tricky category, as anyone who has been placed on a low-sodium diet will tell you. Salt lurks in many unsuspected places. Everybody knows not to salt a country-cured ham at the table because salt is already in there, but you may not realize how much there is in a fast-food milk shake. Salt is the showstopper of the food world; it really makes flavors stand up and be noticed, and you have to understand it and know how to make use of it properly because too much or too little can ruin the careful balance for which you will always be striving.

"Bitter" encompasses the green leafy vegetables: spinach, broccoli, endive, parsley, oregano, and other leafy herbs. I would put coffee into that category as well. Bitterness affects a different zone on the palate, and a masterful use of bitterness, usually in counterpoint to the other major tastes, often can result in a true symphony of flavor. A diet without the bitter taste is like an essay without adjectives.

Pan-Roasted Wild Striped Bass with Roasted Tomato and Broccoli Rabe Medley

SERVES 8

Bitter, salty, sour, and sweet tastes are all well represented here by the harmonic blending of broccoli rabe, fish, tomatoes roasted again in the oven, and honey.

4 tablespoons olive oil

Juice of 2 lemons (squeezed separately)

2 teaspoons salt

1 teaspoon white pepper

2 teaspoons honey

¼ stick (2 tablespoons) unsalted butter

8 Roma plum tomatoes

4 bunches broccoli rabe

2 carrots, cut into julienne strips

2 yellow squash, cut into julienne strips

Eight 5- to 6-ounce striped bass fillets, skin on

Preheat the oven to 400 degrees.

Mix the olive oil, the juice of one of the lemons, the salt, white pepper, honey, and 1 tablespoon of the butter in a bowl, and add the tomatoes, broccoli rabe, carrots, and yellow squash, coating them well with the oil mixture.

Roast the vegetables on a baking sheet until tender.

Heat the remaining 1 tablespoon olive oil in a pan and sear the fish, beginning with skin side down, leaving undisturbed for 2 or 3 minutes, until crispy brown. Turn over and sear the other side of the fish the same way. Cook completely, but do not overcook. (The fish is done when the flesh springs back.) Remove the fish, and let it rest.

Place the remaining 1 tablespoon butter and the juice of the other lemon into the pan, and swirl together to create a butter sauce.

PRESENTATION

Place the vegetable medley on a platter. Arrange the fish on top. Spoon the butter sauce on the fish and medley and serve.

SPICES HAVE BEEN TREASURED SINCE ANCIENT TIMES BECAUSE OF THEIR intense qualities of flavor. There is an infinite number of uses for spices in the kitchen.

Spiciness, as a term related to the "heat" of certain peppers, is an interesting component of flavor that can be inherent to foods or that can be added in a number of different ways. A gentleman named Walter Scoville devised a scale of measurement for the capsaicin in peppers that is widely known to culinarians. It ranks the "heat" of peppers from the mildest, green or red bell peppers, through poblanos, serranos, and jalapeños, to the atomic Scotch bonnets and habaneros. Peppers produce a sort of phantom heat, because they really have less to do with temperature than it does with the chemical reaction that takes place when they come in contact with your mouth. This reaction has a systemic component, which is why you may begin to sweat if you eat a lot of hot peppers, and why they impart a sudden sense of fullness to the body. I feel that there is a danger in using too many Scoville-rated, peppery flavors in my cooking because they have a tendency to dull the tongue and mask the genuine flavors of foods, but when they are properly controlled, as in good chili, jerk chicken, curries, chutneys, and the like, they can be quite marvelous. Balance has to be preserved. That's why when you eat a very hot curry, the traditional *sambals*, or accompaniments, are all sweet and cool. Coconut, cucumber, mango chutney, all help to neutralize the heat and settle everything down.

The opposite of this false heat of peppers might be the artificial cooling sensation brought to the palate by mints and menthols. This sensation can be very refreshing and can be employed to bring a beautiful finish to meat and fish dishes, starches, and astringent dishes, as well as desserts. Mint is widely used in Mediterranean and Middle Eastern cooking, especially Greek cooking, and it adds a flavorful dimension of freshness and liveliness to foods as well as a sense of vitality to the body.

"Pungent" basically refers to spices such as horseradish, ginger, mustard, red and black pepper, cardamom, coriander, chile peppers, paprika, and their brethren, which are featured much more prominently in the ethnic cuisines of China, Thailand, Mexico, and the like. There is a bit of wizardry in spices, of alchemy, which is mostly derived, Merlin-like, from the seeds and barks of mysterious, aromatic plants. Outside of some of the classic spice mixtures— such as curry powder, chili powder, Chinese five-spice powder, garam masala, Old Bay seasoning—the use of spices, from a pinch judiciously added at just the right moment, to the thick pastes and dry rubs used in barbecues, means excitement. Spices are almost always dried, and can be purchased whole or ground. If you can buy and dedicate a small coffee grinder to the purpose of grinding whole spices, do so. You will add a greater depth of flavor to many of your dishes.

"Astringent" may essentially be understood as applying to beans and lentils, and is also a quality found in cabbages, apples, and pears. It refers to the kind of reaction that tannins give to the mouth. If you really want to experience astringency, chew on a slice of persimmon flesh, and have someone you love nearby, because you are really going to pucker up. Again, many Eastern, Middle Eastern, and even European diets, especially around the Mediterranean Sea, rely much more heavily on beans than the typical American diet does. Think of how bean curd or tofu is used in Japanese cooking, or hummus in the Middle East, or the fact that Tuscans were widely referred to as the "bean eaters" of Italy. Beans, or pulses, are a terrific source of nutrition and protein. They are remarkably versatile and flavorful in their own right and are talented transmitters of flavor when married and infused with pork, garlic, onions, molasses, sesame, herbs, and a multitude of other ingredients in purees, baked or simmered, or in soups and stews.

Chicken Tikka Masala

SERVES 4 TO 6

The Indian culture has been exploring the particular qualities of astringent and pungent tastes for centuries. It is never too late for you to start exploring them, too. This recipe features chicken that is marinated for 24 hours, slowly grilled on skewers, then finished in the delicious masala paste.

Place the chicken in a bowl and sprinkle with the lemon juice, salt, and pepper. Mix to coat the chicken thoroughly, then cover and set aside.

Place the onion, garlic, and ginger in a blender or food processor and chop finely. Add the yogurt and strain the lemon juice from the chicken into the blender. Puree until blended, then pour back over the chicken. Cover and marinate in the refrigerator for 24 hours.

Thread the chicken onto kebab skewers, reserving the marinade. Barbecue or grill as slowly as possible until just cooked through (it is important not to overcook the chicken), 6 to 8 minutes. Remove the chicken from the skewers.

Meanwhile, make the masala. Heat the ghee or clarified butter in a wok, add the onion and garlic, and fry for 4 to 5 minutes until soft. Sprinkle in the turmeric, chili powder, and cinnamon. Stir well and fry for 1 minute.

Add the cardamom pods, coriander, and aniseeds, and stir-fry for 2 minutes, then add the reserved yogurt marinade. Mix well and bring to a boil. Add the chicken and cook for 3 minutes. Serve hot.

You can serve this great dish with either a crisp iceberg salad or basmati rice. Enjoy!

A Note on Clarified Butter The use of clarified butter enables you to use butter at higher temperatures than you could otherwise because the milk solids, which have a lower smoking point, are removed from it. Clarify your own butter by starting with 25 percent more butter than you will need for the recipe. Heat over very low heat, scooping off the foam that rises to the top and being cautious not to disturb the water and milk solids that sink to the bottom. Carefully ladle off the clear butterfat into a clean vessel. This is your clarified butter.

FOR THE CHICKEN

4 chicken breasts, skinned, boned, and cubed

Juice of 1 lemon

1½ teaspoons salt

2 teaspoons pepper

1 onion, peeled and quartered

2 garlic cloves, peeled

One 2-inch piece of fresh root ginger, peeled

1½ cups (12 ounces) natural yogurt

FOR THE MASALA PASTE

¼ pound (8 tablespoons) ghee or clarified butter (see Note)

1 onion, thinly sliced

1 garlic clove, thinly sliced

1½ teaspoons ground turmeric

1½ teaspoons ground chili powder

1 teaspoon ground cinnamon

Seeds of 20 cardamom pods

1 teaspoon ground coriander

2 teaspoons aniseeds

THERE IS A FLAVOR THAT IS TALKED ABOUT MAINLY IN CHINESE AND JAPA-nese cooking called *umami*. Chemically, it has to do with the sensation on your palate in response to free glutamates in foods. I have read of it being described as the "savory" taste, and it is referred to in regard to fermented products, such as soy sauce and fish sauce, and in Parmesan and blue cheeses. It is also strongly present in tomatoes, which would indicate a much wider portfolio in the Western sphere of influence, though it is not widely discussed. It is a bit of a mystery—not everyone can clearly name it or sense it in foods—but it bears mentioning when considering flavor. If you are interested in Asian cuisine and influences, it warrants further investigation.

Sesame-Crusted Tuna with Asian Mushroom Salad and Ponzu Sauce

SERVES 6

Mix the soy sauce, vinegar, brown sugar, lemon juice, lime juice, ginger juice, and chives well, making sure the sugar has dissolved. Refrigerate.

Season the tuna with the salt and pepper and sesame seeds. In a large non-stick skillet, over moderate to high heat, pour in the grapeseed oil and sear the tuna for 1½ minutes on each side, or until desired doneness.

In the same pan in which you cooked the tuna, place the olive oil over moderate heat, then add the garlic and brown for 1 minute. Add the mushrooms and the vinegar, shaking the pan to coat the mushrooms with the vinegar on moderately high heat for 2 to 3 minutes, or until the mushrooms are slightly wilted. Turn off the heat. Add the chives, season with salt and pepper to taste.

PRESENTATION

Place the tuna in the middle of a large round plate; top with mushrooms and microgreens. Drizzle lightly with the ponzu sauce and serve the remainder of the sauce on the side.

> *A Note on Raw Tuna* Sashimi-grade yellowfin tuna is referred to as "ahi." It is of a quality suitable for eating raw.

FOR THE PONZU SAUCE

5 tablespoons low-sodium soy sauce

6 tablespoons rice vinegar

2 tablespoons brown sugar

2 tablespoons lemon juice

2 tablespoons lime juice

2 teaspoons ginger juice from a jar of pickled ginger

2 tablespoons chopped chives

FOR THE FISH

Six 6-ounce pieces of ahi tuna (sashimi-grade tuna)

Salt and freshly ground black pepper

5 tablespoons white sesame seeds

5 tablespoons black sesame seeds

4 tablespoons grapeseed oil

FOR THE MUSHROOM SALAD

5 tablespoons (⅔ cup) extra virgin olive oil

1 ounce (2 tablespoons) chopped garlic

6 ounces shiitake mushrooms, stemmed and julienned

6 ounces oyster mushrooms, julienned

6 ounces Crimini mushrooms, julienned

5 tablespoons (⅔ cup) balsamic vinegar

1 ounce (2 tablespoons) chopped chives

Salt and pepper

Microgreens

THERE ARE OTHER ELEMENTS OF FLAVOR THAT I LIKE TO EXPERIMENT with, singly or in combination.

Temperature can have a profound effect, both physiologically and psychologically, on the foods we eat. Consider the difference between iced tea and hot tea, a chilled glass of sake and one served at the more customary temperature, just under one hundred degrees. Cold food that is supposed to be served hot, or hot food that is supposed to be cold, can sometimes produce disagreeable results. Congealed gravy can be pretty unpleasant, and a forcemeat terrine that has been put together above room temperature can be downright scary. But a cooled seared scallop, cold sliced roast beef, cold soups, such as vichyssoise or gazpacho, a warm fruit compote over ice cream, or even a good rice pudding warmed for a few seconds in the microwave can all be revelations in flavor. The vision and talent of the cook should be paramount in deciding which textures and flavors and temperatures are appropriate for any given dish.

I like mixing "hot" and "cold" items on the same plate. Early on in my career, I found myself frequently traveling from tableside to tableside like a missionary, explaining these sorts of ideas to diners and making sure they understood was I was shooting for, and in which combinations to best attack the foods I placed in front of them.

There is an entire matrix of flavors that can be altered and controlled by a skilled cook depending on the degree of *doneness* of a dish or ingredient. This spectrum runs the gamut from raw to "blackened." Raw fish has a delicate flavor that is quite different in degree from that of fish that is broiled, but both can be delightful. Sometimes multiple levels of doneness can be featured in the same piece of food. Seared tuna can be blackened to a crisp with spices on top whilst being left rare to the point of raw in the middle, which results in a delicious contrast in flavors. Steak tartare can be wonderful. Filet mignon should be never be cooked past medium-rare. You can ask me, beg me, offer to pay me, but I just won't do it. A fuller understanding of this will inevitably make you a better cook and lead to experimentation of your own.

Texture certainly has an impact on flavor. There are textures that are perceived to be pleasurable on the palate and some that are not. Most obviously, "tender" is generally the preferred quality when applied to meat, as opposed to "chewy" or "gristly." A steak that has a tender mouthfeel, that "melts in your mouth," is usually more popular than one that offers too great a challenge to the bicuspids and molars. "Moist" is generally preferred to "dry" when it comes to a chicken or turkey breast. A chunky potato soup has a very different texture profile than a silky puree, though the list of ingredients used to prepare them may be exactly the same. A fresh poached fillet of salmon is very different from a salmon mousse, and as a chef it is up to me to decide which texture and flavor profile I wish to present to maximize the pleasure of the diner for whom I am preparing the dish.

The words that describe textures are some of the most evocative in our business, which is why you will often see them so prominently featured on dinner menus. Soft, crispy, tender, chewy, flaky, silky, plump, crumbly, moist, juicy, crunchy, sticky, gooey, and al dente, all denote characteristics that relate to flavor, and choices have to be made on which of these you would most like to feature, depending on what dish, what recipe, what ingredients you are using, and on the audience for whom you are cooking. You may want one texture to be uniformly dominant, or you may wish to combine textures in the same bite. If you are cooking pasta for your Italian mother-in-law, I suggest that you make sure that the pasta is al dente, not soft. I think psychologically these words can prime the palate before the dish ever hits the plate. Compare "cookie" to "chewy, moist, sticky, gooey cookie." This is an instance where anticipation increases the degree of perception and enjoyment.

Sautéed Sea Bass with Crisp Potato Crust

SERVES 4

This is one of my favorite preparations for showing off an irresistible contrast of textures.

Peel and shred or grate the potatoes; ideally, you'll have long, thin strands, but any small shreds will do. (After comparing a box grater, a microplane grater, and the shredding disk on the food processor, our home test cook had the best success creating long, thin strands with a vegetable peeler.) Mix the potato strands with salt to taste, and squeeze out some of their liquid. Sprinkle the fish on both sides with salt and pepper, then make a thick layer of potatoes on each side of each fillet, pressing with your hands to make the potatoes adhere.

Preheat the oven to 200 degrees. (However, if the fish fillets are very thick, say an inch or more, preheat the oven to 375 degrees so you can finish them there.) Heat a 10- or 12-inch skillet, preferably nonstick, over medium-high heat for 2 to 3 minutes, then add the oil and butter. When the butter foam subsides, add the fillets to the skillet. Cook the fillets, turning once, until the potato crust is nicely browned on both sides, about 10 minutes total. Remove the fillets to an oven-safe platter. You might have to cook in batches, but that's okay. Keep the first batch warm in the oven at 200 degrees if necessary whilst you cook the remaining fillets. (However, if your fillets are thick, you may have to actually finish them in the oven for a few minutes at 375 degrees, checking them for doneness. Remember not to overcook—they will continue to cook for another 15 or 20 minutes after you have removed them from the oven. This is called carryover cooking.) Once you touch the flesh and it springs back up, it's cooked.

Once all the fish is removed from the pan, add the wine to the skillet and reduce by half over high heat, stirring with a wooden spoon. Add the shallots and cook for a minute. Add the mustard and salt and pepper, then taste and adjust the seasoning as necessary.

PRESENTATION

Make a small circle of the mustard sauce on each of 4 plates, then place 1 of the fillets in the center of each. Garnish liberally with chives.

2 large baking potatoes (about 2 pounds)

Salt and freshly ground black pepper

Four 6-ounce fillets sea bass, red snapper, or similar fish, skin removed

2 tablespoons extra virgin olive oil

2 tablespoons unsalted butter

2 cups dry white wine

2 tablespoons chopped shallots

3 tablespoons Dijon mustard

Chopped chives

THERE IS MORE THAN A LITTLE SCIENTIFIC METHOD EMPLOYED IN THE search for flavor. Physics is involved, botany, anatomy, and certainly a dollop of chemistry. Sometimes it is desirable to penetrate deep into the tissue of the food item with which you are working. Many of the flavor-enhancing techniques, such as seasonings, salt and pepper certainly, spices, herbs, dry rubs and pastes, and sauces, involve topical applications. Pickling, originally a technique used for food preservation, is a good example of a method that has the effect of changing the flavor profile quite dramatically by working its way into a piece of food.

When you want to get to the heart of the matter, you may wish to use marinades. The use of oils, aromatics, and acids to create a "bath" in which commonly meat or fish are immersed, sometimes for days at a time, to change their flavor, texture, or composition, can be a powerful tool. These days it is not unusual to see a chef wielding a large, scary-looking syringe to inject a marinade deeply into the heart of a piece of meat. In South America, a marination method called *ceviche*, in which raw fish is lightly cooked by the acids contained therein, can take only a few minutes to achieve the desired effect.

Marinated Black Cod with Acacia Honey

SERVES 6

To prepare the marinade, combine the honey, soy sauce, grapeseed oil, and vinegar in a mixing bowl. Reserve about 1 cup of the marinade in a separate container for service. Place the fish fillets in a shallow bowl into which you can nest a tray or utility plate. (Glass pie plates work nicely for this. One will hold the marinade and fillets, the other will sit on top and hold the weight. You may need 4 plates and 2 weights to accommodate 6 fillets.) This is because you will be putting a weight such as a heavy can on top and you need something to hold it. This removes the water from the fish, thereby hastening the marinating process. Give a stir to the marinade and pour over the fish fillets. Cover and top with the weight. Refrigerate for 24 hours.

When ready to cook the fish, preheat the oven to 450 degrees. Remove the fish from the marinade and season all over with salt and pepper to taste. Put the fillets on a baking sheet and cook in the oven until they have a golden dark brown hue and are just cooked through, 7 to 8 minutes.

PRESENTATION

Put a fillet in the center of each of 6 plates. Spoon some marinade over and around the fish. Serve with your choice of vegetables and starch.

2 cups honey (acacia, or your choice of honey; see Note)

1 cup reduced-sodium soy sauce

¾ cup grapeseed oil

¾ cup white wine vinegar

Six 7-ounce black cod fillets

Fine sea salt and freshly ground black pepper

PREPARATION AND COOKING TIME

24 hours to marinate plus 10 minutes to cook

A Note on Honey Of course, you can use any type of honey for the Marinated Black Cod with Acacia Honey. One of the many interesting things about honey is that it reflects the flavor of the floral source from which the bees obtained the nectar. (In fact, it must be closely regulated, since some honey is actually considered toxic to humans because of the toxicity of the floral source.) France is famous not only for its lavender honey, but for acacia honey, which has the additional unique quality of remaining in its liquid state longer than honey from other sources. (In other words, it doesn't crystallize as soon.) Acacia honey may be more difficult to obtain than most. But experiment with different types of honey and see if your palate can detect the difference.

Nantucket Bay Scallop Ceviche

SERVES 6

There are other ways to cook besides heat.

Using gloves to protect your hands, remove the seeds from the jalapeño and discard. Mince the jalapeño very finely.

In a large mixing bowl, mix the jalapeño with the onion, lime juice, lemon juice, mango, papaya, chopped cilantro, and extra virgin olive oil. Then stir in the scallops and season with salt and pepper. Cover and refrigerate for 8 hours.

PRESENTATION

Remove the scallop mixture from the marinade with a slotted spoon and serve in cocktail glasses, each topped with a sprig of cilantro.

½ fresh jalapeño pepper

¼ red onion, diced very small

½ cup lime juice (from about 3 limes)

¼ cup lemon juice (from about 1 lemon)

1 mango, peeled, seeded, and diced small

½ papaya, peeled, seeded, and diced small

2 tablespoons chopped cilantro

¼ cup extra virgin olive oil

1 pound fresh bay scallops

Salt and pepper to taste

6 sprigs of cilantro leaves

OKAY . . . FAT. CONTROVERSIAL? YES. INDISPENSABLE? UNQUESTIONABLY. More has been written attacking and defending fat in foods and cooking than any one person could read in a lifetime. But the lipid is a brilliant little molecule in all of its forms and functions, and I say this with little fear of contradiction from other food professionals: fat is flavor. The role of fat in really good cooking is wide reaching and profound. The body reacts to the presence of fat in some wonderful ways. It aids the digestion and the absorption of essential vitamins. A little bit can give you a sense of fullness. But if fat is your idea of a culinary bad guy, I would refer you to the injunction of Michael Corleone in *The Godfather:* "Keep your friends close, but keep your enemies closer."

Fat is one of the best friends you will ever have in your quest for maximum flavor. As a medium for binding, blossoming, and imparting flavor, it has no equal, save perhaps salt. The glory of the roast; the beauty of browning, sautéing, and searing; the creation of the perfect *fond;* the glisten and sheen of incredible stews and sauces; the exquisite flavor of well-roasted root vegetables cooked in goose fat; duck confit; the hamburger, guacamolé, gravies, sausages, pâtés, cookies, doughnuts, cakes, puddings, creamed *anything,* fried *anything,* even a nice bacon, lettuce, and tomato sandwich, for goodness' sake; they are all *lost* without the incorporation and skillful control of a source of fat. Cherish fat, celebrate it, but do not abuse its favors.

Grilled Maple and Balsamic-Glazed Pork Chops with Three Potato Hash

SERVES 6

This recipe is a great example of how you can take an item like pork chops, leave on just a little bit of fat, and send the flavor through the roof by concentrating and intensifying auxiliary elements of the dish.

To make the glaze, in a small saucepan, combine the syrup, vinegar, orange juice, garlic, and mustard over medium heat. Reduce by half to intensify the flavors and to thicken, and let cool.

Heat the grill. Season the pork chops with salt and pepper. Grill for 5 minutes on each side. Whilst cooking, brush the glaze on the pork chops.

To make the hash, in a sauté pan, melt the butter and sauté the onions until tender. Add the potatoes and sauté for a few minutes. Add the stock. Simmer until the potatoes are tender. Season with salt and pepper. Fold in the oregano, scallions, and bacon.

PRESENTATION

Place the potatoes in the middle of each plate and place a pork chop over the potatoes. Drizzle balsamic glaze over the chops.

FOR THE MAPLE AND BALSAMIC GLAZE

4 tablespoons maple syrup

4 tablespoons balsamic vinegar

3 tablespoons orange juice

2 teaspoons minced garlic

3 teaspoons whole-grain mustard

FOR THE PORK CHOPS

Six 12-ounce bone-in pork chops

Salt and pepper

FOR THE THREE POTATO HASH

½ stick (4 tablespoons) unsalted butter

1 cup onion, diced small

1½ cups diced, peeled sweet potatoes

1½ cups diced, peeled Yukon Gold potatoes

1 cup diced, peeled purple (Peruvian) potatoes

3 cups chicken stock

Salt and freshly ground black pepper

2 teaspoons chopped fresh oregano

2 teaspoons chopped scallions

3 ounces cooked chopped bacon

OLFACTION IS A FUNNY WORD, BUT IT DESCRIBES OUR ABILITY TO TAKE IN and savor the delectable smells associated with food whilst it is being prepared, during the time we are eating it, and in our memories long after. Our sense of smell goes beyond the mere physical process. You have probably heard of the classroom experiment wherein the test subject is blindfolded and given an apple slice to smell as he hungrily bites into a slice of raw onion. The olfactory sense can be temporarily baffled, but in the big picture it is one of the biggest appreciators of good food. The use of aromatics in cooking is foundational. The infusion of fresh aromatic herbs and spices into stocks and sauces, rubs and broths, is near and dear to the heart of any chef. Aroma can be the entire marketing strategy of a good bakery.

I was working on a dinner for Her Majesty, the Queen, and the bill of fare included a rolled Dover sole and a chicken main course. This was at Royal Navel Air Station (RNAS) Culdrose when the Prince of Wales was in residence, and his mother had decided to pay him a visit. I was working directly with Petty Officer Cook "Taffy" Jones, a Welsh guy. I was still a kid, wet behind the ears, and had a healthy respect for a man like him, who obviously knew his way around a kitchen, had a healthy appetite for drink (after hours), was in possession of a fiery Welsh temper, and had easy access to sharp implements. I liked to see him happy.

We had prepped all day, and gotten well ahead of ourselves. Nearly five hours to the seven p.m. dinner, and all that we had left to do was to fillet the fish. My final assignment was simple: to take the bones and skin and add them to the fish stock simmering on the stove. I did so and settled in the back for a leisurely cup of coffee.

I remember it being so peaceful and quiet that I might have nodded off if a great shadow hadn't suddenly descended over me. There stood Taffy, towering, muscles bunched, breathing heavily, eyes filled with a murderous rage. I could read in an instant his desire to bludgeon me to death. I scrambled to my feet, eager to at least double the distance, the critical killing zone, between us. In the loudest possible terms, casting vile aspersions on my intelligence, ancestry, and very Christian soul (which I will respectfully keep out of print for the fainthearted), he chased me back to the stoves to show me what I had done to so incur this deadly wrath. I peered into the pot he indicated, and realized immediately what had set him off. Tragically, foolishly, I had inadvertently dumped my *fish* remnants into the pot where had simmered his meticulously constructed *chicken* stock. It was ruined.

In an earlier, less civilized age, the lash would have fallen. The good old man managed to choke out instructions to me to re-create his chicken stock. With just over four hours left 'til dinner, I had to scramble to get a fresh stock together, but managed it without further incident and in the nick of time. I might like to say at this juncture that I believed that the stock I made was superior even to his, but that might smack of overconfidence, which is probably what got me into trouble in the first place. Not a word was spoken between us for the rest of service and cleanup that night. The silence was deafening.

Before reporting for duty the next day, I took the sensible precaution of downing three beers in rapid succession to steel myself for the abuse that lay ahead. Once inside, I approached Mr. Jones humbly and apologized for my actions of the previous day. To my surprise, he was now in an avuncular mood, the new day having dawned. He addressed me in a kind and soothing voice. Placid and in control, he now appeared every inch the statesman and mentor, a Socrates to my Aristotle.

"Did you *learn* anything from what happened yesterday?" he said. The words "my child" were implied in his tone.

In a rare victory of my mind over my mouth, I suppressed the wise-guy reply "Not really," and instead gave the correct response: "I've got to watch what I'm doing."

"Right. Good. Now go and make me another stock." Go in peace.

I wandered off to do so, gently thanking whatever gods of yeast, hops, and grain had soothed his angry heart the previous night, and took this valuable lesson with me, which has served me well in the kitchen ever since: Follow your nose.

I KNOW SOMEONE WHO CAN WAX POETIC ABOUT MICROCLIMATES AND THE cultivational requirements of each herb. The eastern exposure in her yard allows her to grow copious amounts of thyme, oregano, sage, and mint. She came up with an inventive idea to have a co-op of sorts with her neighbors, who trade for her herbs with the bergamot and chamomile growing in their southwestern exposure and which she loves to have handy for brewing tea. Rinse a handful of herbs and toss them into your roasting pan to fill your kitchen with an incredible olfactory treat. Fresh herbs, ideally just picked from your garden, are among my favorite primary ingredients. I especially love to use infusions of fresh herbs, as in the following recipe for Lemon Thyme–Infused Chicken.

Lemon Thyme–Infused Chicken over a Warm Leek, Asparagus, and Red Bliss Potato Salad

SERVES 6

FOR THE LEMON-THYME CHICKEN

12 sprigs of fresh thyme

5 tablespoons olive oil

Juice of 2 limes

Salt and freshly ground black pepper

Six 6-ounce boneless chicken breasts, skin on

FOR THE WARM LEEK, ASPARAGUS, POTATO SALAD

2 tablespoons Dijon mustard

1 tablespoon whole-grain mustard

1 tablespoon sherry vinegar

¼ cup grapeseed oil

Salt and freshly ground black pepper

¼ pound red bliss potatoes, quartered

1 pound fresh asparagus, cut into 2-inch lengths

2 medium leeks, white and tender green parts only, split lengthwise, then cut crosswise into 1-inch pieces (see Note)

¼ cup snipped chives

PREPARATION AND COOKING TIME (ESTIMATES)

Marinade prep	*15 minutes*
Marinating time for chicken	*4 hours*
Prep time for salad	*40 minutes*
Cook time for warm salad and chicken	*20 minutes*
Prepare dressing and assemble salad	*7 minutes*
Plating	*5 minutes*
Total time	*about 5½ hours*

To make the chicken, take the sprigs of fresh thyme and, with your fingers, strip the leaves from each sprig into a mixing bowl, dropping the stems of the thyme into the bowl as well. Add half of the olive oil, the lime juice, and the salt and pepper, and mix together. Pour over the chicken and let marinate refrigerated for 4 hours.

Before embarking on the actual cooking of the chicken, bring two pots of salted water to a boil to begin cooking the salad ingredients. Mix the dressing for the salad, and then proceed with the cooking of the chicken. See the instructions on making the salad.

Preheat oven to 350 degrees. Heat the remaining olive oil in a nonstick oven-safe pan. Remove the marinated chicken to the heated pan (make sure you remove the thyme stems) and over medium-high heat, cook for 3 to 4 minutes per side until golden brown, and transfer the pan (covered with a lid or foil) to the oven until the chicken reaches an internal temperature of 160 degrees. Remember to use an oven mitt when removing the pan from the oven, since the handle will be hot.

To make the salad, bring two medium pots of salted water to a boil. Add the potatoes to one pot and cook for 15 to 20 minutes. Simultaneously, cook the asparagus and leeks in the other saucepan for 3 to 5 minutes.

To make the salad dressing, whisk the mustards with the vinegar in a large bowl. Then, whisking constantly, pour the oil into the bowl in a thin stream until the ingredients are integrated. Season with salt and pepper and briefly set aside.

Drain the potatoes as well as the asparagus and leeks and pat dry whilst still hot; add to the dressing. Add half of the chives, then season with salt and pepper. (Remember, this salad is served warm.)

PRESENTATION

Place the warm potato salad in the center of each plate with the breast of chicken on top, and sprinkle with the remaining chopped chives.

A Note on Rinsing Leeks Leeks hold a lot of sand, so you must rinse, soak, rinse, soak, and rinse and soak until you are sure none remains. Let the sand fall to the bottom of a large bowl of water and lift the leeks out, thoroughly cleansing the bowl of grit between soakings. Agitating the leeks with your hands sometimes helps.

TASTE MEMORY IS VERY, VERY STRONG IN HUMANS. THOUGH I HAVE NEVER managed the time to read it, I understand that the central conceit of Marcel Proust's epic work *Remembrance of Things Past* is a magnificent series of reveries and recollections that are triggered by a cup of tea and a bite of a petite madeleine pastry. I cannot count the number of times a mother's cherished recipe for meat loaf has been described to me in hopes that I can recapture, if just for the span of a dinnertime, feelings and memories from a long-past childhood. I clearly recall one time when I managed to so accurately re-create a green bean dish that a female patron's mother used to make, that it caused her to burst into tears. Our sense of smell can seemingly imprint flavors straight into our neural network, and a deep, resonant response to the flavors of food is in our genes.

I think that is part of the reason that Italians have such a deep emotional attachment to food and to life in the kitchen: it lies in the tradition of passing recipes from grandmother to mother to son or daughter. In Italian culture, food is fresh and flavorful enough to begin with, but the flavors are reinforced by the nurturance and emotional connection that comes from being integrally involved in the preparation and serving of the family meal from the earliest ages. When the smell of Mamma's red gravy permeates the house, it's not just the fragrance of tomatoes in every room, it's love. When creating new dishes and recipes, I rely a lot on memories of flavor. My mother used to make a carrot and rutabaga smash with lots of butter and fresh ground pepper, and I need only close my eyes and think for a moment to almost taste it. Your taste buds are amazing processing devices, and they store their information in a very real and immediate way that is accessible to you when you are cooking, with just a little concentration and imagination.

You cannot go into a family-style Italian restaurant without seeing a variation of this dish on the menu, and many folks remember when they first jumped off the spaghetti and meatballs and had their first Fra Diavolo. It is easy to make at home, and you can pair it with any kind of pasta. I used a tricolor penne because I think the colors are visually interesting, but the explosive flavors, inspired by "the devil in the dish," remain.

Seafood Fra Diavolo with Tricolor Penne Pasta

SERVES 6

Start a pot of water to boil for the pasta.

In a large sauté pan, heat the oil and sauté the shrimp and scallops. Add the clams and mussels, then the white wine. Add the pepper flakes, garlic, basil,

¼ cup olive oil

1 dozen U/15 shrimp (a per-
pound count of under 15
shrimp per pound)

1 dozen U/10 or 10/20 scallops
(a per-pound count of under 10
scallops per pound or 10 to 20
scallops per pound)

12 top neck clams

12 mussels, cleaned

¼ cup white wine

2 tablespoons crushed red
pepper flakes

1 tablespoon garlic, chopped

1 tablespoon chopped fresh
basil

2 tablespoons chopped fresh
parsley

4 cups marinara sauce

2 teaspoons salt

2 teaspoons pepper

1 pound tricolor penne pasta

parsley, and marinara sauce. Season with salt and pepper. Do not overcook the seafood. The shrimp should be cooked just until pink, and the scallops should be cooked just until opaque. Discard any clams or mussels that do not open.

Salt the boiling water for the pasta and cook the penne al dente.

PRESENTATION

In a large serving bowl or platter, place the pasta on the bottom, and arrange the seafood on top. Ladle the sauce over the pasta. Garnish with chopped parsley.

A Note on Shrimp and Scallops Shrimp and scallops are sold by count per pound. Therefore, the larger they are, the lower the count per pound. The "U" designates the word "under." In terms of size, U/15 shrimp would mean there is a "count" of fewer than 15 shrimp in a pound. 10/20 scallops would have a count of 10 to 20 in a pound.

THE PHYSICAL AND EMOTIONAL CIRCUMSTANCES SURROUNDING THE CRE-
ation and serving of food also contribute to the perception of flavor. If you are
afraid, if you are in a hurry, at a pressure-packed business lunch or a romantic
dinner for two, if you just came in out of the heat or the cold, the same food
can taste different depending on the context. I am sure the taste experience of
the multitude of refugees in South Yemen will differ drastically from your experience at home when you sample my rice and beans. The sound of shelling
and the associated surge of adrenaline had to have made a difference.

If at all possible, I like to talk to people I am cooking for, get acquainted,
have a laugh, build a rapport, and put them at ease. It makes the food taste
better. That is why good restaurants seek the vital element of control, not only
over the food but the colors, the linens, the music, the lighting, the mien of the
service people that you will encounter at every stage of your dining experience.
(And, of course, location, location, location . . .)

As a general guide to the world of flavor and in choosing its building
blocks in your preparations, the closer you are to the source of the flavor,
the better. Natural sugars from fresh fruits, honey, and molasses, and natural cane sugars are generally better than those that are heavily processed,
although those have a place in the modern kitchen in moderation. Sea salt,
fleur de sel, and kosher salt are generally preferable to iodized salt, and an-
chovies, caper berries, oysters, sea urchins are all naturally salty items that
can steer your flavor profiles in that direction. Bitter, pungent, and astringent flavor effects are more easily and simply achieved through the use of
natural products. There is a level of manufacturing to intensify the umami
flavor, especially through the use of fermentation, but in general, the Asian
cuisines in which it is most prominently featured have a high inherent regard for natural sources of flavor. In this regard, I would only warn against
the use of monosodium glutamate, which in my opinion stinks out loud as
an ingredient.

The study of flavor is all about balance, in your overall diet, on a menu,
on the plate, and right down to each individual bite and swallow. I would
love it if you would make and taste all of the following recipes and really
consider the elements of flavor as you eat each one. They contain many elements of everything we have discussed so far: the boldness of the color surrounding the whiteness of the crab cakes; the bitter bite of the bok choy and
the crunch of the cashews; the encompassing richness of the olive oil surrounding the savory tuna; the evocative gaminess of the duck settled in the

comfort of the ragout, its flavorful essence teased even further by the addition of truffles.

What are the relationships between sweet and sour, hot and cold, spiciness and texture, and what is the cumulative effect on the palate and the *mind* of the diner both during and after the experience of eating these dishes? Be careful with your answers; you may be graded later.

Pan-Seared Salmon with Bok Choy Cashew Salad and Orange Soy Glaze

SERVES 8

A well-rounded entrée that encompasses most of the essential flavors: sweet (in the fish); sour (in the citric acid); salt (in the soy sauce); bitter (in the bok choy); pungent (with the ginger).

1 teaspoon ground ginger

Salt and freshly ground black pepper

Eight 4- to 5-ounce salmon fillets

4 tablespoons peanut oil (use canola oil if allergic to peanut oil)

⅛ cup orange juice

⅛ cup soy sauce (low salt)

6 bunches baby bok choy

¼ cup cashews

2 red bell peppers, cut into julienne strips

2 bunches scallions, cut on the bias

½ teaspoon crushed red pepper flakes

Preheat the oven to 350 degrees.

Mix the ginger powder, salt, and pepper. Season the fish with the mixture.

Heat half of the peanut (or canola) oil in a hot sauté pan and sear the fish golden brown on both sides. As each side of the salmon sears, do not disturb for about 3 to 4 minutes to allow the surface of each side to begin to caramelize.

Place the fish on a baking sheet into the hot 350-degree oven to finish the fish. This will take about 5 minutes. Bring out of the oven to rest.

Whilst the fish is in the oven, use the same hot sauté pan to reduce the orange juice and soy sauce by half until a light, syrupy consistency.

Stir-fry the bok choy, cashews, red peppers, scallions, and red pepper flakes in the orange-soy glaze to create a warm salad.

PRESENTATION

Place the salad on a platter and arrange the fish around it. Drizzle the orange-soy glaze onto the fish and around the bok choy salad.

Dungeness Crab Cakes with Lemon Vinaigrette and Asparagus

SERVES 4

FOR THE CRAB CAKES

10 ounces cooked lump Dungeness crabmeat

2 tablespoons finely diced celery

1 tablespoon very finely diced jalapeño pepper (use gloves in handling this)

1 tablespoon chopped fresh flat-leaf parsley leaves

2 teaspoons chopped fresh thyme leaves

Finely grated zest of 1 lemon

½ cup mayonnaise

2 cups panko (Japanese bread crumbs)

2 tablespoons olive oil, for cooking the crab cakes

8 whole crab claws and/or thighs, for plating

Kosher salt and freshly ground black pepper

Extra virgin olive oil

"Sweet" crab, "bitter" asparagus, and a "sour" lemon vinaigrette. "Salty" and "astringent" come along for the ride with the seasonings.

Carefully examine the crabmeat; don't break up the lumps, but make sure there are no bits of shell or cartilage. Gently squeeze with your hands to remove any excess liquid. Be careful; you don't want the mixture to be too dry either. Put the crabmeat into a bowl with the celery, jalapeño, herbs, lemon zest, and mayonnaise. Fold the mixture so that it's just combined and the crab is not broken or mashed. Divide the mixture into 4 portions and shape into cakes that are about 2 inches in diameter and 1½ inches high. Refrigerate the crab cakes. The crab cakes will be cooked immediately before you serve them. Refer to the instructions below for cooking them.

At this point, prepare the asparagus, asparagus vinaigrette, and lemon vinaigrette.

The asparagus spears will be cooked in shallow, simmering salted water in a sauté pan or skillet. Cook until the spears are barely tender, but still crisp and green, 3 to 6 minutes, depending on size. Drain and immerse in a bowl of ice water to stop the cooking. Drain again, then cut the tips off into uniform 3-inch lengths and set aside. Put the asparagus bottoms into a blender and add the chervil and salt. With the lid securely on the blender and the machine running, add both olive oils in a slow stream through the feeder tube. Blend for 1 minute. Strain through a fine-mesh sieve into a bowl. Taste for seasoning. If necessary, add water to give the vinaigrette a pourable consistency. Set aside in a bowl and wash the blender.

Preheat the oven to 350 degrees for the crab cakes.

To make the lemon vinaigrette, put the Meyer lemon pieces, peel and all, into the blender along with the corn syrup, vinegar, and salt, and puree until smooth. With the lid securely on the blender and the machine running, add the grapeseed oil in a slow stream through the feeder tube. Blend for 1 minute. Strain through a fine-mesh sieve into a bowl. Taste for salt and, if necessary, add water to give the vinaigrette a pourable consistency. Set aside.

To cook the crab cakes, pat the panko onto the tops and bottoms of the crab cakes, then heat the olive oil over medium-high heat in an ovenproof skillet. Add the crab cakes and cook for about 2 minutes, or until golden on one side. Flip the cakes over and put the skillet into the oven for 3 minutes to brown the bottom sides.

Remove the crab cakes and let them rest briefly.

PRESENTATION

Place two of the whole claws or thighs in the center of each plate and place the crab cakes on top of them. Make a circle of the asparagus vinaigrette around the crab and arrange 3 or 4 of the asparagus tips in the vinaigrette on each plate. Drizzle the lemon vinaigrette over the crab cakes. Garnish the plate with kosher salt, freshly ground black pepper, and drizzled extra virgin olive oil.

FOR THE ASPARAGUS AND ASPARAGUS VINAIGRETTE

12 to 16 medium-thick asparagus spears, tough ends snapped off and discarded

Salt, for the cooking water

¼ cup loosely packed fresh chervil leaves

¼ teaspoon fine sea salt or kosher salt

¾ cup olive oil

¼ cup extra virgin olive oil

Salt and pepper

FOR THE LEMON VINAIGRETTE

1 Meyer lemon, cut into 8 pieces

2 tablespoons light corn syrup

2 tablespoons champagne vinegar

½ teaspoon kosher salt

1 cup grapeseed oil

Roasted Duck with White Bean Ragout, Truffle Oil, and Shaved Parmesan Cheese

SERVES 6

PREPARATION AND COOKING TIME (ESTIMATES)

Rehydration of cannellini beans	*overnight*
Cleaning leeks/prep time for ragout	*30 minutes*
Cooking and assembly time for ragout	*40 minutes*
Prep time for duck	*5 minutes*
Cook/rest time for duck	*20 minutes*
Slicing duck and plating	*10 minutes*
Total estimated time	*24 hours plus*
	1 hour 45 minutes

Cover the beans with water in a bowl or a pot and soak them overnight. Drain and rinse them. Place in a pot with enough water to cover them, bring to a boil, then simmer until just tender, about 1 hour. Drain, reserving the cooking liquid.

Preheat the oven to 400 degrees.

Place the olive oil in a large oven-safe sauté pan. Cook the bacon until browned. Add the leeks, carrot, celery, garlic, salt, and pepper. Cook for about 8 minutes, stirring occasionally.

Add the drained beans, vinegar, chicken stock, and 1 cup of the liquid from the beans. Place in the oven and cook for about 30 minutes. Allow the oven heat to reduce to 375 degrees. Pull out of the oven, then add the parsley, Parmesan cheese, butter, and truffle oil. Correct the seasoning with salt and pepper as needed.

In a heavy skillet over high heat, add the oil. Season the duck breasts with salt and pepper and place in the pan, skin side down. Sear for 3 to 4 minutes, or until golden brown. Turn over and cook for another minute.

Take the duck out of the pan, place on a baking sheet, and place in the oven for 6 to 8 minutes at 375 degrees, or until desired doneness. Let the duck rest before slicing.

PRESENTATION

Spoon the beans in the middle of each of 6 plates. Slice the duck breasts in half (each serving will be half of a duck breast). Then slice each half in ¼-inch slices and place over the beans. Drizzle with truffle oil.

A Note on Leeks The root word of blanch means "whiten." "Blanch"—the cooking term that means to cook briefly in hot water—is derived from the process of scalding nuts, such as almonds, to remove the skin and expose the white part underneath. Cooks aren't the only people who blanch things. Gardeners, farmers, and Mother Nature also blanch vegetables by shielding them from the sun, thereby keeping parts of the plant white. In the case of cauliflower, the process occurs naturally to an extent because of its natural covering of leaves. The stalks of leeks are buried in sand to keep them white. The result: lots of sand in leeks that must be removed before cooking. Soak them in a bowl of cool water to let the sand drop to the bottom. You may have to repeat the process a few times to get the leeks thoroughly clean.

FOR THE WHITE BEAN RAGOUT

1 cup cannellini beans

1 tablespoon olive oil

4 ounces chopped raw bacon

1 leek stalk, white part only, diced small

1 carrot, minced

1 celery stalk, finely chopped

6 garlic cloves, minced

Salt and freshly ground black pepper

1 teaspoon balsamic vinegar

½ cup chicken stock

2 tablespoons chopped parsley

4 tablespoons Parmesan cheese

2 ounces (4 tablespoons) unsalted butter

1 ounce truffle oil

FOR THE DUCK

2 tablespoons salad oil

3 large duck breasts

Salt and freshly ground black pepper

Lobster Salad with Spicy Cucumber Gazpacho

SERVES 6

I love recipes that can surprise you with their complexity and their simplicity at the same time. This one draws virtually all of the texture out of what you think gazpacho is supposed to be like, reducing it to its most essential flavors, yet it takes more than a full day to prepare.

Chop four of the cucumbers, the tomatoes, jalapeño, onion, celery, and add the juice of one of the lemons in the food processor for 10 to 15 seconds. Place the mixture in cheesecloth and tie. Place the bundle in a large strainer over a container. Let rest overnight with a weight on top of the cheesecloth so the liquid will drip into the container. (One way of doing this is to nest a stainless-steel bowl, which fits into the strainer, on top of the cheesecloth bundle, and put a jar or can into the bowl as the weight.)

Take the cooked lobster and chop into ½-inch pieces. Remove the seeds from the two remaining cucumbers and dice. To make the lobster salad, combine the lobster and cucumber with the mango, papaya, crème fraîche, juice of the remaining lemon, chopped chives, salt, and pepper.

Squeeze all the excess liquid out of the cheesecloth and discard the solids. To the liquid add salt, pepper, and rice wine vinegar.

PRESENTATION
Place portions of cold lobster salad in the middle of each plate. Drizzle with the gazpacho. Garnish with chopped chives.

6 large cucumbers, peeled

10 large ripe tomatoes, diced large

1 jalapeño pepper, seeded

1 large onion, diced

2 celery stalks, diced

Juice of 2 lemons (the juice from each will be used separately)

Two 1½-pound lobsters, cooked and broken down

1 mango, peeled and diced small

1 papaya, peeled, seeded, and diced small

1½ cups crème fraîche

2 tablespoons chopped chives

Salt and freshly ground black pepper

2 tablespoons rice wine vinegar

3 tablespoons chopped chives

PREPARATION AND COOKING TIME

30 minutes to prep the dish

24 hours to extract the gazpacho liquid

Tuna Poached in Olive Oil over Shrimp and Yukon Gold Mashed Potatoes

SERVES 6

FOR THE POTATOES

4 large Yukon gold potatoes, peeled and quartered

4 ounces (8 tablespoons) unsalted butter

4 ounces (½ cup) sour cream

1 ounce (⅛ cup) chopped chives

4 ounces cooked chopped shrimp

FOR THE TUNA

8 cups olive oil

1 tablespoon freshly ground pepper

2 tablespoons fennel seeds, coarsely ground

2 tablespoons coriander seeds, coarsely ground

Six 6-ounce tuna fillets

2 tablespoons (⅛ cup) kosher salt

1 cup shaved fennel

Juice of 1 lemon

2 tablespoons olive oil (from the oil used to poach the tuna)

Salt and freshly ground black pepper

1 cup micro fennel greens

Fennel fronds

Fleur de sel (a sea salt; see Note)

EQUIPMENT

A deep fryer

A ricer

Boil the potatoes until soft in enough salted water to cover. Run the potatoes through a ricer and mix with the butter, sour cream, chives, and chopped shrimp. Keep warm.

Heat the olive oil in a deep-sided pot or deep-fryer to 180 degrees. Mix together the ground pepper, fennel seeds, and coriander seeds. Place the ground spices on a plate and press the tuna into the spices to coat.

Drop the tuna into the heated oil and cook for 5 minutes. Remove each portion from the oil carefully with a slotted spoon onto paper towels.

Toss the shaved fennel with lemon juice, oil, and salt and pepper.

PRESENTATION

Place the potatoes in the middle of the plate. Top with the tuna and place the shaved fennel on top of the tuna. Drizzle with the olive oil in which the fish was cooked. Toss the microgreens together with the fennel fronds and place on top of the shaved fennel. Sprinkle with fleur de sel.

A Note on Fleur de Sel Fleur de sel is a gray-colored salt crystal hand-harvested in the Camargue region of France near Provence. Only the top layer of salt is gathered from pans of seawater.

As a chef, I can tell you, each and every one of us wants to be the best. It's the human way. Our ambition to achieve excellence is rekindled anew every few moments, whenever we face a new tray or bowl or cupful of ingredients. It is in our nature both to conform to the traditions in which we have been schooled, and to search tirelessly for new ways to make them different, to change them, to improve and improvise and build our repertoires, and maybe to come up with something extraordinary. The universal appeal of eating in restaurants is to taste perfected dishes, the perfectly seared steak, the perfectly fired chicken, the most ethereally light soufflé, the most perfectly balanced crème brûlée. The universal appeal of cooking is someday to leave your unique and indelible mark upon the profession, to create a dish or a style that will be forever enrolled in the canon. That is why we worship at the altar of flavor.

5

POINT AND COUNTERPOINT

Competing in the most dangerous sport in the world
and frank talk on how best to eat

FEATURING . . .

IN STRIKING OUT TO ACHIEVE BALANCE IN YOUR DIET, IT IS IMPORTANT not only to learn about your personal taste cravings and palate but also to know your own body.

I have taken a certain pride and interest in being fit and in good health since I was a young man. My father was a professional soccer player and I had an early inclination toward sport. I played soccer and rugby, and at about age thirteen, I met a man whose example has inspired me since, a Welsh gym instructor named David "Dye" Jones. Dye was a great motivator and a great teacher of leadership, both in words and by example. He started me lifting weights and I trained religiously with him, and with his son. David Jones, Junior, two years my senior and also called Dye, was a tremendous athlete who served with distinction in the Air Force and played rugby professionally for the Salisbury club. They instilled a work ethic and a sense of discipline in me that I still carry and rely on every day.

In 1988, I hit my peak physically when I competed for the Royal Navy Command of Portsmouth in the Annual Field Gun Competition at the Royal Tournament in London. If you are not a native of the British Isles there is an excellent chance that you have never heard of this revered institution, but it is a brutally grueling sporting competition that is assayed only by fanatics, and may rightfully live up to its reputation as the toughest team sport in the world.

The origins of the field gun competition hearken back to a legendary engagement in the Second Boer War in South Africa in 1899. The British were under siege and outnumbered in the town of Ladysmith, sorely pressed by the Dutch Transvaal Burgher Army, a nasty bunch to be sure. Anchored off Cape Town were HMS *Powerful* and HMS *Terrible* (in those days they really knew how to name ships). The commanders knew that the long guns on board, especially the devastating twelve-pounder field guns, might tip the balance in favor of the Ladysmith garrison. The guns were dismantled, shipped as far as possible by light rail, then by oxen cart, but the final stage was only navigable on

foot over very difficult terrain. The sailors from the naval brigade strained their guts and fortitude to the limits of human endurance to wrestle the hardware and guns, some of which weighed more than eight hundred pounds, over inhospitable topography and an impassable chasm over which they rigged a wire traveler, to come to the rescue of the forces at Ladysmith and win the day. Her Majesty, Victoria Regina, personally thanked the men for their superhuman efforts.

The object of the modern field gun competition for teams of Navy sailors is to re-create this historic event over an elaborate obstacle course that represents the original terrain. It starts with a five-foot-high "home wall" over which the equipment is hauled in the first leg of the race, called the "run out." The 120-pound wheels, the gun carriage, and the vintage 12-pounder gun itself must be manhandled over the wall. The gun barrel alone weighs a slippery nine hundred pounds. From here it's up a steep ramp and across a twenty-eight-foot chasm, which must be crossed on a wire assembly by all, down a ramp, and through a hole in the opposing wall. Then the gun is assembled and three rounds are fired at the "enemy."

Big guns come from wielding the meat mallet . . . and curls, of course.

The second section is called the "run back." The gun carriage and barrel must be hefted back over the enemy wall in one piece. Its combined weight is in excess of 1,250 pounds. Once the last man is over the wall and across the chasm, the rig is collapsed, a process not unlike toppling two telephone poles, and three rounds are fired in a "rear guard" action.

This culminates in the "run home," which means forcing everything and every man through a hole in the home wall, getting the wheels and the pins on the assembly in seconds, and ending in a final flat-out sprint to the finish line.

It takes eighteen men a side, working with split-second timing, clockwork precision, and unshakable teamwork, to achieve the course. In my day, men from Portsmouth, Devonport, and the Fleet Air Arm competed, and enthusiasts from all over England would come to cheer us on.

I was a "wheel man"; Wheel Man #4, to be precise. I was stationed on the HMS *Maxton,* a sweeper up in Scotland, when I was drafted for the Portsmouth Field Gun Crew in 1988. This was a prestigious appointment and pleased me no end, but the level of physical and mental toughness required was a shock to the system, to say the least. We were dropped into a parallel universe of extreme physical exertion. We would arise at six a.m., eat, then run. We ran in the ocean, ran in the heat and rain and mud and sand, ran uphill and uphill (I honestly don't ever remember running downhill). We ran with logs and sandbags strapped to our shoulders, and then we trained with the gun itself, over and over and over and over again. Our uniforms consisted of heavy black pants, gaiters, and a white tunic. As a wheel man, I was responsible for slinging a 120-pound wagon wheel over my shoulder, running like Man o' War, and swinging like Tarzan with it over the battlefield, and variously slapping it on or pulling it off of the assembly as we attacked the course. I padded both my shoulders with foam padding and piles of gauze bandages before each session, but the wheel inflicted innumerable welts and bruises that just would not be denied.

To compete successfully in field gun, each competitor must have the strength of a rhinoceros, the lung capacity of an Olympic sprinter, the stamina of a locomotive, and the determination of a crazed madman. In the original adventure, the men of the *Powerful* and the *Terrible* took days to cross the wicked landscapes of South Africa. In the field gun competition, the entire course must be traversed in less than four minutes or you are disqualified. My crew routinely recorded runs in less than three. The field gun competition is about as close to real war as you can get in sport, and men have suffered smashed bones, bloody gashes, shredded tendons, even death on the grounds of the Royal Tournament. We trained incessantly prior to the matches, with a

manic single-minded dedication and discipline. No matter how fit you thought you were, nothing could prepare your body for the sheer pain of the contest itself.

One care that I was able to leave behind during this period of time was worrying about what I was going to eat. We ate everything in sight. Our training tables seemed to consist of anything and everything we could lay our hands on. I would start the day with an archetypal English breakfast of eggs, bacon, sausages, bread and butter, and tomatoes, all broiled and piled high. That opening salvo would prime the engine to run beautifully, as long as it was further fed by a minimum of five to six full table-busting meals over the course of the rest of the day. We ate proteins, starches, and sweets indiscriminately, constantly hungry for anything that would provide calories. We took to carrying whole roasted chickens around with us in case of emergencies; sharks used to tell their children scary stories about us; small animals and birds scattered at our approach.

This story is illustrative in terms of thinking about one's body type and personal physical makeup when looking at the big dietary picture. I was at what I would consider to be my maximum capacity for physical exercise in those days. I exercise and keep to a pretty busy schedule today, but if I ate every week what I ingested in a typical week back then, I would either

Above: Robert, Wheel Man #4 in Portsmouth Field Gun competition; that's me at center with my backside to you

Above left: My picture in the Field Gun competition program

become sick or, if I could manage to stick to it, would eventually weigh five hundred pounds.

The health of the body is inextricably linked with the foods we choose to put into it. This seems a matter of common sense. Yet, today, in this ten-thousandth year or so of human civilization, eating for health and fitness seems more of a conundrum than ever before, especially in the Western world.

If you are desperately searching for a system of eating that will give you unbridled health and eternal slimness, and that will create an irresistible gravitational pull to the opposite sex, just sit down at your computer, call up a search engine, and type in the word "diet."

There, that was easy, wasn't it?

As you sit and consider the literally millions of entries that flash before your eyes, many of which flatly contradict one another, you can begin to scratch the surface of the scope of the problem.

I would posit that as the universe of dieting theories, food fads, processed snacks, fast foods, health gurus, nutritional trends, and breakthrough studies expands, so do our collective waistlines. We suffer from a limitless menu of food choices, not only in terms of dishes and ingredients but of an astonishing availability of food kinds and combinations, but we have no regard for rational or recognized systems of culinary thinking; plates ordered in "family friendly" restaurants arrive in serving sizes of staggering, absurdist proportions. Portion sizes have become a running joke: "The food isn't that great, but they sure give you plenty of it!" We live among an embarrassment of culinary riches, whilst we struggle, awash in a sea of food gimmickry and of revolutionary diet plans that promise to whack off anywhere from ten to thirty pounds a week, without ever seeming to ask, at least in their screaming headlines, where those extra pounds came from in the first place.

One key concept has been lost, and it can be summed up in one word: *balance*.

It would be remiss of me to just quote you the word "balance" without mentioning a second word that is as linked to the concept of achieving balance in your diet as is the word "cause" to "effect" and, with due deference to Mick Jagger, that word is *satisfaction*. Balance and satisfaction are the point and counterpoint of sensible eating.

The concept of balance goes back at least as far as the Greeks, who espoused in all things moderation as the path to health and happiness. In a perfect world, we would grow hungry, we would eat a variety of foods as close to their natural states as possible, and once we were *satisfied*, we would stop and go for a walk. Balance has been achieved when your body tells you that it has been properly satisfied. If we could learn to feed properly and listen to our bodies' messages, there would be no need for starvation diets, or diets that insist that we gorge ourselves exclusively on carbohydrates *only*, or on veggies or fruits *only*, or on fats and proteins *only*, or diets that seek to effectively eliminate one food category, such as sugar or fat or salt.

Foods taste good together for a reason. There is an innate wisdom of the body that *knows* what is good. This wisdom can be recognized consciously and can be cultivated, if we only decide to pay attention to it. When the healthy body* is fed properly, it responds with a message of health and well-being, of *satisfaction*, not with conflicting messages of discomfort or bloating, of stunned, immobilized, overpacked fullness, of acid reflux and indigestion, of lingering ill-temper and bad disposition or, over time, of unhealthy weight gain, bone density loss, eating disorders, or food addictions.

Greens taste wonderful with olive oil, a sprinkling of salt and pepper, maybe a few shavings of Parmigiano-Reggiano, for a reason. Throw in a fresh, ripe tomato and some cured olives, pair your salad with a lean protein, say grilled lamb or chicken, squeeze the juice of a lemon over the top of it all, and add some freshly harvested herbs, like oregano or thyme, and you have the basic Mediterranean diet. Eat as much of this as you want until you are *satisfied*, and you will be doing your body a lot of good. Conversely, eat three fast-food burgers a day, dripping with "special sauce," paired with a bag of fries and a sugary soda, and by the end of a week you'll feel as if you're ready for a trip to the emergency room.

---

* I specify a "healthy" body because in some conditions, like diabetes or celiac disease, or in the case of food allergies, for example, the body offers a metabolic or systemic resistance to "healthy" eating. In the case of celiac disease, affected people may continue to gorge on certain foods because they are prevented from absorbing the nutrients in them. The body's intolerance to gluten disables the nutrient-absorbing villi in the small intestine and only after a period of abstinence and healing can the body's craving be satisfied. Again, try to listen to your body. If you suspect you have a problem, consult your physician so you know what you may be up against.

The body craves a sense of completeness and balance from the fuel we feed it, and I strive to integrate this idea whenever I construct a recipe. I try to pair hot with cold, moist with crispy, savory with sweet in the same way that a painter controls color, or a composer controls tone and rhythm.

The body's instinctual response to this input from the foods we eat, if we eat them in the correct proportions, is to send signals to the brain to stop eating when satisfaction has been reached and when the body's needs have been provided. Even a little bit of pungent red cayenne pepper added to a dish sends an earlier signal of "fullness" to the brain than simply salting or buttering a dish will provide. The body wants and needs to experience the bitter with the sweet, the astringent with the salty. What is the reason that the body requires all of these tastes to be healthy? It is another facet of the pleasure provided by eating, really, because it provides the pleasure of being in balance, physically and even spiritually, with the foods you eat.

I know of a study that was conducted wherein restaurantgoers were given either butter or olive oil with their bread at table before a meal. Upon observation, it was determined that whilst diners sopped more olive oil per slice than the butter spreaders used butter, they ate fewer pieces of bread and consumed substantially fewer calories, by *choice*. Food psychologists felt that this may be because the olive oil has a stronger, more complex flavor than butter, and that diners felt more satisfied more quickly with the olive oil than with the butter.

Compare the experience of reading a great story or listening to a great piece of music, of watching a great movie or TV show, with the vacuous feeling of sitting and clicking on channel after channel with your remote control, that feeling of "500 channels and nothing's on." You fill the same amount of minutes with your remote control, but the experience leaves you empty and depressed. Feeding on an entire carton of ice cream, a bag of potato chips, or a box of chocolate chip cookies has the same dulling effect. There's an expression in computer programming called GIGO, or "garbage in, garbage out." These scenarios apply to your diet as to anything else in life. Search your feelings about how you eat, observe your own eating behaviors, get in touch with your body, and you will soon be able to determine what works for you and what doesn't.

Pan-Seared Salmon, Haricot Vert Salad, and Herbed Mustard Dressing

SERVES 6

This recipe is one of my all-time favorites and actually came to me in an unusual way. I was attending what many people know as a progressive dinner. Each course is served at a different participant's home—or at a different restaurant—and the party travels from one place to another within a close proximity. This one was organized by a yacht club at the New Jersey shore, on a bright sunny day by the water. (How much better does it get?) Anyway, I had visited one of the homes and tried this bean salad, which I thought really had some promise. Apparently the recipe had been handed down from one friend to another over some generations, and was quite good, although I thought a couple of other ingredients would put this into orbit, flavorwise.

So, after many tries to perfect what I thought the correct texture and flavor profile should be, I finally got there—A GREAT BEAN SALAD! I think this recipe has great balance and is a good gauge to help determine your own level of eating satisfaction.

FOR THE BEAN SALAD

1 pound haricots verts
(very thin string beans)

1 medium red onion,
finely diced

2 tomatoes (seeds removed),
finely diced

FOR THE MUSTARD DRESSING

2 limes

¼ cup fresh chopped rosemary

⅛ cup fresh chopped tarragon

¼ cup fresh chopped cilantro

3 tablespoons stone-ground mustard

⅛ cup rice wine vinegar

1 tablespoon chopped
fresh ginger

½ cup grapeseed oil (or your choice of olive oil or canola oil)

2 ounces bottled water

Sea salt and pepper to taste

First, blanch the haricots verts in salted boiling water until al dente (or cooked to your liking). Once this is done, drain the beans into a strainer or colander, and then they should be shocked by dunking the strainer of beans into a waiting bowl of ice water to stop the cooking process, which will also help them retain a great color. Drain and set aside in the refrigerator until needed.

Place one of the limes in a small microwave-safe bowl and microwave it until the essential oils in the skin are released. (This usually takes 30 seconds to 1 minute. Listen while it is microwaving and you will actually hear the "whoosh" sound when the oils are released, after which you can remove it and see the oils in the bottom of the bowl.) Then repeat with the second lime. I am having you microwave them one at a time because the ripeness and size of each lime may be different, requiring a different amount of time for the "whoosh" to occur for each. These limes will be hot coming from the microwave, so you can let them cool enough to handle before squeezing them. Make sure you use the oils in the bottom of the small bowl, as well as the juice that is squeezed.

Turn on the blender and through the feed tube, add the rosemary, tarragon,

6 salmon fillets (8-ounce size
for dinner or 5-ounce size for
lunch)

Coarse sea salt and freshly
ground pepper

Oil

Microcelery, for garnish

Fresh lime slices, for garnish

EQUIPMENT

A blender

A large bowl of ice water

cilantro, stone-ground mustard, rice wine vinegar, and fresh ginger, and blend together until a smooth paste has formed.

At this point the limes should be cool enough to squeeze. With the power on, add the lime juice through the blender feed tube, and then very slowly add the oil and water until the mixture thickens and can coat the back of a spoon.

Adjust the seasoning with salt and pepper. Set aside in the refrigerator until needed. (When chilled, the dressing should resemble something like mayonnaise.)

Reserve some of the dressing to drizzle on the plate later. Then, mix the beans, onion, and tomatoes with the dressing (adjusting the amount to your preference), and refrigerate for only a couple of hours. *(Don't mix too far ahead, because the salad ingredients will bleed and you will have a very runny dressing.)*

To prepare the salmon: season the fillets with salt and pepper. Place a little oil into a sauté pan and bring to the smoking point (you need a hot pan in order to get a crispy outside).

Cook the salmon, skin side down, undisturbed for about 5 minutes, or until the skin begins to get crispy, then turn and begin cooking for 5 minutes more. (You may need more time on the salmon depending on the thickness). You can, if you wish, finish the salmon in the oven at 375 degrees. However, *do not overcook the salmon*. Once you touch the flesh and it springs back up, it's cooked. Remember, the fish will continue to cook a further 15 to 20 minutes after it is removed from the oven. This is called carryover cooking.

PRESENTATION

To plate, take a little haricot bean salad and place it in the center of a plate, top with the crispy salmon, and drizzle with some of the herbed mustard dressing. Place the micro-celery and fresh lime slice on top of the salmon. Yummy! A truly amazing dish any time of the year!

THE FOODS YOU EAT SHOULD SERVE NATURE'S PURPOSE TO PROVIDE EQUI-librium within the body. How purely pleasant it is to arrive at the dinner table with a healthy appetite, enjoy a balanced meal that features a symphony of the tastes and textures that you are hungry for, and then to feel not crammed to the point of bursting, but completely satisfied. The sound you are aiming for is not a strained, painful "oooohh"; it's a contented "aah."

Listen to your body and pay attention to it when it's trying to tell you it is fully sated and happy. This is the last time I'll say it: respect your food, respect your body, and do not overeat!

Mixed Vegetable Curry

SERVES 4 TO 6

3 tablespoons vegetable oil

1 teaspoon fennel seeds

2 onions, sliced

1 teaspoon ground coriander

1 teaspoon cumin seeds

1 teaspoon chili powder

2 teaspoons chopped fresh
root ginger

2 garlic cloves, crushed

1 small eggplant, thinly sliced

1 potato, cubed

1 green bell pepper, deseeded
and sliced

2 zucchini, sliced

One 14-ounce can chopped
tomatoes

2 fresh green chiles, deseeded
and chopped

2 ounces frozen peas

Salt

**PREPARATION AND COOKING
TIME**

Ingredients prep: 15 minutes

40 minutes to cook

Heat the oil over medium-high heat in a large wok or heavy-bottomed saucepan, stir in the fennel seeds, and cook for 1 minute, stirring constantly. Add the onions and cook for 5 minutes until lightly browned. Lower the heat, add the coriander, cumin, and chili powder, and stir-fry for 1 minute. Add the fresh ginger, garlic, eggplant, and potato, mix well, and cook for 15 minutes.

Add the green pepper, zucchini, tomatoes with their juice, chiles, and salt to taste. Bring slowly to a boil, then simmer, stirring occasionally, for 10 minutes.

Stir in the peas and cook for 3 minutes. Season with salt as needed. Transfer the curry to a warmed serving dish and serve at once with naan or chapati.

A Note on the Breads Naan is a leavened bread eaten in North India and environs. Chapati is a flattened disk of Indian bread eaten in South Asia. (See my recipes for Chapati with Onions and Pork Vindaloo.)

Rogan Josh (Lamb with Tomatoes and Almonds)

SERVES 4

I am fascinated whenever I get into a discussion about ayurvedic principles of eating with someone who knows what they are talking about. Many of the Indian notions of balancing hot with cool, with understanding your body type and metabolism, and matching foods that will help to keep you on an even keel mentally and physically, resonate deeply with what I think I know and understand about food. And as a true Englishman, I have never turned my back on a good curry.

First, make the masala: Grind the ginger, garlic, mace, nutmeg, cloves, peppercorns, almonds, the two cardamom pods, saffron, and poppy seeds, adding them one at a time through the feeder tube of a food processor, then adding a little water at a time to make a fine paste.

Heat the ghee or clarified butter in a wok and fry the onion until browned. Add the three cardamom pods, and stir in the masala paste. Fry for 2 minutes, taking care not to burn the mixture. Add the turmeric, chili powder, cumin, paprika, and coriander, and fry for 2 minutes more. Stir in the yogurt and tomatoes. Stir in the lamb and a little salt.

Cover and cook over a gentle heat for 40 to 50 minutes, sprinkling with a little water if necessary. Serve garnished with chopped cilantro leaves.

A Note on Peeling Fresh Ginger Peeling fresh ginger is the easiest thing in the world. You don't even need a knife. Simply take a teaspoon, flip it so it's "tip down" to the surface of the gingerroot, and scrape the covering off.

FOR THE MASALA PASTE

1 tablespoon fresh root ginger, peeled

6 to 7 garlic cloves

1 blade of mace (¼ teaspoon ground mace)

¼ teaspoon ground nutmeg

4 whole cloves

12 peppercorns

2 ounces almonds, blanched

2 large cardamom pods

Pinch of saffron threads

1 tablespoon poppy seeds, dry-roasted

FOR THE LAMB

2 ounces (⅛ cup) ghee or clarified butter

1 onion, finely chopped

5 small green cardamom pods

½ teaspoon ground turmeric

1 teaspoon chili powder

1 teaspoon ground cumin

1½ teaspoons paprika

1 teaspoon ground coriander

¼ pint (4 ounces) natural yogurt

One 8-ounce can tomatoes, finely chopped

1 pound boned leg of lamb, cut into 1-inch cubes

1 teaspoon salt

Chopped fresh cilantro leaves

EQUIPMENT

A wok

A food processor

PREPARATION AND COOKING
TIME

30 minutes to prepare

1 hour 20 minutes to cook

A Note on Clarified Butter The use of clarified butter enables you to cook at higher temperatures than you otherwise would be able to do with butter. This is because the "clarification" process separates out the milk solids, which have a lower burning point than the butterfat. To clarify your own butter, take whole butter in an amount that is about one-quarter more than what is called for in clarified form. Melt it over low heat and scoop out the foam that rises. Then, spoon off the clear butterfat to a clean bowl or container, being careful not to disturb the water or milk solids at the bottom. Voilà! The clear portion is clarified butter. (Ghee is clarified butter that is heated a little longer to impart a nutty flavor.)

A Note on Mace "Blades" This is the term for the delicate outer covering of the fruit, which yields both mace (the fruit portion) and nutmeg (the nutlike seed portion).

Chapati with Onion

MAKES 12 CHAPATI

A type of bread eaten in South Asia.

8 ounces (1 cup) all-purpose or whole-grain flour

1½ teaspoons salt

4 teaspoons melted ghee, or unsalted clarified butter

7 ounces water, approximately

2 onions, very finely chopped

2 fresh green chiles, very finely chopped

Sift the flour and 1 teaspoon of the salt into a large mixing bowl. Make a well in the center and add 2 teaspoons of the melted ghee or clarified butter, together with enough water to make a supple dough. Knead for 10 minutes, then cover with a damp tea towel, and leave in a cool place for 30 minutes.

Mix the onions and chiles with the remaining ½ teaspoon salt. Place in a sieve and squeeze out any liquid.

Knead the dough again, then divide into 12 pieces. Roll out each piece on a lightly floured surface into a thin round. Put a little of the onion and chile mixture in the center, fold the dough over, and form into a ball, then roll out carefully into a round.

Using the remaining 2 teaspoons ghee or clarified butter, as needed, to grease a skillet; brown the rounds on the burner at high heat on both sides. The rounds should puff up. Use tongs to remove them safely from the skillet.

A Note on Traditional Chapati Preparation Traditionally, chapati is held briefly over an open flame so that it will puff up.

A Note on Clarified Butter Do you remember when you were a little kid and you saw those tiny pots that your mother or grandmother had in the cupboard—or you even saw them for sale in a store—and you wondered why a grown woman would want a little toy pot like that in her very grown-up kitchen? Well . . . clarifying butter is one of the uses for those tiny pots. In order to let heat and gravity do their work in letting the foam rise to the top and letting the milk solids drop to the bottom so you can spoon off the middle clarified layer of butterfat, there has to be a small enough space in the container in which that can happen. Since most people don't require huge amounts of clarified butter at any one time, the very small pots are useful to successfully clarify the butter in your home kitchen. When you use the small pot, you can reminisce about your Easy-Bake Oven days.

PREPARATION AND COOKING TIME

Prep and kneading time
10 to 15 minutes

Dough resting time
30 minutes

Assembly/cooking time
15 to 20 minutes

Total time
about 1 hour

EQUIPMENT

Tongs with rubberized handles (so you won't get burned)

Pork Vindaloo

SERVES 4 TO 6

Pork Vindaloo (*rear*) with
Chapati with Onion (*front*)
and rice (*left*)

Blend 1 tablespoon of the vinegar in a bowl with some water and rinse the pork in this mixture. Drain and pat dry with paper towels.

Put the onion, cumin seeds, mustard seeds, garlic, ginger, cloves, cinnamon, and peppercorns into a blender or food processor with a little of the remaining vinegar and puree to a thick paste. Place the pork into a large bowl, add the paste, and mix thoroughly. Cover and set aside to marinate for 15 to 20 minutes.

Heat the ghee or oil in a wok or frying pan and fry the curry leaves until golden brown. Add the marinated pork, tomatoes, and turmeric, and keep stirring until the tomatoes are broken up. Add any remaining vinegar and a pinch of salt. Cover and simmer for 40 to 50 minutes until the pork is tender. The sauce is intended to be fairly thick in this dish; however, a little water may be added during cooking if necessary. Serve hot, garnished with coriander leaves.

> *A Note on Coriander and Cilantro* Coriander and cilantro come from the same plant. "Cilantro" is the term commonly used for the leaves, and the seeds are usually referred to as "coriander."

> *A Note on Ghee* Ghee is clarified butter that has been heated to impart its nutty flavor. Both ghee and clarified butter allow for cooking at higher temperatures because of the absence of the milk solids, which have a lower burning point.

FOR THE PORK VINDALOO

½ cup vinegar

1½ pounds lean pork, cubed

1 large onion, roughly chopped

1 teaspoon cumin seeds

2 teaspoons mustard seeds

5 to 6 garlic cloves, peeled and crushed

½ ounce fresh root ginger, peeled, or ½ teaspoon ground ginger

4 cloves

1-inch piece of cinnamon stick or 1 teaspoon ground cinnamon

6 to 8 peppercorns

1½ ounces ghee or 3 tablespoons oil

6 to 8 curry leaves

1 pound tomatoes, peeled and chopped

½ teaspoon ground turmeric

Salt

2 to 3 sprigs of fresh coriander (cilantro) leaves, chopped

PREPARATION AND COOKING TIME

30 minutes to prepare the ingredients
15 to 20 minutes to marinate the pork

1 hour to cook

VEGETARIANISM IS A STANCE THAT MANY PEOPLE UNDERTAKE, EITHER for health, philosophical, or religious reasons. Whilst I do not subscribe to it in my daily life, I respect those who do, if for no other reason than it shows that they are thinking deeply about what they put into their bodies. Here are a few recipes just for them.

Roasted Vegetable Crepes with Roasted Red Pepper Sauce

SERVES 6 (2 CREPES PER SERVING)

FOR THE FILLING

2 zucchini, finely diced

2 carrots, finely diced

2 yellow squash, finely diced

1 eggplant, finely diced

2 green bell peppers, finely diced

1 yellow bell pepper, finely diced

2 ounces olive oil

Salt and freshly ground black pepper

2 garlic cloves, chopped

4 ounces Boursin cheese or goat cheese

2 teaspoons chopped fresh parsley

2 teaspoons chopped fresh basil

FOR THE CREPE BATTER

2 cups flour

Pinch of baking powder

Salt and white pepper to taste

1½ cups milk

FOR THE SAUCE

¾ stick (6 tablespoons) butter

3 tablespoons flour

1½ cups vegetable broth

2 roasted red bell peppers, seeded and peeled

1 garlic clove

6 sprigs of parsley, chopped

Preheat the oven to 350 degrees. In a mixing bowl, coat the zucchini, carrots, yellow squash, eggplant, green peppers, and yellow pepper with olive oil. Add salt and pepper to taste and the chopped garlic. Toss and place on a baking sheet. Roast until very golden brown. Cool. Add the Boursin cheese, parsley, and basil.

To make the crepes, sift the flour, baking powder, and salt and pepper together, and slowly whisk in the milk. If the batter is still a little thick, dilute it with a bit more milk.

Heat a small sauté pan, lightly oiled (or use spray). Place a small amount of batter, about ¼ cup and swirl the pan around to cover the bottom. When the bottom is cooked, the edges will be a little brown. Remove and flip, then let cool on a tray.

To make the sauce, melt the butter; add the flour, then the vegetable broth. Add the bell peppers and garlic. Simmer 30 minutes. Pour the mixture into a blender and blend until smooth.

PRESENTATION

Heat the crepes in the oven. Spoon the filling mixture into each crepe; fold into a triangle shape. In a hot sauté pan, lightly sauté the crepes until golden. Place all the crepes on a platter, ladle the sauce on top. Garnish with chopped parsley.

Vegetable Barley Risotto Style

SERVES 6

Bring the vegetable broth to a simmer. In a separate large saucepan on an adjacent burner, heat the oil and add the barley. Lightly sauté; you actually are toasting the barley.

Add the zucchini, yellow squash, carrot, and onion to the barley and sauté until translucent. Add the bay leaf and garlic.

Begin slowly adding the broth, one ladleful at a time, to the barley/vegetable mixture, stirring as you go: this will bring out the starch in the barley. As the mixture absorbs the broth, ladle more into the pan. When all of the broth has been ladled into the barley pan, slowly simmer until the barley is soft and creamy. Add butter as the last step for more flavor and creaminess to the risotto. Remove the bay leaf.

6 cups vegetable broth (warm)

⅛ cup canola oil

One 1-pound bag pearl barley

1 zucchini, medium diced

1 yellow squash, medium diced

1 carrot, medium diced

1 red onion, medium diced

1 bay leaf

1 garlic clove, chopped

¼ cup unsalted butter

IT SEEMS ALMOST SELF-EVIDENT THAT IT IS A GOOD IDEA FOR THE BODY TO eat seasonally, that is, eat wintry foods in the winter, autumnal foods like squash in the fall, and freshly harvested foods in the spring and summer. Here are two great dishes to enjoy in the winter and summer months.

FOR THE SALAD

1 small eggplant

1 red bell pepper

1 yellow bell pepper

1 zucchini

1 yellow squash

1 large white onion

2 portobello mushrooms

Salad oil

Salt and pepper

FOR THE PESTO DRESSING

2 cups fresh basil leaves, packed

1 ounce pine nuts, roasted

3 garlic cloves, finely minced

3 ounces grated Parmesan cheese

½ cup extra virgin olive oil

Freshly ground black pepper

1 ounce 8-year balsamic vinegar

6 basil sprigs

A few pieces of shaved Parmesan cheese

Grilled Winter Vegetables with Pesto Dressing

SERVES 6

Cut the eggplant into ½-inch-thick slices. Quarter the red and yellow peppers and remove the seeds and stems. Slice the zucchini and squash lengthwise into ¼-inch-thick slices. Cut the onion into ½-inch-thick disks. The portobello mushrooms will be left whole, but clean the black gills off the portobellos. Brush all the vegetables lightly with oil, salt, and pepper.

Place the eggplant, red pepper, yellow pepper, zucchini, yellow squash, onion, and mushrooms on a grill and cook over medium-high heat, turning occasionally until tender and slightly charred, 10 to 12 minutes. Remove the vegetables from the grill. Cut the portobellos into 1-inch strips. Cut the peppers into ¾-inch strips.

To make the pesto dressing, place the basil in a food processor, add the pine nuts and garlic, and blend. Add the Parmesan cheese. With the food processor running, add the oil slowly through the feed tube. Stop and scrape down the sides, and add black pepper to taste. Blend the pesto until it forms a thick, smooth paste.

Basil pesto will keep in the refrigerator for one week.

To assemble the dish, place all the grilled vegetables in a mixing bowl. Add enough pesto dressing to coat.

PRESENTATION

Serve in a large bowl and drizzle with 8-year balsamic vinegar. Garnish with basil sprigs and shaved Parmesan cheese.

Summer Tomato Soup

SERVES 4

Heat the olive oil in a large, preferably stainless-steel saucepan or flameproof casserole.

Add the onion and carrot, and cook over medium heat for 3 to 4 minutes until just softened, stirring occasionally.

Add the tomatoes, garlic, thyme, marjoram, and bay leaf. (Remember to reserve a marjoram sprig for garnish.) Reduce the heat and simmer the

1 tablespoon olive oil

1 large onion, chopped

1 carrot, chopped

2¼ pounds ripe tomatoes,
cored and quartered

2 garlic cloves, chopped

5 sprigs of thyme, or
¼ teaspoon dried thyme

4 to 5 marjoram sprigs
(reserve 1 for garnish), or
¼ teaspoon dried marjoram

1 bay leaf

3 tablespoons crème fraîche
(or sour cream or yogurt) plus
a little extra to garnish

Salt and freshly ground
black pepper

soup, covered, for 30 minutes. Remove the bay leaf. Add 2 cups water if necessary.

Pass the soup through a food mill or press through a sieve into the pan. Stir in the crème fraîche (or sour cream or yogurt) and season with salt and pepper as needed. Reheat gently and serve garnished with a spoonful of crème fraîche and a sprig of marjoram.

IN MY OPINION, THE MOST IMPORTANT THING IN MAINTAINING NUTRI-tional health is to strive for balance. I am not a diet guru and I am not a health advocate, I am a chef. I believe in food. I believe that the body responds to the skills of the chef, in his or her discrimination and judgment of ingredients, menus, methods, combinations, and timing. Know your food, prepare it with care, and listen to your body, and your body will tell you, visually, physically, emotionally, and spiritually, when you are feeding it well. When it tells you, you will know it. You will be satisfied.

THE FRENCH GODFATHERS

One man's guide to surviving an education at the
merciless hands of French master chefs

FEATURING . . .

Robert, George Kralle, and George Galati

I T IS TREMENDOUSLY IMPORTANT TO KNOW AS MUCH AS YOU CAN ABOUT the foundations of your profession and, if at all possible, to learn from the best. I received the beginnings of a good culinary training in the Navy, and I expanded my horizons whenever I could through experimentation, reading, and talking to other cooks and to the people who ate my food. At twenty-two, I realized that I needed a grounding in classic French cuisine if I were truly to forge a career for myself in my chosen trade, so one day I took my leave from the tables of the Royal Family and somewhat naively showed up at the door of the Waterside Inn in the village of Bray, on the River Thames.

Anyone who is familiar with the culinary scene in England and the genesis of fine dining in the modern era in the British Isles will immediately recognize the name of the Waterside Inn. The proprietor of the establishment is a man named Michel Roux who, with his brother Albert, introduced the very soul of perfected

French cooking to Great Britain when they emigrated in the sixties. After a period of time spent cooking exclusively for the Cazelet and Rothschild families, they opened Le Gavroche in 1967. With that groundbreaking institution and later with the Waterside Inn, they were the only three-star Michelin chefs in England for decades. Marco Pierre White, Marcus Wareing, and Gordon Ramsay have all been through their kitchens, and so have I.

If you took Don Corleone, made him French, and multiplied by two, you would end up with Michel and Albert Roux. They were the undisputed godfathers of haute cuisine in England.

I made my way to the Waterside Inn, knocked on the door, and talked to the chef who was running the kitchen that day. I explained that I would like to see if I could work in with them sometime soon, because I wanted to learn from the best. I think he might have heard that line a time or two before, but he asked me to call him back later in the week and suggested that I come in that night for dinner.

I returned that night with a date. It seemed like a good idea to take a look around and at the same time impress a girl with good food, fine wine, and beautiful decor. The table settings, the ambience, the dress and demeanor of the waitstaff, right down to the busboys, was so pristine and elegant it was almost intimidating. I don't remember the girl's name, but I do remember the food. I had aubergine and chicken-liver galettes in a buttery tomato sauce, Dover sole with a red pepper coulis ringed with finely diced yellow peppers, a mille-feuille of melon, and raspberry Pavlova. I am not sure what I was expecting. I was about to spend nearly five hundred pounds, an amount equal to many multiples of my regular weekly pay packet, so my expectations were pretty high. If the fish came out looking like Carmen Miranda's hat ringed with exploding firecrackers, that wouldn't have surprised me at all. Instead of lots of flash and showiness, the truth of their food dawned on me slowly. It started when I noticed the way the yellow peppers that ringed the sole were cut. They were shaped like little diamonds, a lozenge cut, and they were each absolutely, exactly the same size. The flavors worked on you vaguely at first, then crept through your entire system. When I was a kid, a sauce was something like ketchup; you plopped it on something else without thinking about it, usually to improve something that was bland or overcooked to begin with. Here, the sauces worked as a counterpoint to perfection. The sole was fresh, lovingly presented as the essence of what sole should taste like; the coulis did not distract from the experience, it sweetened it, aided by the texture and freshness of the peppers. They had me.

I persisted, and checked in at the restaurant every free moment I had away from the Royal Family. I was allowed into the kitchen a week later. In fact, it is surprisingly easy to present yourself for apprenticeship to French master chefs for training. Once you have wrangled an invitation into the kitchen, you simply have to be prepared to work endlessly at the most menial tasks imaginable whilst being heaped with the most creative and lovingly confected abuse, if you are noticed at all, for an indeterminate period of time of their choosing, not yours, that inevitably stretches into years. Chefs need extra hands, they need workers, they need disciples, and on some level they need worshipers, and they will take you on. They will make it clear to you that you are not worth a bag of dirt from their home country. The dirt from their homeland can produce truffles. As far as they know, you are only good for scrubbing and carrying, until you prove otherwise. They will not pay you . . . in money. But if you show them persistence and talent, they will reveal their treasures to you, and they will teach you, and they will make damn sure that their teaching sticks.

I spent the first eight weeks cleaning vegetables. Early on, "*Pah!*" was the phrase they most often applied to my fevered efforts. I was so unceasingly compared unfavorably to execrable matter, I was tempted to change the name on my passport to Robert "*Merde!*" Irvine. They had a favorite word in the Queen's English. Many of the letters in this word are contained in "firetruck" and "fruitcake," and I believe it may be rendered *fûcque* in the medieval Gallic. Their accents were thick and French, like a good hearty bisque, and they would often shout for my amusement, "What the *firetruck* do you think you are doing?!"; or "Who the *fruitcake* told you to do it that way, you piece of execrable matter?!"; "You are absolutely the *fruitcaking* worst I have ever seen!"; "*Firetruck* you!"

Under the tutelage of Albert and Michel, I learned nearly everything that matters in the life of a professional culinarian. The Brothers Roux were tyrannical, methodical taskmasters, and their food was brilliant. Albert could most often be found at Le Gavroche; for most of my tenure, I was with Michel at the Waterside. It didn't matter where they were physically; philosophically they were of one mind. Michel was very specific with me about knife skills. You would try something new, show it to him, and he would send it back. He sent everything back. When you tournéd a carrot, you wanted to end up with a barrel cut, with pieces approximately fifty millimeters long, with seven equal facets. The word "approximately" was not in his vocabulary, and you would end up doing it a *million* times.

In the first year, I progressed from vegetables to fish to sauces. They taught you to keep everything and use everything, from bones, skins, and peels and ends of vegetables for stocks; to meat and seafood trimmings, which were built into terrines and galantines; to eggshells, which were used to clarify stocks. I often brought Michel coffee or tea and made his lunch. Every dish you made for him was a test. He would demand *"Coquilles St. Jacques,"* and if the plate you brought back fell short of his standards, into the garbage it went. And make no mistake, the standards were theirs, not yours. You were not permitted to vary an iota from their recipes.

The Rouxs focused on bringing out two qualities to a finely honed edge in their pupils: consistency and discipline; Everything else could be left to your native culinary talent, but if these two qualities were absorbed, they could be satisfied that you would always be of some use in a kitchen. In my second and third years, I learned the preparation of stocks, the methods of building them over hours of patient attribution, and proper techniques for the cutting of vegetables with machinelike precision; I learned mother sauces, béchamels and veloutés and their offspring, béarnaises and Mornays, the entire complicated and ethereal catalog; I learned emulsions and forcemeats and the arts of the *pâtissier*, the *rôtisseur*, and the garde-manger. I learned to create both *pâté à choux* and *pâté en croûte* by reflex, to sauté by nerve memory, to butcher and fillet on automatic pilot, to create a menu in my sleep.

There was precious little sleep in the four years I spent running out to Bray on practically every available minute of leave time I had from dishing up dinners to the Royals. In my fourth year, I had a personal breakthrough when I was working sauces for the Rouxs. I had produced a *sauce marzan*, a hollandaise variation with olives and cucumbers, silky and slightly salty, which was to accompany sole. I assembled it and tasted it. It was as if I felt a click in my head and I breathed in deeply. There are so many things that can go wrong with a sauce that when *everything* goes right, it can take your breath away. This was probably the best sauce I had made to that point in my life. But you couldn't just run up to Michel with a spoon in your hand and say, "Dude, you *gotta* try this!" When you had finished the sauces for the day, you would line them up and place a small silver tasting spoon in front of each one, each spoon pointing straight to the sauce with military precision. He would dip in each spoon, taste, and if he said nothing to you, you knew that it was ready for service. I lined up *the* sauce last in the rank, and I took a chance. I left an extra tasting spoon just slightly off to the side, just slightly at an off angle, to suggest that it had been left there oh-so-inadvertently. Michel tasted each sauce in turn. When he came to *the* sauce, he tasted and I swear I saw a flicker in his eye. Maybe he breathed in just a little more deeply. He rested the first spoon on the white linen placed there for the purpose. And then he reached for the second spoon. He tasted again. He told me I had done a good job, patted me on the back, and walked away. Patted me on the back. Pure, unadulterated triumph.

The day finally dawned when the brothers declared me eligible for my final Master Chef's testing. Clearing this hurdle can be a momentous achievement in a chef's career, especially in a European kitchen. A Master Chef's rating can mean the difference between a one-star placement and a three-star placement. My first reaction was "I'm not ready." The peremptory response was "Yes, you are." It wasn't put as a request; nothing in their kitchen ever was. This was to be a command performance.

In the time I had spent with them, I had cleared certain benchmarks along the way at their gentle mercies. I had passed my charcuterie, was judged able to make an acceptable terrine, a passable dodine, galantine, and mousseline (when I say passable, that means it passes muster with two three-star Michelin chefs; that means that they found pleasure in seeing and eating it), and make cold aspics and jellies. I had mastered the lozenge, rondelle, and tourné cuts for decorative vegetables. I could roast, I could braise. I managed my time properly and did not create excessive waste when I worked. I understood not only the substance of the foods I worked with, their critically measured and calibrated relationships to one another, but I understood context, the visual appeal of food, the use of aromas, of proper delivery to table, neither too hot nor too cold nor too long a wait. I also knew what foods were needed when in the kitchen. I was organized; I had skills.

The final push lasted about four days, and the Roux brothers judged my performance along with a third Master Chef, who graded dish after dish, forkful after forkful, bite after bite. I would receive an order, go off to the kitchen, and work as hard as I possibly could, to come as close to perfection as I could possibly manage. The days were sixteen to eighteen hours long and I was a nervous wreck. There was no running update, no conversation, no encouragement. You put the dish down and walked away. Some of the dishes I created along strictly classic lines; in others, I allowed for inspiration based on what was at hand, or on forms and flavors suggested to me by the food itself, its freshness, its texture, the time of year, informed by the preferences and prejudices of the men for whom I was preparing the food.

They had watched me come along for four years. In the end, after dissection, criticism, consultation, comparison and, most of all, after tasting, they awarded me my Master Chef certificate and medal. Apparently, I could cook.

Years after I achieved my master's certification with the Rouxs and left the Navy, I joined Celebrity Cruises as executive chef. In those days, I was out to make a mark for myself. In some cases, we were turning out 25,000 meals a day, and I was in charge of purchasing, organization, quality control, and menus. I was learning quickly about life in kitchens that weren't necessarily filled with young British guys. I worked with enough Ecuadoreans to learn how to say incredibly nasty things to people in a tongue other than my native English. We cruised all over, from Philadelphia to the Panama Canal, and in each port, I was taking the opportunity to source local ingredients for use on our ships. My food was consistently judged by our passenger satisfaction rating with a score of 9.9 out of a possible 10.

Albert and Michel were hired as consultants to the line, and their familiar menu items started to appear from headquarters. The menus and recipes were very good, of course, but in my new station in life, I felt confident enough to change them as I saw fit. I changed their marinades and cuts; I served variations on their recipes, their trout in pastry with saffron sauce, tournedos of beef with goose liver pâté en croûte. I introduced specials on the menu each day of my own creation, and I even put liver and onions on at lunch because it was a favorite of mine.

One brilliant sunny day, *Don* Michel himself showed up in the kitchen on my ship, the SS *Meridien*. "What the *fruitcake* are you doing here?" he said. "I'm your chef," I said with a smile. The look on his face, of artfully practiced contempt and instinctive skepticism, was mixed with, maybe, a hint of paternal pride, and it made my day.

The next few recipes are well served by the foundations I learned at the Waterside Inn. I hope you enjoy this small catalog of applied knowledge.

Cold Leek and Potato Soup

SERVES 6 TO 8

Vichyssoise serves in the public consciousness by its use in the movies and in literature as the ultimate representation of elegant dining. So in honor of true elegance in dining, as taught to me by the Brothers Roux . . . ladies and gentlemen, I give you . . . the queen of all soups.

Put the potatoes and broth in a saucepan and bring to a boil. Reduce the heat and simmer for 15 to 20 minutes.

Make a slit along the length of each leek and rinse well under cold running water. Slice thinly.

When the potatoes are barely tender, stir in the leeks. Season with salt and pepper and simmer for 10 to 15 minutes until the vegetables are soft, stirring occasionally. If the soup appears too thick, thin it down with a little more broth or water.

Puree the soup in a blender or food processor, in batches if necessary. Or better yet, use a handheld blender (known in some circles as a "boat motor") and puree it right in the pot. If you would prefer a very smooth soup, pass it through a coarse sieve. Stir in most of the cream (reserving some for garnish), cool the soup, and then chill. To serve, ladle into chilled bowls and garnish with a swirl of the reserved cream and chopped chives.

1 pound potatoes (about 3 large), peeled and cubed

6 cups chicken broth

4 medium leeks, trimmed

Salt and freshly ground black pepper

⅔ cup crème fraîche or sour cream

3 tablespoons chopped fresh chives

A Note on Rinsing Leeks If vegetables lived in a feudal society, a leek would be "King of the Sand Castle." So you must rinse, soak, rinse, soak and rinse, and soak some more until you are sure no sand remains. Agitate the leeks in a bowl of cold water and let the sand fall to the bottom. Lift the leeks out by hand (as opposed to draining in a colander) so the grit stays at the bottom of the bowl. Then thoroughly cleanse the bowl between soakings.

I HOPE YOU ENJOY THE FOLLOWING TRIO OF ENTRÉES, EACH FEATURING more than what immediately meets the eye.

Duck Breast Stuffed with Apples and Chestnuts and Roasted in Bacon

SERVES 4

A treat for the senses with warm beckoning aromas and a visual surprise inside.

PREPARATION AND COOKING TIME (ESTIMATES)

Butterflying duck breasts	*15 minutes*
Prep time for apples	*10 minutes*
Roast time for apples alone, overlaps with prep time for chestnuts and celeriac	*20 minutes*
Remaining roast time for apples with chestnuts added (10 minutes), overlaps with remaining cooking time for celeriac (10 minutes) during which you can begin sautéing the ingredients for the duck sauce	*10 minutes*
Whilst duck sauce is simmering for 25 to 30 minutes, remove the apple-chestnut mixture from the oven and puree the celery root (10 minutes); start assembling duck "packages"	*30 minutes*
Begin cooking duck on the stovetop	*8 minutes*
Whilst duck is in oven, strain duck sauce and begin plating	*15 minutes*
Total time	*1¾ to 2 hours*

FOR THE ROASTED APPLES

4 tablespoons unsalted butter, melted

¼ cup water

1 tablespoon sugar

½ teaspoon kosher salt

2 Fuji apples, peeled, cored, and each cut lengthwise into 8 wedges

12 to 16 peeled whole chestnuts, fresh or frozen

2 teaspoons fresh thyme leaves

FOR THE CELERY ROOT PUREE

1 (1-pound) celeriac (celery root), peeled and cut into 2-inch pieces

Kosher salt

4 tablespoons unsalted butter

Preheat the oven to 350 degrees. Combine the butter, water, sugar, and salt in a bowl. Add the apples and toss to coat. Spread the apples out on a rimmed baking sheet and roast, stirring frequently, for 20 minutes. (During this time you may want to begin cooking the celery root as described below.) Add the chestnuts and roast for 10 minutes more, or until the apples and chestnuts begin to brown and the butter and water have been absorbed. Remove from the oven, toss with the thyme, and set aside to cool.

To make the celery root puree, put the celery root into a large saucepan with generously salted water to cover and add 2 tablespoons of the butter. Bring to a boil, decrease the heat to maintain a simmer, and cook for about 20 minutes, or until the celery root is soft when pierced with a knife. Drain, then transfer the celery root to a blender with the remaining 2 tablespoons butter. Puree until smooth and season with salt if necessary. Set aside for up to 1 hour at room temperature and rewarm before serving.

To make the duck sauce, heat the olive oil in a saucepan over medium-high heat. Add the apple, shallots, and garlic, and cook for about 6 minutes, or until they begin to caramelize. Add the Calvados, increase the heat to high, and cook until almost all the liquid has evaporated. Add the peppercorns, thyme,

FOR THE CALVADOS DUCK SAUCE

2 tablespoons olive oil

1 cup thinly sliced unpeeled Fuji apple (about 1 apple)

¼ cup sliced shallots

2 garlic cloves, crushed

1 cup Calvados or good-quality brandy

6 black peppercorns

2 thyme sprigs

1½ cups dark chicken stock

FOR THE DUCK BREASTS

4 boneless, skinless duck breast halves, about 6 ounce each, butterflied (see Note about butterflying)

24 thin slices bacon

¼ cup grapeseed oil or olive oil

PREPARATION AND COOKING TIME

Several of the elements of this meal can be prepared in advance to varying degrees and are thus noted in the description. Allow 1¾ to 2 hours if you are preparing everything before mealtime. (This encompasses times during which preparation can be done whilst some of the cooking is under way.)

and chicken stock, and simmer for 25 to 30 minutes, or until thickened to the consistency of a heavy cream sauce. (Whilst the duck sauce is simmering, you may want to begin assembling the duck breasts as described.) Strain the sauce through a fine-mesh sieve into a small saucepan. Refrigerate for up to 2 days and reheat before serving.

To prepare the duck, increase the oven temperature to 375 degrees. Working with 1 breast at a time, spread a butterflied breast, skin side down, on a work surface. Place 4 apple wedges down along the center and fill in between with the chestnuts, using about 4 per breast. Fold the breast meat over onto itself to form a roll. Place 4 overlapping slices of bacon lengthwise on the work surface and place 2 slices perpendicular to the 4 slices so they overlap by 1 inch to form a cross. Place a duck breast in the center, parallel to the 2 bacon slices, fold the bacon over the duck, then roll it up to make a neat package. Repeat with the remaining breasts and bacon. (These can be assembled in advance and refrigerated for up to 8 hours.)

To cook the duck, heat the oil over medium heat in a large ovenproof sauté pan. Carefully place the bacon-wrapped duck breasts in the pan and cook on all sides for about 6 minutes to render and brown the bacon. Drain off most of the fat from the pan and put into the oven to finish the cooking, about 15 minutes for medium-rare. Remove the pan from the oven and let the duck breasts rest for 5 to 8 minutes.

PRESENTATION

To serve, place a ½-cup mound of celery root puree in the center of 4 warm dinner plates and spread out with the back of a spoon into 4-inch circles. Trim off about ¼ inch from the ends of each duck breast and then cut each breast crosswise in half. Place these two halves of the duck "roulade" in the center of the celery root puree and spoon a little of the sauce over. Drizzle some of the remaining sauce around the puree.

> *A Note on Butterflying Poultry* The butterfly cut allows the flesh of the poultry breast to be of a thinner, more uniform thickness, which is conducive to stuffing and rolling as in a roulade.
>
> Place the breast on your work surface, skin side down (it is usually already skinned at this point, but this means to put the curved side of the breast "face-down". With a sharp knife make strategically placed incisions (without cutting all the way through the breast), which will allow you to spread the flesh open to a "single" contiguous thickness of about ¼ to ⅜ inch thick.

Chicken Roulade with Prosciutto, Spinach, and Sun-Dried Tomato Stuffing, Served with Tomato Demi-Glace

SERVES 6

Chicken cutlets and a few key ingredients translate into a memorable entrée with a spiral-designed stuffed interior. Prepare earlier in the day, and freeze to make it easier to handle.

Six 6-ounce boneless chicken breasts, skin on

Salt and freshly ground black pepper

6 slices prosciutto

18 leaves fresh spinach

24 pieces sun-dried tomato

3 to 6 whole eggs, or as needed

1 to 2 cups half-and-half, or as needed

2 cups flour, or as needed

2 cups Italian flavored bread crumbs, or as needed

1 quart canola oil

Mashed potatoes, as an accompaniment

1 teaspoon chopped garlic

¼ cup red wine

2 cups beef stock

¼ cup tomato puree

1 cup demi-glace (brown
sauce)

½ stick (4 tablespoons)
unsalted butter

1 teaspoon chopped fresh
thyme

EQUIPMENT

A large cutting board

Plastic wrap to cover the
cutting board

A meat mallet

A deep fryer

Before you proceed, realize that your objective in butterflying the chicken breasts is to be able to flatten them with the meat mallet so you will have a single piece of chicken breast for each serving that is thin enough to accommodate a layer of stuffing, which can then be rolled up (into your roulade).

Lay a long piece of plastic wrap over the cutting board and tuck it underneath the sides of the board. The chicken breasts should be placed on the covered cutting board, skin side down, with enough space between them so they can lie flat after you butterfly them. To make the butterfly cut, carefully slice open the chicken breasts (without slicing them all the way through) and spread the flesh of the chicken. Season the breasts with salt and pepper. Then put another length of plastic wrap over the seasoned chicken breasts to keep the mess down when you pound them with the meat mallet. Pound the chicken to integrate the seasonings into the flesh and to make the breasts thin. Then remove the top layer of plastic.

Lay 1 slice prosciutto on each breast. Add 3 leaves spinach and 4 pieces sundried tomato on each breast. Fold in each end and roll tightly. Place on a sheet tray and freeze until firm. (The chicken should not be allowed to freeze completely hard, but freezing it slightly makes it easier to handle when breading.)

Whilst the chicken roulade is hardening in the freezer, prepare the tomato demi-glace. In a saucepan, sauté the garlic and then deglaze the pan with the wine. Add the beef stock and tomato puree. Boil over medium heat until reduced by half. Add the demi-glace (brown sauce) and let simmer until thickened ("medium thickness").

When the chicken is firm, set up a breading station. Whisk together 3 eggs and 1 cup of the half-and-half for the egg wash. (Begin with this amount and whisk more together if needed.) Then set up a bowl each of flour, egg wash, and Italian bread crumbs. Evenly coat the rolled frozen chicken with flour (not too much or the bread crumbs won't stick). Dip the floured rolled chicken into the egg wash, then into the bread crumbs. In a deep-fryer, lightly fry golden brown. Finish in a 325-degree oven for 15 minutes until completely cooked firm. Let rest.

Reheat the tomato demi-glace, and to finish, remove from the heat and immediately whisk in the butter and fresh thyme.

PRESENTATION

Slice each chicken roll to expose the beautiful stuffed interior. Place mashed potatoes in center of each plate and lay the chicken roulade over the potatoes. Drizzle the tomato demi-glace on top and serve with your favorite vegetables.

Roasted Rack of Lamb, Stuffed with Summer Ratatouille

SERVES 8

Preheat the oven to 350 degrees.

Heat ⅛ cup of the olive oil in a sauté pan. Season each rack of lamb with salt and pepper. Place the lamb into the hot pan and sear the meat all around. Remove and let sit.

In the same hot pan, sauté the zucchini, yellow squash, eggplant, and olives.

¼ cup olive oil

2 racks domestic lamb, cut and trimmed (leave racks whole)

4 teaspoons salt

2 teaspoons freshly ground black pepper

1 zucchini, medium diced

1 yellow squash, medium diced

1 small eggplant, medium diced

¼ cup pitted Kalamata black olives, cut in half

2 tablespoons chopped fresh basil

3 tablespoons tomato puree

4 tablespoons Boursin cheese

1½ pounds fingerling potatoes

EQUIPMENT

A meat thermometer

A boning knife, or something similar to make the "tunnel" (see page 201)

Remove from the heat and stir in the basil, tomato puree, and Boursin cheese. Let sit to rest and to become cool enough to handle.

Coat the potatoes with the remaining ⅛ cup olive oil and salt and pepper. Place on a baking sheet and roast until golden brown.

With a boning knife, create a long hole going straight through the lamb rack from one end to the other. Begin a small incision at one end as deep as you can make it reach into the center, and then make another cut from the other end that will meet up to create a long "tunnel" into which you will stuff the vegetable mixture ratatouille. (Each slice will have ratatouille "stuffing" in the meat.)

Take the ratatouille and stuff it into the lamb racks. Place the lamb in a roasting pan and roast in the oven until done to your liking, 8 to 10 minutes for medium-rare, or to an internal temperature of 125 degrees (this means that because of the 5 to 8 minutes of carryover cooking whilst the lamb rests, you pull it out at 120 degrees so it will end up at 125 degrees for medium-rare). Remember, only you know your oven—it may take longer. Doneness—the way you like it—is more important than time.

Remove the lamb to a utility platter and let rest.

PRESENTATION

Place the potatoes on serving platter. Slice the racks of lamb in between the bones. Each slice will have ratatouille in the center. Place around the potatoes.

KNOWLEDGE IS POWER. SIMPLE STATEMENT, BUT IT SURE COVERS A LOT of territory, especially in the world of cooking. In cooking, everything proceeds from the simple to the complex, and the road to really fine dining is paved with knowledge. Baby Einstein knew that two plus two equals four. Much, much later, after years of learning, Professor Einstein figured out that $E = mc^2$. In that same vein, the path to cooking knowledge proceeds from the simple to the complex. Let's start with the simple end of this paradigm: plain. I am actually taking a quick step past the very beginning of the line, because for the moment I am going to skip over "raw." Raw encompasses ingredients in their completely natural state: wheat as opposed to flour, for instance. "Plain" I would define as "unadorned."

There is a pretty famous diner scene in the film *Five Easy Pieces*, wherein Jack Nicholson's character tries, initially without success, to order plain toast from a waitress. She, a stickler for the rules, refuses him, because there are no sides of plain toast written on the menu. Instead, he orders a chicken salad sandwich on toast; hold the lettuce, hold the tomato, hold the mayonnaise . . . and hold the chicken. "Hold the chicken?" she asks with great indignation. Suffice it to say that his rather rude suggestion of where exactly she should hold the chicken leads to a melee and a classic moment on the silver screen, but it underscores the point that the unadorned don't always come easy. Sometimes you just want it plain.

There is a path to be traveled by every cook from the plainest recipes to the more complex. At one end is a freshly picked tomato with a little salt; farther on is a marinara sauce, a coulis, or a soup. Simple, a plain boiled potato; more complex, vichyssoise. Simple, a nice plain hamburger; more complex, beef Wellington. The coin of the realm on this journey is knowledge.

Consider the egg. The humble chicken's egg should prove a terrific case study for demonstrating how knowledge applied to a single ingredient can make all of the difference. There is a kitchen legend that says that the immaculately white chef's toque and its many pleats represents nothing less than how many ways a chef can prepare an egg. The more knowledge you acquire, the more you will be amazed how much promise this little white sphere holds. Let's pass on eating it raw out of the shell, unless you're really into it or are a die-hard *Rocky* fan, and let's go straight to unadorned.

Even if you claim to know nothing about cooking, chances are that you know how to boil water. That is a very powerful piece of knowledge. In a very fundamental way, it marries the concept of heat to your ingredient of choice, and you can, at last, start cooking. Boil the egg.

If you boil the egg for 3 minutes, you will be able to enjoy a nice soft-boiled egg, which is lovely with a little salt and pepper. You may already have the knowledge and equipment necessary to cook up a nice slice of the aforementioned toast. You pair the toast with your newly cooked egg, and now you've created a dish. You can see how things can steamroll if you are not careful.

Suppose you let your egg boil a little longer. In 10 minutes you will have a hard-boiled egg on your hands. Careful peeling it . . . it's hot! Nice on its own, but you realize you can chop this into just about any kind of a salad. Paired with mayonnaise, it's egg salad. Hold it . . . mayonnaise.

Once you know how, mayonnaise is easy, an emulsification of vinegar, oil, and eggs. Now you can take your hard-boiled egg, mix it with this new element, mayonnaise, and create an egg salad sandwich or deviled eggs. Leave that baby to cure in brine for a while, you have a pickled egg.

Try poaching an egg *out* of its shell in your gently boiling water. Pair this up with another emulsified dressing that requires another bit of expertise to go along with your eggs, hollandaise sauce. Nip the poached eggs on top of an English muffin, throw on a little ham and parsley, and suddenly you and your storehouse of knowledge have mastered eggs Benedict. Swap the muffin and ham for tortillas and beans, and you're in for huevos rancheros.

With only the tiniest adventuresome leap, you can fry two of your eggs with bacon and potatoes, and you've made another variation on breakfast. Scramble them, add a little cheese and veggies, fold carefully, and you have an omelet. Leave it unfolded, and you've likely made a frittata. Mix them up as if you are going to scramble them, dip in some bread instead, and make French toast. Combine some eggs with cream and scramble, slip them into a pie crust, and you will have made quiche Lorraine. Mix them up with a little flour and a fork, and if you know what you are up to, you can whip up a big bowl of fresh pasta.

Once you are feeling confident, it is not going to kill you to try your hand at the skill and timing required for creating a savory soufflé. All it takes is a little know-how and a little practice.

We foolishly neglected the promise of those raw eggs until one fine day we learned that they can be used to make a Caesar salad, spaghetti alla carbonara, or steak tartare.

When it's time for dessert, you can really start strutting your stuff. Cookies, cakes, pies, custards, ice creams, pastries, are all within your reach, all of them with your little round friend. You just have to take the time to learn how. As you become more accomplished, you may feel from time to time that you have left "plain" far behind in your rearview mirror; please always try to remember that the simpler the preparation, the more the skill, refinement, taste, and judgment of the cook may shine through. You may proudly and rewardingly live your life in search of the perfectly risen soufflé, the perfectly folded omelet, or the perfectly poached egg. (Go out, buy a few dozen eggs, and increase your knowledge.)

Asparagus Parmesan Frittata

SERVES 4 TO 6

1 pound thin asparagus

Salt

2 tablespoons extra virgin olive oil

3 medium shallots, minced

6 large eggs

½ cup freshly grated Parmesan cheese

¼ cup shredded fresh basil leaves

Freshly ground black pepper

6 to 12 whole fresh basil leaves

Bring a quart of water to a boil in a medium saucepan. Snap and discard the tough ends from the asparagus. Slice the asparagus diagonally into 1-inch-long pieces. Add the asparagus and salt to taste to the boiling water and cook until almost tender, about 1½ minutes. Drain and set aside. Preheat the broiler. Heat the oil in a large nonstick skillet with an ovenproof handle. Add the shallots and sauté over medium heat until translucent, about 3 minutes. Add the asparagus and cook for 30 seconds. Lightly beat the eggs, cheese, basil, and salt and pepper to taste in a medium bowl. Add the egg mixture to the pan and stir gently with a fork to incorporate the vegetables. Cook over medium-low heat. Continue cooking until the frittata is set, except for the top, about 8 minutes.

Place the pan directly under the broiler and cook just until the top is golden brown and set, 1 to 2 minutes. Make sure the frittata rises, but do not burn it. Being sure to use an oven mitt when grasping the very hot handle of the pan, invert the frittata onto a large platter. Garnish with whole basil leaves, cut into wedges, and serve.

Black Angus Beef Tartare with Toasted Brioche and Fried Quail Egg

SERVES 6

This may seem primarily like a beef dish, but for my money, in terms of flavor, texture accent, and visual interest, the eggs, from both quail and chicken, play a starring role.

¾ pound Angus beef filet

1 large egg yolk

1 tablespoon chopped gherkins

1 tablespoon chopped capers

1 tablespoon chopped shallots

2 tablespoons chopped chives

Splash of Tabasco

Splash of Worcestershire sauce

Splash of sherry vinegar

Salt and pepper

1 tablespoon unsalted butter

6 slices formed brioche bread, ¼ inch thick and 1½ inches in diameter

6 quail eggs

Olive oil

1 head frisée lettuce (aka frisée greens)

6 slices prosciutto, cut into thin strips

¼ cup extra virgin olive oil

Juice of 1 lemon

1 tablespoon chopped chives

EQUIPMENT

A 1½-inch-diameter circle cutter (biscuit cutter)

Prepare the beef with a sharp knife, chopping it very fine (tartare). Mix the egg yolk, gherkins, capers, shallots, and 1 tablespoon of the chives. Season with Tabasco, Worcestershire sauce, and sherry vinegar. Season with salt and pepper, and set aside briefly.

Heat the butter in a pan, add the brioche slices, and fry until golden brown. Cut the slices with the biscuit cutter. Using the cutter as a ring mold, form the tartare into circles the same size as the brioche, and place on top of the brioche. Fry the quail eggs in a little olive oil and place on top of the tartare on the brioche.

Toss the frisée, prosciutto, lemon juice, and olive oil. Season with salt and pepper. Place the salad next to the tartare and garnish with the remaining chives. Drizzle with olive oil.

Apricot Ravioli with Sabayon

SERVES 4

Take care with the quality of your eggs for this recipe. The better and closer to fresh, free-range, and organic they are, the better the taste and texture of your ravioli will be.

In a medium saucepan, add the apricots, cover with boiling water, and set aside for 1 hour. Add the apricot brandy and cook over low heat for 20 minutes, or until the apricots are very soft. Remove from the heat and set aside to cool in the liquid. Strain, chop finely, and set aside.

4 ounces dried apricots

2 tablespoons apricot brandy

6 ounces fresh egg pasta dough

Mint leaves

Confectioners' sugar

3 sprigs of mint, steamed and minced

FOR THE SABAYON

2 egg yolks

2 eggs

4 tablespoons granulated sugar

¼ cup apple juice

¼ teaspoon ground cinnamon

Juice of ½ lemon

EQUIPMENT

A pasta machine

A double boiler

A cookie cutter in a shape that will accommodate a filling

Roll the pasta dough through a pasta machine until it is at its thinnest setting. Arrange mint leaves on half of the rolled-out piece of dough and fold the other half over the mint to enclose. Roll the dough again until it is through the finest setting, and place on a lightly floured work surface. Cut into shapes with a cookie cutter (I like leaf shapes for this recipe), place on a parchment-lined sheet pan, and set aside. On half of the cutout dough shapes, place 1 teaspoon of the apricot filling in the center of each, and lightly brush the edges with water. Cover the filling with the remaining cutouts and press the edges to seal. Cover the ravioli with a towel and set aside for 2 hours. Bring a large saucepan of water to a boil, add the ravioli, and cook for 1 minute. Remove the ravioli with a slotted spoon, drain on a paper towel, and keep warm.

To make the sabayon, fill the bottom of a double boiler with 2 inches of water and bring to a simmer. Using the top of the double boiler as your mixing bowl, whisk together all of the ingredients, then place over the saucepan. Reduce the heat and cook, stirring constantly, until the sabayon is thick enough to coat the back of a spoon. Remove from the heat and set aside.

PRESENTATION

To serve, arrange the ravioli on a plate, slicing one open to reveal the filling. Spoon some of the sabayon on the plate and garnish with confectioners' sugar and a sprig of fresh mint.

A Note on Making Your Own Fresh Pasta If you were enamored of Silly Putty as a kid, then making pasta from scratch is for you. Technically you can do this with a rolling pin, but if you love pasta enough to make your own, set yourself up with a pasta machine—and get one with an electric motor so you won't have to crank.

You will need: 3 cups all-purpose flour, 3 eggs at room temperature, and 1½ teaspoons olive oil.

Mound the flour in the center of a clean room-temperature work surface, like a large wooden cutting board. Create a crater in the center of the mound. Crack the first egg into the center of the crater and add ½ teaspoon of the olive oil. With a fork, gently begin to scramble the mixture within the confines of the crater, whilst integrating the flour from the sides of the crater as you carefully beat the egg. Once the first egg is mostly mixed in, shore up the sides of the mound again with flour, maintaining the crater shape. Repeat the process with the second egg and ½ teaspoon olive oil, and again with the third egg and the remaining ½ teaspoon olive oil. Start kneading the dough with your palms, allowing the warmth of your hands to impart elasticity to the dough. Knead for a count of about 400 strokes, or until you feel you have created a cohesive mass. Wrap the dough in plastic wrap and allow it to rest for about 30 minutes. Work with one-third of the dough at a time—keeping the balance wrapped in plastic wrap to prevent it from drying out. Use a pasta machine to gradually roll each section of the pasta down, successively reducing the setting on the machine until it is at its thinnest setting.

A Note on Cookie Cutters Get into the habit of collecting stainless-steel cookie cutters in various shapes for your repertoire. You've seen them not only in cooking supply stores but in gourmet shops of all kinds as well as in gift and souvenir shops. The stainless-steel ones last forever and are usually quite affordable. Adding the touch of seasonal shapes of dough atop your holiday pie, cutting the tea sandwiches into interesting designs, or—as in the Apricot Ravioli recipe— going the distance to beautify filled pasta, will begin to give you the reputation of a culinary artist.

Bacon and Cheese Quiche

SERVES 8

FOR THE CRUST

1¼ cups all-purpose flour

½ teaspoon salt

¾ stick (6 tablespoons) cold unsalted butter, cut into pieces

3 tablespoons cold margarine, cut into pieces

3 to 4 tablespoons ice water, as needed (have a glass of ice water standing by)

FOR THE FILLING

4 ounce medium-thick bacon slices

3 eggs

1½ cups whipping cream

1 cup grated Swiss cheese

⅛ teaspoon grated nutmeg

Salt and pepper

This is my variation on quiche Lorraine, a classic dish that looms large in the legend of the egg.

To make the pastry shell, sift the flour and salt into a bowl to aerate the mixture. Cut in the butter and margarine with a pastry blender until the mixture resembles coarse crumbs. Stir in just enough ice water to bind.

The pastry dough can also be prepared in a food processor equipped with a dough blade. To do so, you put the sifted flour, salt, butter, and margarine into the processor bowl and press the "pulse" button. Pulse until the mixture resembles coarse bread crumbs. Then, whilst drizzling the ice water sparingly through the processor tube into the flour mixture, pulse just until the dough comes together. Then stop—you don't want to overwork the dough. This method has the advantage of reducing the likelihood of overworking the dough, because the "X factor" of the warmth of your fingertips is removed from the equation.

Gather the dough into a ball, wrap in wax paper, and refrigerate for 20 minutes.

Place a baking sheet in the center of the oven and preheat the oven to 375 degrees.

Roll out the dough ⅛ inch thick and transfer to a 9-inch tart pan. Trim the edge. Prick the base all over with a fork to keep the base from bubbling up. Line with parchment paper and fill with pie weights. Bake for 12 minutes. (Whilst the shell is baking, begin frying the bacon.) Remove the paper and weights from the pastry shell and continue baking until golden, about 5 minutes more, to dry out the base.

Maintain the oven temperature at 375 degrees.

Fry the bacon until crisp. Drain, then crumble into small pieces. Sprinkle in the pie shell.

Beat together the eggs, cream, cheese, nutmeg, salt, and pepper. Pour over the bacon and bake until puffed and brown, about 30 minutes. Serve the quiche warm.

A Note on Tart Tins or Flan Pans Making a successful quiche, tart, or flan (of the "tart" variety as opposed to the "custard" variety) is expedited by the use of a tin with rippled sides whose secret is its removable bottom. They are available in gourmet cooking stores in either a standard or a nonstick variety. You can also use a flan "ring," which necessitates using it on a baking tin to support the bottom of the pastry crust as it bakes. A long spatula with a blade that's not too thick is helpful to help you disengage your "flan" crust from the bottom of the flan tin and to slide it gently to its destination. However, if it starts to break apart (as is more of a risk with one large flan than with smaller individual ones), the nearly invisible base of the flan pan enables you to use it for service with little consequence to your presentation.

Pear Soufflé

SERVES 6

3 ripe pears, peeled, cored, and quartered

1 vanilla bean

Up to ½ cup fructose for pear puree (adjust according to ripeness of pears, see Note after recipe) plus 1 tablespoon for beating with egg whites

1 cup water

1 tablespoon pear liqueur

2 egg yolks

1 tablespoon unsalted butter, for buttering ramekins

7 egg whites, at room temperature

¼ teaspoon cream of tartar

1 pint of vanilla ice cream or crème fraîche

EQUIPMENT

A blender or food processor

A mixer

A large copper or stainless-steel bowl

Six 8-ounce individual soufflé dishes or ramekins

If you have never before made a soufflé, I urge you to challenge yourself with this delicious dessert soufflé. You may find that soufflés are not as difficult to make as you've heard. The pear puree in this recipe serves the role of what we call the "base" in a soufflé. In traditional soufflés the base is usually pastry cream.

Place the pears in a saucepan, and then slice the vanilla bean open lengthwise and scrape the vanilla seeds over the pears. Leave the vanilla pod in the pot whilst the pears cook. Add half the fructose and the water, and cook the pears uncovered over medium heat until very soft, adding more water if necessary to keep the mixture from burning.

Remove the vanilla pod and drain the pears through a strainer to remove any excess liquid. Transfer the pear mixture to a food processor and process until smooth. Remove the puree to a bowl and stir in the pear liqueur and additional fructose if necessary. (I would suggest adding fructose gradually to taste in 1-tablespoon increments since it can quickly get too sweet.) Add the egg yolks and combine well. Set aside and reserve.

Preheat the oven to 450 degrees, with the rack placed at the middle position or just below the middle position of the oven. (If the rising soufflé gets too close to the heating coils it may fall.) Butter 6 individual soufflé dishes lightly and set aside. With the mixer beat the egg whites and cream of tartar in a copper or stainless-steel mixing bowl, starting on low and gradually increasing speed. When soft peaks form, add 1 tablespoon fructose and continue to beat until stiff but not dry.

Gently stir one-quarter of the beaten egg whites into the pear puree just until the color is fairly uniform. (This will lighten the density of the puree base to increase the likelihood that the egg white will remain filled with air.) Then fold in the remaining egg whites.

Fill the soufflé dishes and smooth the tops with a spatula. Run your thumb around the inside edge of each dish. This will form the "hat" on the soufflé and it will also eliminate the need for a collar.

Place the filled soufflé dishes in the oven and close the door gently. Reduce the oven temperature to 400 degrees. Bake for 7 to 8 minutes and serve immediately with ice cream or crème fraîche.

Note: If you have a strong preference about the firmness of the inside of a soufflé, you can safely test it without making it fall.

Keep the oven light "on" in the last few minutes of baking time to monitor the situation through the oven window. Once you see that the top is nicely browned and cracked, you can use a long skewer inserted at an angle from the side to test the doneness of the inside. If you like the inside firmed-up inside rather than soft, bake until the skewer comes out clean. Keep in mind that even if a soufflé falls, it is still delicious.

A Note on Fruit Sugar If you have difficulty finding fructose (fruit sugar), be aware that it is sold in dry form, and some stores stock it with dietary specialties (like diabetic foods and gluten-free flours, etc.).

A Note on Whole Vanilla Beans Whole vanilla beans are sold usually 1 or 2 to a jar in the spice section of the store. They are very expensive, but are the "gold standard" in vanilla taste (which is why I call them "black gold"). Split them in half lengthwise and scrape the small vanilla seeds into the mixture, then put the pod into the cooking pot to extract its flavor. Remove the pod before serving.

Wild Mushroom Soup

SERVES 6 TO 8

1 ounce dried wild mushrooms, such as morels, cèpes, or porcini

6 cups chicken broth

2 tablespoons unsalted butter

2 onions, coarsely chopped

2 garlic cloves, chopped

2 pounds button or other cultivated mushrooms, trimmed and sliced

Salt and freshly ground black pepper

½ teaspoon dried thyme

¼ teaspoon ground nutmeg

2 to 3 tablespoons flour

½ cup Madeira or dry sherry

½ cup crème fraîche or sour cream

Snipped fresh chives

Put the dried mushrooms in a strainer and rinse very well under cold running water, shaking to make sure all the sand has been removed. Place them in a saucepan with 1 cup of the broth and bring to a boil over medium-high heat. Remove the pan from the heat and set aside for 30 to 40 minutes to soak.

Meanwhile, in a large, heavy saucepan, melt the butter over medium-high heat. Add the onions and cook for 5 to 7 minutes until they are well softened and just golden. Stir in the garlic and fresh mushrooms, and cook for 4 to 5 minutes until they begin to soften, then add the salt and pepper, thyme, and nutmeg, and sprinkle the flour over the mixture. Cook for 3 to 5 minutes, stirring frequently, until blended.

Add the Madeira or sherry, the remaining chicken broth, the dried mushrooms, and their soaking liquid and cook, covered, over medium heat for 30 to 40 minutes until the mushrooms are very tender.

Puree the soup in batches in a blender or food processor. Strain it back into the saucepan, pressing firmly to force the puree through the sieve. Stir in the crème fraîche or sour cream and sprinkle with the snipped chives just before serving.

W HEN YOU ARE A YOUNG BRITISH SUBJECT AND TRAVELING AROUND WITH members of the royal household to exotic ports, supervising their food, it is easy to get a swollen head and start thinking you are a pretty cool guy. I traveled to some amazing places throughout America and Europe, the Far East, and the South Pacific. I particularly remember staying at the Al-Bustan Palace Hotel, which is virtually carved into a cliffside in Oman, and being astonished at the opulence as I stared up at the glittering golden central foyer that cuts through the entire building. I blushingly admit that there, as well as in other posh locales, I often entered with one suitcase and left with two, the second filled with robes, slippers, towels, and other souvenirs of the good life.

On one occasion, I and a small advance team were installed in the Old

Winter Palace Hotel in Egypt, situated right next to the Temple of Luxor. I had hoped to have a chance to view the artifacts from King Tut's tomb, but found out that they were in fact on display at London at the time. Whenever we were in a truly foreign city, we were routinely instructed, "Don't eat the food and don't drink the water." It was late in the day and we had been traveling a long way. I was in no mood to heed the usual warnings. I was ready for a couple of beers and something to eat. I called down to room service and managed to communicate my desire for drink and the makings of a sandwich, or so I thought. After a long wait, the food arrived.

I was disgusted. They had delivered what to me looked for all the world like a pile of stale flat bread, a stack of cold camel meat, and coffee with some sort of strange-smelling liquid that I guessed was goat's milk. In my arrogance, I salvaged the two beers from the tray, walked the rest over to the unshuttered windows, and tossed the lot down into the street below.

I am, after all, my mother's son, and I immediately regretted doing something so stupid. I leaned out the window and looked to make sure that nobody had been hit down below. I am ashamed to say that what I saw was a number of people down in the street, some children and some older, scrambling and fighting for the food I had discarded, picking it up off the street as part of their or their family's next meal. They were so poor, it must have seemed like manna from heaven. I have never forgotten that moment, and my determination to have respect for the people for whom I cook, whenever and wherever I have the privilege, took a leap forward that day. Pay attention—not all of the lessons take place in the kitchen.

My memories of that experience in Egypt sometimes remind me of the incredible bounty we take for granted at our fingertips. In many cultures, soups take one simple ingredient and skillfully elevate it to the point of sustenance for many people at once. This thought put me in the mind of the following recipe, which concentrates, almost to the exclusion of anything else, on the singular and essential earthy flavor of mushrooms, which I adore.

7

I'M PASSIONATE ABOUT *PASSION*

Jamaican escapades, George and George, and
the art of running Donald Trump's kitchens

The American Academy of Hospitality Sciences "Five Star Diamond Award"

I AM OFTEN ASKED VARIATIONS ON THE QUESTION "WHAT MOST ATTRACTS you to the cooking profession?" I have given lots of different answers, but over time, I have narrowed it down to three keys: "people, pleasure, and passion."

Most of the time, I truly believe it is passion that drives the boat. When you're up before the crack of dawn, or awake late, late at night, long after everyone else has eaten and gone home to bed, and you are cleaning or scraping, or slicing or stirring, and your bones are on fire and the arches in your feet are disintegrating, and you can hardly bear to look at another scrap of food, it is only passion that keeps you going.

There are times when cooks have to do whatever it takes to get dinner on the table, and no one illustrates this point better than my old friend Guppy.

I had left the employ of the Royal Family and the British Navy, and had landed a plum spot at the Jamaica Grand Hotel in Ocho Rios as their executive chef. I was gradually finding my land legs and being christened to life on the beautiful island of Jamaica.

It had been decided by management that every Thursday we would make a superlative amount of noise, live music, and fun for our guests by throwing a big bash called "Jump Up!" For the first one, we were expecting a crowd of about two thousand and I was planning a huge amount of food, an endless buffet that would feature in the starring roles Jamaican classics that I was rapidly stockpiling recipes for, including bammies, codfish and ackee, and of course, Jamaican jerk pork and chicken, a local favorite that I had been happily devouring and enjoying in my travels around the island.

By Tuesday evening, it was full steam ahead, though I was still learning the ins and outs of properly organizing my Jamaican staff as I went along. Everything in Jamaica is "Irie, mon!" which is a cheerful way of saying, "Everything's cool; don't worry!" Your underwear can be on fire, and the response might easily be "Irie, mon! Don't worry. Just take 'em off; they'll settle down. Have a beer and rest awhile. Or you can wait 'til the rain comes to put them out; it always comes, sooner or later . . ."

Anyway, things were rolling along as smoothly as could be expected and I had a game plan for making the jerk marinade that I had shared with one of my cooks, an entirely pleasant guy named Guppy. (It's important to note that even though his name was spelled G-u-p-p-y, a fact that I confirmed with him, it was indeed pronounced with a soft *g*, as in "Juppy.") He was an industrious little guy, an extremely hard worker, and was in charge of all of the marinades for the meats, chicken, and fish. I was in my office doing paperwork when I noticed that something had changed in the kitchen. There is a rhythm and a distinctive sound to a working kitchen, and when it changes, you had better know why.

I walked out and silently observed Guppy performing what looked to me for all the world like some strange island ritual. He had a large roll of plastic wrap and was dividing it into long strips. Many of his coworkers were watching him intently, and had become quiet, as if in a kind of nervous anticipation of this ceremony. Once the entire roll had been divided, he solemnly began to take one of the strips and wrap it around his head, like a bandana. I was curious, but also wanted to be respectful of whatever was going on. Some obscure branch of voodoo, perhaps? Far be it from me to question somebody's superstition or religious practice, especially in a culture that was new to me. Work seemed to be progressing, just more quietly, so I went back into the office.

About eight minutes later, I heard the whine of a large mechanical chopping machine.

Two minutes after that, I was under attack.

I began coughing uncontrollably, my eyes were streaming with acid, my nose was running, and my throat was on fire. I felt panic heave me up out of my chair and hurl me out of the office.

I bolted out into the kitchen and was horrified by what I saw next. The place was completely deserted. I turned at a sound behind me, and through squinting, painful eyes, I saw an inhuman figure waggling toward me that for the world looked like a Plastic-Wrap Ninja come to finish me off. It was a mummified creature, bound head to toe in thick sheets of glistening plastic, shouting something that was completely muffled by the wrap across its mouth, just below its airholes. It grabbed me by the arm and gently led me, hacking and coughing, out the back door to fresh air.

In the excruciatingly bright sunshine, all of my workers, who had sensibly cleared out of the danger zone a few minutes before, placidly watched whilst I concentrated on breathing and recovering what was left of my composure. Guppy reached up and began to peel the plastic wrap off his head with hands that wore five pairs of food-service gloves under a pair of yellow marigold dishwashing gloves. He smiled at me apologetically.

He had been responsible for pulverizing four *20-pound cases* of hot Scotch bonnet peppers for the jerk, and with the thick, evil cloud of capsaicin vapor they produced, he had innocently teargassed me to within an inch of my life. Had I been able to put two and two together, I would have gladly begged to crawl into his plastic-wrap cocoon with him before the conflagration.

This recipe is dedicated to all of the great people I worked with in Jamaica, and especially to Guppy. "Irie, mon!"

Jamaican Jerk Chicken

SERVES 8

Jamaican jerk can also be done using either dry rubs or thick pastes, which can be absolutely mind-blowing. I chose to marinade the raw meats simply because I feel that you can control the heat and flavor better. If you like it hot, you can add a couple more Scotch bonnets. Just be careful: **wear gloves when handling Scotch bonnet peppers. They will hurt you if you don't.** **You have been warned!**

Place one of the limes in a small microwave-safe bowl and microwave it until the essential oils in the skin are released. This usually takes 30 seconds to 1 minute. Listen for the "whoosh," after which you can remove the bowl and see the oils in the bottom of the bowl. Reserve these oils. Then repeat with each of the limes. I am having you microwave them one at a time because the ripeness and size of each lime may be different, requiring a different amount of time for the "whoosh" to occur for each lime. These limes will be hot coming from the microwave, so you can let them cool enough to handle before squeezing them.

Using a blender (or a food processor), blend the allspice, nutmeg, cinnamon,

This recipe accommodates about 8 pounds of cut-up chicken—say (depending on the size) 8 to 12 drumsticks and 8 to 12 thighs with the following marinade.

FOR THE MARINADE (YIELDS ABOUT 6 CUPS, WHICH CAN BE USED FOR PORK OR BEEF TOO)

4 limes

4 teaspoons ground allspice

3 teaspoons ground nutmeg

3 teaspoons ground cinnamon

⅛ cup fresh thyme leaves

2 white onions, finely chopped

1 cup chopped scallions

2 hot Scotch bonnet peppers

2 cups low-sodium soy sauce

EQUIPMENT

A blender

A coffee grinder to grind your own spices

Plastic, latex, or rubber gloves to protect your hands from the hot peppers (some people wear safety goggles and a face mask also, depending on their sensitivity)

thyme, onions, scallions, and peppers (whilst wearing gloves) together to make a pulp. Return to the limes and squeeze the juice into the blender through the feeder tube. *Make sure you use the lime oils that were released by microwaving, as well as the juice you've squeezed.* Then add the soy sauce through the feeder tube. Mix well.

Place the chicken pieces and lime skins in a container that you will be able to cover tightly. Pour the marinade over the chicken and let rest in the refrigerator overnight (or a minimum of 4 hours). *Keep the chicken tightly covered and away from other foods, as it will taint them.*

The best way to cook jerk is over an open-flame barbecue. For authentic flavor, you need some pimento wood—or hickory would do as a substitute. To get the best flavor from this dish, the chicken must be cooked slowly, turned and basted regularly.

If you don't have a barbecue grill, then cook it in the oven, as you would roasted chicken, say, in a covered pan at 300 degrees for 2 hours plus another 30 minutes, uncovered, at 400 degrees. The important thing is that you check for doneness. When the chicken is done, the flesh will feel firm and the juices will run clear. You can also use a meat thermometer, which should register an internal temperature of at least 180 degrees.

You can use other kinds of peppers or add hot sauce.

I love to eat this with creamy coleslaw along with either a beer or a drink called Ting, which is a grapefruit soda famous in Jamaica—almost as famous as Red Stripe beer.

Enjoy!

A Note on Grinding Your Own Spices If you can grind the spices fresh, they will have more flavor—use a coffee grinder. Many people have a dedicated coffee grinder just for this purpose.

GOD KNOWS THE PAIN GUPPY HAD GONE THROUGH BEFORE HE SETTLED on this unusual prophylactic approach to food prep, but the point is that he came up with a way to do what he had to do to get the job done. That was one of a few scares I had in Jamaica, though not all of them took place in the kitchen.

At the beginning of my time at the Jamaica Grand, just prior to my encounter with Guppy and the Great Scotch Bonnet Gas-Out, I found myself at loose ends. I had arrived on the island with a passel of great ideas, a metric ton of energy, and a boatload of confidence. I was a Master Chef. I had served (literally, breakfast, luncheon, and supper) my Queen and country with some distinction, and I was prepared to have some fun. I was ready, willing, and eager to report for work on my first day, but I hadn't actually received my work permit from the government.

My days were relegated to walking the beautiful property, basking in the sun, and pretty much kissing babies and running for office whilst I took copious notes on the people and the setup. About 5:30 in the afternoon, after a day of casing the joint, I decided to tour one of the kitchens that had recently been remodeled, after enjoying a quick snack of bammies, conch chowder, and Red Stripe at a neat little shack next door.

I entered the kitchen through a large swinging door and started back toward the chef's office, tucked way in the back. Halfway down on the right was the butcher's shop, presided over by an exceedingly large gentleman named Mr. Enormous (I have changed his name to protect the innocent, namely me). He simply beamed when he saw me and flashed a benevolent smile, cleaver in hand. Seemed an absolutely charming young man.

There was a metal door just beyond the butcher's shop for deliveries. A well-organized squad of young men in street clothes, none of whom I recognized, looked as if they were competing on an episode of *Supermarket Sweepstakes*. They were grabbing armfuls of whole chickens, legs of lamb, beef roast, slabs of bacon, and anything else they could get their hands on.

"Hey, what are you doing?" I shouted. I rushed toward them, and they bolted out the back door, laden with the hotel's goods, past the laundry and to the water's edge, where a motorboat sat waiting, revving its engines for a fast getaway. With the crystal blue skies and the tropical vistas of Jamaica behind them as they made good their escape, I felt as if I were in a James Bond film, specifically *Dr. No*. I think I could have caught them with my jet pack (from *Thunderball*), but it wasn't readily available. They had beaten me!

I called security and rang the police. I gave what I thought were cracking good descriptions of the desperadoes, gave them my version of events, and that was that, or so I thought.

The next morning, whilst I was getting ready in my apartment in the hotel for my first official day on duty, I received a call from security. They wanted to meet me right away in the chef's office. I rushed to get ready. Perhaps the criminals had already been caught and justice was about to be done! Moments later, I entered the office and was confronted by five grim-looking local policemen and a frightened-looking security staff.

"Who's been shot?" I asked, with my most authentic, "00" agent dry wit. The atmosphere in the room became even colder.

One of the officers strode forward and told me that they were there on a report that I was keeping a firearm. This was a serious transgression, and suddenly I flushed with anger and a wave of fear. I had been on the island barely a week and I was already in a confrontation with the local constabulary. They had orders to search my room, and security called someone from management and housekeeping to open it up for them.

This was bad. My mind was racing. There was a hotel maid who had complete access to my room. She could have planted the Crown Jewels in my apartment and I'd have never known about it. In my imagination, betting was running ten to the dozen that she had stashed an Uzi under my mattress.

They didn't exactly toss the room. After a cursory look around, they seemed satisfied that I wasn't hiding an arsenal and let me off with a warning and a look that said, "Keep your nose clean and we won't have any more trouble, mon."

Shaken, but not stirred, I made my way back to the kitchens. To make a long story a bit shorter, I soon found out through the grapevine that none other than Mr. Enormous had dropped the dime on me. Turns out he was the black market "Big Mack Daddy" of the hotel and was sending me a signal that nothing, but nothing, got done behind the scenes at the Grand without his say-so.

Over the course of my time in Jamaica, I learned to get along well enough with Mr. E, who always greeted me with the same warm smile. We eventually established a policy of mutual respect, based on the concept of laissez-faire, or live and let live, which lasted without incident as long as his extracurricular activities no longer ate into the proper operation of my kitchens. These kinds of situations are sometimes the price you have to pay just to get in the front door; I hadn't yet cooked so much as a piece of toast. Eventually I was able to team up with the food and beverage director, Anthony Corbin, and bring those great ideas of mine into reality. It just took a lot longer than either of us had imagined. Perseverance, my friends, always perseverance.

Chicken Mushroom Barley Soup

SERVES 6

It's an amazing sight, really, to see a grown man trying to get away with an armload of whole chickens. If you manage to get your hands on some, try this . . .

Place the chicken in the water with the whole vegetables (celery, carrots, onion, and parsley) and simmer for 1 hour to make the broth.

Cook the barley until tender and set aside.

Remove the chicken to a utility platter or bowl to let it cool. Strain the broth into another pot, and retrieve any remaining chicken pieces and vegetable pieces from the strainer to reserve for the soup.

Heat the butter in a pan and sauté the diced celery, diced carrots, and diced onions gently to make a mirepoix. Add this mirepoix to the pot of broth and simmer for 30 minutes. Whilst this is simmering, pick the meat from the now-cool chicken. The chicken and the whole vegetables should be cut into bite-sized pieces for the soup.

Add the bay leaves, chopped thyme, chopped parsley, chopped garlic, and sliced mushrooms to the pot of broth. Let simmer for 30 minutes more. Remove the bay leaves, add the cut-up chicken and vegetables and the precooked barley, and serve. Season with salt and pepper as needed.

1 whole frying chicken

2 quarts water

3 celery stalks, left whole

3 carrots, scrubbed and peeled but left whole

1 onion, peeled, roots removed

½ bunch of parsley, rinsed

4 ounces pearl barley, precooked

2 tablespoons unsalted butter

5 celery stalks, medium diced

1 carrot, medium diced

3 onions, medium diced

2 bay leaves

1 teaspoon chopped fresh thyme

2 teaspoons chopped fresh parsley

2 teaspoons chopped garlic

8 ounces mushrooms, sliced

Salt and freshly ground black pepper

PREPARATION AND COOKING TIME

About 2½ hours

MY ENORMOUS ADVENTURE" WAS ONE OF THE FIRST LESSONS I LEARNED out in the real world in the fine art of survival skills that have little or nothing to do with cooking. The better acquainted you are with your own strengths and weaknesses, the more you can work to improve on them, to maximize the former and to minimize or eliminate the negative impact of the latter. When I first entered the service and began my early military training, I worked hard and excelled. I was physically active and mentally disciplined; I finished most of the tasks I was assigned easily and usually ahead of my fellow recruits; my bunk was neater and cleaner, my shoes were shinier. Anytime I felt that I was ahead of the curve, I would cruise to the finish line and somewhat arrogantly wait for my fellows to catch up. I was soon informed by my superiors that there was a good chance I wasn't going to make the cut and the likelihood that I would have *to repeat* the training.

I was stunned and angry. I thought that I was better than most of the men I was training with. What was the meaning of all this? The answer was as clear to them, if not readily to me, as if it had been printed in ink across my forehead: I was not a team player. Sure, you could bounce a satellite transmission off the reflective surface of my shoes, but, they wanted to know, how about the guys who might be falling behind? How was I going to get *them* up to that level?

My first response, which I was savvy enough to keep to myself, was "It's not my problem." True enough maybe, but I could also see that calculation wasn't going to get me over in their eyes. My second response was to attack the problem by personally polishing every pair of shoes in the barracks to a high-gloss shine. That made me temporarily popular enough with my bunkmates, but my superiors just rolled their eyes. It took me a while, but eventually I saw what they were aiming at. They saw a potential in me, a leadership potential, and it was their job to nurture and develop it, so that it could be exploited in Her Majesty's service, but also to ensure my development, ideally, into an officer and a gentleman. I soon found it within my grasp to lead by example, by encouragement, and by inspiring discipline and respect in those with whom I served.

These lessons came in handy when I went to work for Donald Trump at the Taj Mahal in Atlantic City. I worked at the Taj for four years, most of those as executive chef, and from the beginning to very near the end of my tenure there, going in to work every day was like going into Tombstone before Wyatt Earp came to town.

I will say this for Donald Trump: He does not spend a lot of time visiting you and having tea and looking over your shoulder to see if things are moving along satisfactorily. In my time there, I believe we were in the same room only a handful of times. But he expects results, and in this case, results meant running a tight ship and improving the bottom line of the food-service units at the casino and hotel. I had been contacted by a headhunter whilst at the Jamaica Grand, and I had been thinking about working in the United States for a while. This was to be my first big job stateside, and I was determined to make a success of it.

Things had fallen to a low state in the food-service sector of the business, which encompassed all of the restaurants, buffets, banquets, special events, and room service, and management knew it. When I arrived, I was given a list of forty employees who were to be let go immediately. I made the determination that I would be the one to investigate who was fit to stay and who to go, according to my own discretion.

Before long it was evident that catastrophic problems with organization, discipline, supply lines, cleanliness, waste, out-and-out bad workers, thievery, and drugs taking were out of control and systemwide. I hit the ground running and instituted cost-and-inventory controls right away. I started tracking every delivery that came into the hotel, which often meant meeting a shipment at the loading dock, visually inspecting it, and personally walking it to its final stop. Prior to my arrival, deliveries would be just as likely to disappear as to reach their destinations. I began policing employees' time cards. More than once, I would come into the kitchen searching for an employee who had punched in at the time clock, only to be told he had "gone to the bathroom," or was "out for a smoke." There I stood at his station, waiting patiently for his return. After forty-five minutes and a no-show I made sure he was gone forever.

The bathrooms were a drugs playground. I would surreptitiously enter a stall and just wait, taking notes on conversations and noting faces, matching them up with their drugs of choice, usually sniffables or injectibles, and as soon as possible, I found ways to relieve the offenders of their duties permanently. I kept up with my workout schedule religiously because I never knew when I might be embroiled in a physical confrontation. I was threatened with lawsuits, bodily harm, and early demise. My car was vandalized so often in the parking lot that I began leaving my real car at home and driving an ancient, lemon-yellow junkyard bomb in to work. Security was obliged to escort me in and out of the property on a daily basis.

Of the original 38 chefs who worked there when I first arrived, I kept on 5. Before I left, I had fired a total of 322 people. I was aptly nicknamed "the Terminator."

In their places, I brought in chefs and cooks from all over the country. Word spread that change was in the air, and I was eventually able to build a team that I trusted. First and foremost, I wanted chefs who could *cook*. I brought in new blood, people who were young, energetic, and enthusiastic about the situation and about each other. I wanted them to know that I was interested in them and what they thought as well, and that I was open to their ideas.

Instead of being stuck in the mud with old institutionalized menus, I was constantly changing the bills of fare, using everybody's influences. I instituted a policy that enlisted everybody's creativity when we made a major menu change. First, I would decide on the elements of the dish. Say it started with an 8-ounce filet mignon with braised eggplant. That would be paired with Dauphinoise potatoes, roasted asparagus, and fried leeks; the sauce would be a port wine demi-glace; and let's say I wanted tobacco onions, very thinly sliced onions deep-fried with flour and paprika.

Five chefs would be nominated to assemble these elements into an integrated plate. Each one might start by searing the fillet and finishing it in butter, but the Dauphinoise potatoes, which are a layered dish, kind of like a potato lasagne in a cheesy custard, could be prepared and presented any number of ways. They could be piled, molded into a ring, served under the fillet or on the side. Same with the vegetables. Some chefs might like to highlight the green color of the asparagus; others might take it past the bright green for a different flavor element. Their placement of all of the ingredients on the plate would be different and individual. We would all dissect and discuss what we saw and tasted together, and then I would make a final determination as to whose was the best. Then everyone would learn it, and we would take pictures of it to hang up over the line for reference. Once this was all decided, you had consensus and team spirit prebuilt into the mix every time that dish was made.

For a while, overseeing the Taj Mahal was really fun. We elevated our cuisine to the point where we could host *Chaine de Rôtisseurs* dinners, events put on by a Parisian-based food and wine society that had the highest standards for service and creativity. We put on some really exciting events and started to get some great press, including a chef's dinner where we turned a ballroom into a tropical rain forest, with over three thousand live plants and a section of a real airplane fuselage.

I did a lot of learning on the job, but in the end I applied the same principles I had learned in the military. Honesty and hard work were rewarded; slacking and dishonesty were ruthlessly cut off. This was a new era in my life in dealing with large numbers of staff and employees. Ultimately, 650 people reported to me. I would like to send out a word of thanks and regard to Rudy Prieto, president at the time, who supported me through it all (he was eventually fired by Donald Trump on Christmas Eve, 1999). Food service and culinary awards began to pile up as the negative trends reversed and we actually got down to the business of cooking. Before I left, we were doing group-wide revenues of more than $80 million per year.

The day I tendered my resignation and announced that I was leaving and taking a position across town at Caesar's, as their new executive chef, I was given exactly fifteen minutes to clear out my belongings and vacate the premises. Corporate policy, I'm sure. My guys helped me pack a few boxes, and that was that. It was a tough job, but somebody had to do it.

Well, on that note, let's finish with something sweet.

Pear Apple Crumb Pie

SERVES 8

FOR THE CRUST

1 cup flour

½ teaspoon salt

⅓ cup cold shortening, cut into pieces

2 tablespoons ice water (have a glass of ice water handy)

FOR THE PIE FILLING

3 firm pears

4 tart cooking apples

¾ cup sugar

2 tablespoons cornstarch

¼ teaspoon salt

Grated zest of 1 lemon

2 tablespoons fresh lemon juice

½ cup raisins

¾ cup flour

1 teaspoon ground cinnamon

6 tablespoons cold unsalted butter, cut into pieces

EQUIPMENT

A shallow 9-inch pie pan

Combine the flour and salt in a bowl. Add the shortening, and cut it in with a pastry blender until the mixture resembles coarse crumbs. With a fork, stir in just enough water to bind the dough. Gather the dough into a ball and transfer it to a lightly floured surface. Roll out to about ⅛ inch thick.

Transfer to a shallow 9-inch pie pan and trim to leave a ½-inch overhang. Fold the overhang under for a double thickness. Flute the edge with your fingers. Refrigerate.

Place a baking sheet in the oven and preheat the oven to 450 degrees.

Peel and core the pears. Slice them into a bowl. Peel, core, and slice the apples, and add to the pears. Stir in ⅓ cup of the sugar, the cornstarch, salt, and lemon zest. Add the lemon juice and raisins, and stir to blend.

To make the crumb topping, combine the remaining sugar, flour, cinnamon, and butter in a bowl. Blend with your fingertips until the mixture resembles coarse crumbs. Set aside.

Spoon the fruit filling into the pie shell. Sprinkle the crumbs lightly and evenly over the top.

Place the pie on top of the baking sheet in the oven and bake for 10 minutes, then reduce the heat to 350 degrees. Cover the top of the pie loosely with a sheet of aluminum foil, and continue baking until browned, 35 to 40 minutes more.

A Note on Food Processor Pastry To prepare the pastry dough in a food processor equipped with a dough blade, you would put the sifted flour and salt along with the shortening (or butter) into the processor bowl and pulse the food processor. Do this until the mixture resembles coarse bread crumbs. Then sparingly drizzle the ice water through the processor tube into the flour mixture and pulse only until the dough comes together. Many home cooks use this method with much success because it minimizes the amount of time you work the dough with your hands (so you are less apt to overwork it). The less you work the dough, the flakier it is.

A Note on Pie Pans Shallow pie pans hold about 2 cups. Standard pie tins accommodate 3 cups. Deep dish pans hold 4 cups.

I HAVE AN OUTGOING NATURE, AND I ENJOY ENCOUNTERING PEOPLE ON every level, professionally, in the kitchen, in the dining room, and beyond. Providing pleasure at the table is an ongoing source of motivation. But without passion, the fire dies, the pleasure diminishes, and the people drift away.

Passion can be described as a fire inside. I consider myself a lucky man in that I discovered my passion for cooking at an early age. I never really had to stoke the fire, or bank it or conceal it, or watch it die to a flicker or a spark and then fight to rekindle it. I found that I had the interest and the ability early on and opportunities came my way, by chance or intention, which allowed me to follow my passion. In my profession, no chef is an island, however.

Each person in the chain has to have a vested interest and each person has to be accountable. Each person has to act like an owner, like a stockholder in every meal that is placed before a customer. Pride in craftsmanship is essential, whether you are cooking for a thousand or putting a meal on the table at home, even if you are eating alone. It begins with showing up to work on time, in clean clothes, teeth brushed, hair combed, ready to put your best effort forward. You can try to motivate people, incentivize them, train them, threaten them even, but man, woman, boy, or girl, if there is no fire in the belly for the task at hand, your pains will most likely be in vain.

I like seeing passion in people; I respond to it, and I have to believe that the reverse is true. When passion is present, anything is possible, and you must train yourself to recognize it and fan the flames whenever and wherever it is encountered. I like to think that in my kitchen, a passionate dishwasher can rise to the level of a passionate chef; indeed, my good friend Ruben Espinal is proof of that. He started at the back of the kitchen, made himself indispensable, and argued passionately for a chance to learn. When given the chance, he responded with talent and hard work, and has never given less than his best efforts. And a chef he is today, at Resorts in Atlantic City.

Today, my right and left hands in the kitchen and in my various travels are both, by a strange and happy coincidence, named "George." They both came to me at different times, and I recognized their potential in different ways. George Kralle, whom we laughingly call "Little George" (only in comparison to the other George, as you would readily see if you ever happened to be stuck in an elevator between the two of them), appeared in my kitchen looking for a position when I had none available. He had a solid background in working at hotels and country clubs and had been part of the team that opened Trump's first hotel, the Trump Plaza. He had an intensity and an eagerness that was apparent, but in reality, the reason I hired him was the appearance of his shoes.

For someone who takes cleaned and polished shoes as seriously as I do, hearkening back to my days in the Royal Navy, I looked upon his lustrously shined footwear as an indisputable endorsement of his character, discipline, and self-respect. I took him on at my own expense until I could find a spot for him, and have never regretted it.

George Galati, "Big George," came to me with a great background as well. He had been a sous-chef at Tavern on the Green and head chef at Max's Grill in Florida, and had been voted Chef of the Year in 1993 by the North American Chefs' Association. He came to me with an agenda similar to the one that carried me to the doors of the Waterside Inn and the gentle ministrations of the Brothers Roux. He wanted to learn and to become a top executive chef. I have to admit I responded to his willingness to learn much more than his desire to rise in rank. The former is a process that you can throw yourself into heart and soul; the latter is a result. Whether the desired result comes about or not, it is the process of learning that will always remain a vital and meaningful part of your life. George has the talent and the drive to become anything he wants, and will always feel the benefit of a culinary education passionately pursued, every time he properly organizes a complex task, arrives fifteen minutes early for an appointment, insists on excellence over mediocrity, fries an egg properly, or enjoys a well-prepared meal. I play to the particular strengths of the Georges as much as possible. For instance, George Kralle is very good at hot foods; George Galati excels at cold foods, salads, and the like. In this manner, they are like yin and yang in the kitchen, perfectly complementary in many ways. I have placed many challenges in front of both of these men, and they have always worked hard to pull through with the highest marks.

There is a trick to passion, and that is never to let the pursuit of your passion become stale. For me, as for many in the profession, teaching is critical to keeping the true spirit of cooking alive in yourself and in those with whom you work. Giving of yourself, investing in whatever you are doing beyond the mere fact of just showing up, inspires passion. You have to be fully present in the moment that you are teaching, preparing, planning, ordering, or doing any and all of the things required for great cooking. The attitude and internal compass should remain the same whether you're in the back of the house or out front taking curtain calls.

Especially in the chef culture of today, people want to see you, to talk to you, and to feel they know you. They want to invest themselves in you. Nobody just wants to eat these days; they want an experience, they want a story to tell, they want a memory of having had something special, they want to be seduced, to be educated, to see something and taste something that they can carry away and try at home, to be entertained. They want to be fulfilled, not just full, at the end of a meal.

Many's the time when I have made a deal on the spot with someone attending a dinner or a banquet to jump off the menu and run back into the kitchen to make them something special; not because of the challenge, not to show off, and not because I am usually standing around in the kitchen at a banquet with a lot of time on my hands, but because it is what they asked for. That's part of the pact: *"Come to me and I will feed you the best way I know how."* Keeping that attitude fresh for yourself, that you will do your best in whatever your job may be, helps to make sure that the passion stays alive.

I do not want to be known for preparing the same food over and over again. I do not want people to say, "If you go to see that fellow Irvine, you've got to have his *famous* fill-in-the-blank, chipotle something, spicy whatever, insert dish here à *la Robert*." Picasso had his blue period, but he never went back to it again; da Vinci only painted the *Mona Lisa* once. Frank Sinatra stopped singing "Strangers in the Night" altogether. I would rather have it be said, "Go to see Irvine; you don't know what you're going to get, but it's going to be great."

Our profession demands hard work, and we all hope that hard work will result in advancement. Everyone wants to be the boss. In many ways, in the kitchen I am like the master of a ship, but that is a sword that cuts both ways. The captain is responsible ultimately for the fate of each member of his crew. He may command, but in a very real sense he is the servant of everyone on board, and he will, if he is worth his salt, go down with the ship as the last man on board. I had good early lessons in service in my life and career, and over time I have learned to submit myself to authoritarian situations without feeling chafed or subordinated. We can strive for perfection and plan for gaining authority, but we must also have a passion for service.

Service is passion tempered with humility. We cook *for* people, not *at* them. There is a notation under the heading for each of my recipes: "Serves 4," "Serves 6," "Serves 8 to 10." Mark it well.

Green Peppercorn Steak au Poivre

SERVES 4

Here is a deceptively simple preparation that maximizes the flavors available in freshly ground peppercorns.

Preheat the oven to 200 degrees (so you can keep the steaks warm).

Put 2 tablespoons of the butter and the oil in a large skillet, and turn the heat to medium-high. Season the steaks with salt and pepper. When the butter melts, add the steaks and turn the heat to high. Sear on the first side for about 3 minutes, then turn and sear on the second side for 2 to 3 minutes. Lower the heat and cook until just short of your chosen level of doneness, about 7 minutes total for medium-rare. Remove to a utility platter and keep warm in the oven whilst you make the sauce.

Pour out any fat from the skillet, leaving the brown bits in there. Add the remaining butter and shallots, and cook over medium-high heat, stirring occasionally, until the shallots are soft, about 3 minutes. Add the green peppercorns and cook for 30 seconds. Add the mustard, cream, and demi-glace, and cook, stirring for 30 seconds.

Pour the sauce over the steaks and serve.

3 tablespoons butter

1 tablespoon neutral oil, such as canola oil or grapeseed oil

Salt and coarsely ground black pepper

Four 6- to 8-ounce tenderloin steaks

2 shallots, chopped

2 tablespoons canned green peppercorns

1 tablespoon Dijon mustard

2 tablespoons cream

1 cup demi-glace (brown sauce)

ANOTHER WAY TO KEEP YOUR PASSION FOR COOKING ALIVE IS TO FOLLOW this dictum: "Challenge yourself!" I am certain that you have things you do well in the kitchen, have an expertise in certain dishes that produce delicious results, but you should always ask yourself, "Where are the limits of my abilities, and how much fun can I have overcoming them?"

You should have fun in the kitchen, because discovery is fun, and only in cooking do you actually get to feast on your new accomplishments with your friends and family. Cooking should never be a dry exercise in measuring, spooning, and heating. It should be joyful and funny and exciting and thrilling and satisfying. If you are good at sautéing and roasting, become a baker. If you can bake a cake, you can make a soufflé. Go beyond pigs-in-a-blanket the next time you are deciding on the list of hors d'oeuvres for your upcoming affair and find something to do with that tin of caviar you've been denying yourself for years. If your time in the kitchen has become rote and boring, challenge yourself, shake up your routine, and get ready to taste what happens next.

The following is a challenging recipe, but a more flavorful sense of complete satisfaction at the end you will seldom find.

Tea-Smoked Chicken with Chilled Sour Brussels Sprouts Salad

SERVES 6

This dish takes a little more planning due to the production of the sauce, so we will begin there. This can also be done the day before and, in fact, the sauce benefits from sitting overnight in the refrigerator.

You are making your own stock for the sauce. This can be done the day before or, if you do not have the time to make a stock, use a good bouillon cube. However, if you have made your own stock before, you know that there is nothing quite like the results. If you have not done so before, I encourage you to challenge yourself to achieve this skill.

FOR THE SAUCE

2 tablespoons grapeseed oil

8 sprigs of fresh thyme

6 garlic cloves, peeled and chopped

2 large red onions, finely diced

One 750-mL bottle chardonnay wine

2½ pounds duck or chicken bones (see "A Note on Bones for Stock," page 242, and information on butchers)

1 gallon water

3 pieces star anise

½ teaspoon black peppercorns

Salt and pepper

Up to 3 ounces (6 tablespoons) unsalted butter

FOR THE RUB

1½ tablespoons sea salt or kosher salt

1 tablespoon peppercorns (black, green, or pink)

FOR THE CHICKEN

Six 8-ounce chicken breasts

Please be sure to review the equipment list for *Tea-Smoked Chicken* on page 242.

To make the sauce, in a stockpot, heat the oil. Add the thyme, garlic, and red onions, and sauté until tender.

Deglaze the pot with 2 cups of chardonnay and reduce until the liquid is almost all gone.

Add the duck bones and water to form a stock. Bring to a boil, then reduce the heat, cooking for a further 3 hours. The liquid needs to be reduced by half of what you started with to intensify the flavor.

Strain the liquid through a fine strainer or cheesecloth and reserve.

In a new saucepan, add the remainder of the wine, the star anise, and the peppercorns, and cook until it also is reduced by half.

Then combine the two liquids together (the stock liquid plus the wine reduction), and again reduce this combination by half. Strain and refrigerate before reheating just before serving (or finish as indicated below, if serving it immediately).

To finish this sauce, *just before serving* add about 3 ounces of butter to the heated sauce and immediately remove from the heat, continuing to whisk.

To prepare the rub, place a large sauté pan or wok on medium to medium-high heat, add the salt and peppercorns, and roast *slowly*, stirring constantly. (If the peppercorns pop out of the pan, the heat is too high.) Roast slowly until the mixture begins to smoke. This should take 15 to 20 minutes. If you don't see wisps of smoke at the 18-minute mark, then turn up the heat a bit.

Allow the mixture to cool, then blend this mixture in a coffee grinder until thoroughly combined. Rub into the chicken breasts, cover, and refrigerate for at least 4 hours. However, the longer the breasts are rubbed, the better the flavor, preferably 24 hours.

To prepare the salad and dressing, in a large bowl, combine the Brussels sprout leaves, hot pepper, and salt, and refrigerate.

In a small saucepan, mix together the peppercorn oil and garlic. Sauté for a couple of minutes, add the sugar and vinegar until the sugar dissolves, then allow to cool. Pour this mixture over the refrigerated Brussels sprout leaves and refrigerate for a couple of hours.

To make the basting liquid, in a small saucepan, heat the oil, add the shallots, and sauté until brown, about 2 minutes. Remove from the heat and add the soy sauce, vinegar, and sesame oil. Set aside to have ready for the roasting pan for the chicken.

To smoke the chicken, first, in a mixing bowl, combine the flour, sugar, rice, and tea leaves.

Prepare to make a small stovetop smoker with a wire rack:

1. Line the bottom of your smoking vessel with heavy-duty aluminum foil on which you will put the smoking mixture. (This is important because the mixture contains sugar, which, when melted, will make everything stick like glue to the surface.)

2. Spread the smoking mixture in the bottom of your smoker.

3. Put the wire rack into the smoker and assemble the rubbed chicken pieces on it. Ensure that the rack sits high enough in the smoking vessel to provide enough clearance for both the smoking mixture on the bottom *and* the chicken pieces, which will sit on the rack. (Remember, a lid will be put on the smoking vessel atop the chicken.)

4. Put on the domed lid, which must provide enough clearance for the chicken to fit on the rack and still be securely covered.

5. Cooking this dish will make your kitchen smell wonderful, but it's probably a good idea to turn on the fan in the range hood and possibly open the kitchen window in case you have a very sensitive smoke detector.

6. Turn up the heat to high for 5 minutes. Reduce the heat and smoke for an additional 10 minutes. (Meanwhile, preheat the oven to 350 degrees.)

7. Turn off the heat and leave the chicken for a further 10 minutes.

8. Remove the chicken from the smoker and set aside.

To finish the chicken, use tongs to put the smoked chicken pieces in a roasting pan and coat on both sides with the prepared basting sauce. You will be finishing the chicken in the oven at 350 degrees. *Remember, the turning can only be judged when you check the chicken. Ovens are calibrated differently from each other, and some chicken breasts are thicker than others.* Continue to baste as you check the chicken for doneness to your liking. (Our test cook left the chicken in her oven for an additional 50 minutes! But only you know your oven.)

PRESENTATION

Strain the Brussels sprout leaves from the liquid, and place on the center of the plate. (Please remember, these leaves are served chilled.) Top with the chicken breasts (or slice the breasts), cover with the finished sauce, and spread cilantro leaves on top.

Oh, yes . . . bask in your sense of accomplishment.

FOR THE SALAD

1 pound Brussels sprout leaves only, separated from cores

1 hot pepper, finely diced (use gloves when preparing the pepper)

About 1 teaspoon salt

FOR THE SALAD DRESSING

¼ cup peppercorn oil (available at Asian stores)

4 garlic cloves, peeled and thinly sliced

1 tablespoon sugar

¼ cup rice wine vinegar

FOR THE BASTING LIQUID

2 tablespoons grapeseed oil

2 shallots, finely diced

2 tablespoons light soy sauce

2 tablespoons balsamic vinegar

1 tablespoon sesame oil

Fresh cilantro, about a handful

FOR THE SMOKING MIXTURE

(These ingredients will be burned for the smoke—they will *not* be consumed.)

½ cup all-purpose flour

½ cup sugar

½ cup white or brown rice

½ cup leaf tea (your choice; however, since loose tea is becoming a rarity, please note that the contents of about 24 tea bags yields ½ cup)

EQUIPMENT

A stockpot

Plastic, latex, or clean rubber gloves with which to prepare the hot peppers

A coffee grinder to grind the spices (some people have a dedicated grinder for this purpose)

A wok with a domed lid, or something similar to serve as the stovetop smoker

A wire rack to support the chicken, which will fit inside the smoker with enough room to clear the smoking mixture on the bottom as well as provide enough clearance for the chicken between top of the rack and the domed lid. (Review the smoking instructions in the body of the recipe to make sure you have the proper arrangement.)

Heavy-duty aluminum foil to line the bottom of the smoker (*important* for cleanup purposes)

A roasting pan for the chicken

A Note on Bones for Stock In the event that you are unable to obtain bones for the chicken stock, buy wings, legs, and/or thighs (or use the necks you have stockpiled in the freezer from the roasters you have bought), and cook them down. Your butcher should accommodate your need for the bones, but in today's world some supermarket butchers are disinclined to provide individual attention for real cooks like you.

The local butcher of our home test cook for the Tea-Smoked Chicken recipe recently retired after nearly fifty years in the business. This neighborhood butcher had achieved nearly godlike status because of his helpful, knowledgeable, and friendly service. To a regular customer, he would have given the chicken or duck bones for the stock. This, of course, is nearly unheard-of today, and most customers would be willing to pay for the bones anyway. A message to all you entrepreneurs out there: real home cooks need real butchers and real fishmongers! There are plenty of real home cooks who really cook and who aspire for excellence. They need your services. Remember, in *Fiddler on the Roof*, Tevye made a match for his daughter with the village butcher so she would never be hungry. This wasn't because the would-be couple would be "eating up" the profits, but because a local butcher who treats customers like valued individuals can easily achieve a loyal following, which translates to a successful business. And . . . in the case of our cook's recently retired butcher, adoring fans. Future meat purveyors should follow his example.

Pan-Roasted Black Bass with Prawns over Cauliflower Risotto

SERVES 4

This recipe takes a little patience, because the deconstructed cauliflower microflorets act as the risotto. And never underestimate the power of a good, well-made stock (or, in this case, fumet.)

Remove and discard the outside leaves of the cauliflower, cut out the cores, and separate the heads into florets. Using your hands, break apart half of the large florets into the tiniest possible florets, or what we call "microflorets," and set aside. Put the remaining large florets, about 4 cups, into a large saucepan with generously salted water to cover and bring to a boil over high heat. Lower the heat to maintain a lively simmer and cook for 8 to 10 minutes, or until tender. Drain and *reserve the liquid*. Let the cauliflower cool for a few minutes, then put 2 cups of the large florets and ½ cup of the reserved cooking liquid into a blender with the butter and puree until smooth. Transfer to a bowl and set aside. Bring a pot of water to a boil and cook only the tiny florets for about 1 minute, or until slightly tender but not mushy, and set aside.

Peel the prawns and set aside, reserving the shells and heads for the sauce. Heat 1 tablespoon of the grapeseed oil in a skillet over medium-high heat. To make the sauce, add the shells/heads and cook for about 2 minutes, or until they turn pink, then add the fumet. Simmer until the liquid has reduced by half. Strain through a fine-mesh sieve into a bowl, discarding the shells and reserving the liquid. Melt the 1 tablespoon unsalted butter over medium heat in the same skillet, add the shallots, and cook for 1 minute. Add the wine and thyme sprig, and the reduced fumet, and cook until reduced again by half. Decrease the heat to low and whisk in the ½ cup cut-up butter one piece at a time, adding each piece only after the previous one has melted. Strain through a fine-mesh sieve into a small bowl and season with salt and pepper. Set the bowl into a small saucepan of hot water to keep warm.

Clean the skillet and heat the remaining 1 tablespoon grapeseed oil over

FOR THE CAULIFLOWER RISOTTO

2 large heads of cauliflower

Salt

6 tablespoons unsalted butter, at room temperature

FOR THE SAUCE AND PRAWNS

¾ pounds medium heads-off prawns or other fresh shrimp, or 1 pound shrimp with heads on

2 tablespoons grapeseed oil

1 cup fish stock (fumet)

1 tablespoon unsalted butter

2 tablespoons chopped shallots

¼ cup dry white wine

1 sprig of fresh thyme

½ cup cold unsalted butter, cut into ½-inch pieces

Kosher salt and freshly ground black pepper

FOR THE BLACK BASS

2 tablespoons olive oil

Four 4-ounce pieces black bass fillet, skin on

Kosher salt and freshly ground black pepper

Chopped fresh flat-leaf parsley leaves, for garnish

medium-high heat. Add the prawns and cook, stirring frequently, for about 2 minutes, or until just pink. Set aside.

Heat the oil in a large skillet or sauté pan over high heat. Season the flesh side of the fish with salt and pepper. Put into the pan, skin side down, and cook for about 3 minutes, or until the skin has crisped. Using a spatula, turn the fish over and cook for 2 to 3 minutes more.

PRESENTATION

To serve, reheat the cauliflower cream (the pureed mixture) in a small sauce-pan, add the microflorets, and warm over low heat. Put a spoonful of this "risotto" in the center of 4 warm dinner plates and top with the fish. Spoon a ring of warm sauce around the fish and arrange the prawns in the sauce. Then drizzle a little more sauce over them and sprinkle the parsley over all.

A Note on Fumet Fish stock—fumet—is required for the Pan-Roasted Black Bass with Cauliflower Risotto. There is nothing like the results obtained from making your own stock, fish or otherwise. Besides being a skill that proficient cooks should have, there is something almost spiritual about it—in the shamanic sense of wholeness. The use of the entire fish with little or no waste is admirable at the very least—and can even be considered responsible. In your freezer, you can stockpile the shells of raw or cooked shellfish, and bones and trimmings from lean (not oily) fresh fish, all of which can be used to make your own fumet. (You can also use whole fish that's not too expensive.)

About 2 pounds of fish parts will yield approximately 2 cups of stock. Sauté a chopped onion and half a dozen parsley stems in some butter. Add a dash of salt, about a teaspoon of lemon juice, a cup or so of white wine, and enough cold water to cover the ingredients. Bring to a simmer and skim off the unwanted surface material. Simmer for a further 30 minutes to reduce by half and strain through a fine sieve. Store the labeled stock in the freezer in 1-cup increments for use as needed.

FINALLY, FEED YOUR PASSION BY KEEPING SOCIETY WITH LIKE-MINDED individuals. Seek out people you can who share your passion. If possible, meet the very best; get to know them. If you can't meet them, follow their exploits, read their theories, consider their work and opinions, and let them inform your own. I would like to take a moment to refer you to two of the best examples I know of professionals in the pursuit of excellence.

Michel Richard has achieved the status of legend in our field. A magnificent Frenchman who came to America as a baker and basically conquered the country, his impact on cuisine in the United States, and especially on California cuisine, which has become the seminal movement in American cooking since the early days of Chez Panisse, has been as profound as that of his countryman Lafayette on the art of political revolution. Still, he refuses to sit on his laurels, though he has earned enough to stuff an entire sofa. His restless mind needs to be fueled by constant experimentation. He still amazes me to this day with the cross-pollination he achieves between baking methods and cooking methods. He is able to isolate and employ suspension agents typically found only in baking to create textures and flavors in hot food that I am still not sure I completely understand. I love to visit his restaurants not only because I know that the food and hospitality will be of the very highest order but because I know I will always learn something. He is one of the most brilliant culinarians I have ever known. He never lets it get old.

Roberto Donna, both as friend and as inspiration, has no peer. The first time I met Roberto was at the Madison Hotel at a Beard Foundation dinner. Somehow, no food had been prepared to feed the chefs who had cooked the main dinner of the evening. Without missing a beat, Roberto appropriated half a dozen prehistoric-sized cuts of beef from the walk-in and cheerfully prepared salt-crusted prime rib with trimmings for us all. I would affectionately describe him as a happy warrior in the kitchen.

He now presides over the dining room at his restaurant, Galileo, in the nation's capital. Everything he does is filled with passion, as anyone who has ever worked in one of his kitchens will attest. His kitchen is not a quiet place, especially if his wishes are not immediately and flawlessly carried out. As magnificent as Galileo is, with its homemade cotechino sausages, agnolotti, mousses, and terrines; its universe of excellent pastas and sauces, cheeses, and risottos; and its vibrant and memorable soups and desserts, the real action, as in Rick's place in *Casablanca*, is in the back room. That is where, in his private dining workshop, his culinarian's lair, *Il Laboratorio*, he labors to find perfection. Here he creates ten- and twelve-course tasting menus for his clients in an intimate venue, featuring not just fine Italian food but fine dining experiences to compete with any in the world. His flawless technique may be on full display in his Roasted Duck Liver with Cherry Sauce, but the effort and skill he puts into garnishing it with a single zucchini flower, which he stuffs and poaches whilst managing to keep every petal of the flower intact, is wondrous to behold. If passion is in the details, then my good friend is passion personified.

Decide what *you* are going to obsess over. Great cooking is seeing to the details.

STYLE AND SUBSTANCE

The importance of doing it with style
and my road to the White House

Robert and Big George heating things up in the kitchen

IN THE RUNNING GUN BATTLE BETWEEN STYLE AND SUBSTANCE, IT IS PROB-ably true that style gets all of the good press whilst substance does all of the work. Style has all of the fun; substance does all of the planning and scheduling and even does the washing up afterward. Now, in any good fable, style usually gets its comeuppance, as in "The Tortoise and the Hare," or "The Ant and the Grasshopper," but in reality I think that the two are inextricably linked, like tea and crumpets, fish and chips, or love and marriage (at least in the best ones).

I had been invited to attend (as a guest) a gala luncheon charity event given by the Ladies Professional Golf Association, or the LPGA, which was being held at the Atlantic City Convention Center. I decided to walk over from the Taj Mahal to take a look. I was especially intrigued by the invitation because the cooking was going to be done by Charlie Trotter, out of Chicago.

Charlie Trotter is one of the best in the business. He is a consistent five-star Mobil chef, a multiple James Beard Award-winner, a chef who has had a real impact on the trade itself. He is a pioneer in the renaissance of the tasting menu, and his exacting standards and the perfect judgment and balance in his dishes can make a single bite seem like an adventure. I had brought a friend of mine along, another chef, named Robert Caracciola, and we were looking forward to seeing and tasting what was on offer, and to a rare and well-earned day off. There's also no question that the "nosy" side of me wanted to poke around and see what was going on.

We arrived early, hoping to squeeze in a bit of reconnaissance, and there literally seemed to be *nothing* going on. I found one of the lovely ladies who was to be in charge of the event, and she looked much more worried than happy to see me. Apparently, due to a miscommunication of some kind, the stage for the presentation was practically bare, and nothing was ready for the impending arrival of the impresario, Mr. Trotter. No pots, no pans, no water, not a single chopped onion, not a towel or a spoon. Realization and panic were setting in for her at the same time. "I need your help," she said. "What am I going to do?!"

There is nothing like rallying to the rescue of a damsel in distress to whet your appetite before a big dinner, and I'm generally happier in a setting where *I* can be the boss, for at least part of the evening anyway, so Bobby and I took off our jackets and set to work. We worked together at the Taj Mahal, and we ran across the boardwalk and raided the Taj's kitchens for carts full of everything we thought *we* would want at hand to put on a show. We arranged for Trotter's cooking gear, utensils, pots and pans, mise en place, even put nice clean liners in the garbage cans. Charlie arrived later than expected, due to a flight delay, and when he arrived was in no mood for hugs and kisses, so we backed off and stayed out of his way. He is very strict and nothing was really the way he had asked for it to be, but at least we had given him a fighting chance. We had stuck to rule number one: get the food on the plates. And it helps when the guy's a genius . . . his food was fantastic.

Having made a favorable impression, I was asked to put the LPGA event together on my own a couple of years hence, and I was in a mood to do it with some style. This was one of the events that started to build my reputation for putting on splashy parties. I brought in a number of chefs, including my old friends Ming Tsai and Marcus Samuelsson of Aquavit; about forty in all. My theme was "Chefs of the (Salad) Greens," and I paired a fantastic chef with each of the golfers on the tour. The event was for the benefit of about twenty charities bundled together, so the facilities and the arena at the Taj Mahal had been donated, and therefore I actually had a respectable budget to work with, and I took advantage of it. The chefs took over management of their own stations, and were charged with producing the most incredible dishes they could devise. For the setting, I provided miniature "golf holes" with pin flags and *real grass* for each station. We laid fresh sod down over the entire ballroom floor.

I have a friend who lived near me at the time named Vivat Hong Pong, who is a wonderful guy and also happens to be the world's greatest ice sculptor. He is the Michelangelo of the chain saw, and he came and carved *golf carts* out of titanic blocks of ice that looked big and detailed enough to drive away in. The printers at the Taj had the bills of fare printed up to look like score cards. We raised lots of money, made a big splash in the South Jersey press, and had a heck of a lot of fun with it all. Sometimes you want a simple understated dinner for two, but at other times you have to pull out the big guns and throw a *party*.

WITHOUT SUBSTANCE, THERE IS NO "THERE" THERE, AND THE CONVER-sation never really gets started. That is why we slave over technique, search for the best combinations, write them into recipes, seek out only the finest, freshest ingredients, and refuse to compromise on quality. But all of this preparation seldom rises to the level of true greatness without style. Style adds a little flair, a little flourish, the tip of the hat, the gleam in the eye, the perfect remark to the perfect person at the perfect moment. It's the lady in the tramp, and the little bit of tramp in the lady. There is both high and low style, and every kind in between. The epitome of high style is probably Fred Astaire in anything, Cary Grant in *It Takes a Thief,* Princess Diana at the White House. An excellent example of low style is Brigadier General Anthony McAuliffe's reply to a surrender demand from the German forces when surrounded in the Battle of the Bulge at Bastogne: "Nuts." In both cases, you know it when you see it.

Whatever your personal "it" may be, you had might as well do it with style.

Sometimes style can mean just doing what comes naturally when the opportunity presents itself. When the time had come to leave the Taj Mahal, I remember interviewing for the executive chef position in Atlantic City at Caesar's and had just sat down to lunch with their top-tier executive team. They ordered a number of appetizers, among them a clam dish in a light savory sauce with garlic and herbs. I knew upon sampling the first bite that a mistake had been made. The clams had a weird metallic taste; the base of onions and garlic and herbs had been processed in a mechanical chopper of some kind and had imparted a metallic taste to the clams. I excused myself, made my way back into the kitchen, and quickly recooked the dish (with a few of my own touches), but this time I prepped the ingredients by hand. I brought the dish to the table and had my interviewers compare the results whilst I explained. They signed me up on the spot. A bit of knowledge and experience applied at the proper moment, with just a dash of style, clinched the deal.

Lobster Risotto with Clams

SERVES 6

The preceding story put me in mind of one of my favorite clam dishes. Really, the only secret to a delicious risotto is patience. Make the commitment to stir the Arborio rice constantly whilst it is cooking. Maybe try to remember the lyrics to "Stairway to Heaven" to pass the time when you are doing it; if you can manage to remember them all without cheating, the timing should be just about right.

Put the lobster stock in a pot and keep _just below boiling_. ("Just below boiling" is the true definition of "simmering" in classical cooking.) On an adjacent burner, heat the olive oil in another large saucepan. Add the shallots to the oil and cook until soft. Stir the rice into the pan with the oil and shallots. Stir the rice until it becomes translucent, then pour the wine into the rice to deglaze the pan. When most of the liquid has evaporated from the rice pan, add one ladle of stock at a time to the risotto from the simmering pot of lobster stock on the next burner. The method is to let the risotto absorb the lobster stock gradually before you add the next ladleful to it. Once all the stock has been added and absorbed (after 15 to 25 minutes), add the heavy cream.

Remove the risotto from the heat. Stir in the lobster meat, cheese, butter, basil, and lemon juice. Season with salt and pepper to taste.

Place the clean clams in a saucepan; add the garlic, shallots, thyme, and white wine. Cover and bring to a simmer. Cook, covered, until the clams open. (Discard any clams that do not open). Swirl in the butter and parsley.

PRESENTATION

Mound the risotto in the center of each of 6 shallow bowls. Place 4 clams on top of each serving and drizzle the liquid from the clam pot. Garnish with a sprig of basil and shaved Parmesan.

**A Note on Cooking with Wine** Cook with a wine you wouldn't mind drinking! You only need ½ cup for the Lobster Risotto with Clams, which means you can drink the rest with your meal. (Or while you're cooking—but don't stop stirring that risotto!)

FOR THE RISOTTO

2½ cups lobster stock

1 tablespoon olive oil

1 tablespoon chopped shallots

1 cup Arborio rice

¼ cup white wine

2 ounces heavy cream

¾ cup diced lobster meat, cooked

3 tablespoons freshly grated Parmesan cheese (plus a piece to shave for garnish)

2 tablespoons unsalted butter

1 tablespoon chopped fresh basil

Juice of 1 lemon

Salt and pepper

FOR THE CLAMS

24 littleneck clams, well scrubbed and rinsed

1 tablespoon minced garlic

1 tablespoon minced shallots

1 sprig of fresh thyme

¼ cup white wine

3 tablespoons unsalted butter

1 tablespoon chopped fresh parsley

6 sprigs of fresh basil

In GREAT COOKING, STYLE HAS A LOT TO DO WITH COMMUNICATION. STYLE can run hot or cold. Some cooks like big, hearty preparations that will feed an army, and others only want you to have an impeccably crafted bite or two before they are ready to take you in another direction. Style is always a reflection of personality. In the old days, the kitchen was walled off from the dining room, except in rare cases, and seldom the twain did meet. But Escoffier was able to pay exquisite homage and an everlasting compliment to a great singing diva of his day, Nellie Melba, with his creation Pêche Melba. They never really even had to meet. He said all he wanted to say with warmed peaches, silky ice cream, raspberries, and red currant jelly. He could have remained forever in the back of the house and she would have understood completely.

I like to communicate with food, in the way it is presented, and with special or unlikely ingredients. I will design an evening dress for a beautiful woman made entirely of fiberglass and fitted with shelves for an assortment of spectacular hors d'oeuvres, and have her circulate through the room before dinner service. I will plant fireworks in your food for presentation if I think you will be duly impressed and entertained. I will spend tens of thousands of dollars to build a replica of an Italian village in a hotel in Atlantic City to serve you a plate of spaghetti (and it will be very good spaghetti). I really want you to have a good time, in style.

It is epigrammatic in the business that "you eat with your eyes first." It's true. The mix of colors on a plate, the arrangement of items, evocative composition—all are important to the experience. There should always be a certain amount of "come hither" on the plate, an invitation to pleasure. I think that the presentation on the plate should delight the eye, like fine sculpture or painting, as well as reflect the sensibilities of the artist, that is to say, the chef.

These four words, which I drill into the heads of my chefs, are the essence of my style of presentation on the plate:

High
Tight
Clean
Centered

"High" means that I like to give the food a certain height off of the plate. For my Blackened Tenderloin of Beef, I will create a firm base with, say, a Sweet Corn and Potato Hash, and top that with the filet. From there, I can bake a crust of blue cheese on the filet and top that with a crown of delicately fried onions. I like to make the food sit up and be noticed.

"Tight" means that I don't like to see the food spread out all over the place, as in the "three-plops-and-down" method, where the meat's at six o'clock, the veg is at ten, the starch is at two, and the sauce is working its way into a bit of everything. If I have a 10-ounce piece of fish, I will cut it or fold it so it stays within the structure that I have determined will work best for that dish. When I say "stay put," I mean it.

"Clean" means that I like you to be able to see the elements of the dish. If I give you a roulade of chicken stuffed with prosciutto on a bed of saffron risotto, I will slice the roulade so that you can see the ingredients in the center and appreciate their integration into the dish. I add saffron to the rice not only for the flavor, but so that the color is harmonious with the rest of the dish and calls out for attention. I might add the dusky red of a bite of sun-dried tomato in the roulade to recall the color of the saffron threads. It all gives you a sense of inclusion on my plan for the dish, a sense of "aha! I see what he's up to!" Then, moments later, when you smell and taste the white truffle oil, it comes as a pleasant surprise.

"Centered" means just what it says. I like to put the food in the direct center of your range of sight, usually with an expanse of white plate around it for contrast and to accentuate its beauty. I may subtly pool a sauce around the base of a centered dish to create a halo of color, but if I do so, I will make sure that the texture of the sauce is firm, not runny, so it doesn't spread and mess up the plate.

With this presentational matrix, you cannot help but give a focal point to the eye. It communicates precision, but can also make room for a sense of playfulness. In my Maine Lobster Salad, you won't have any problem figuring out that it is a *lobster* salad; the presentation of the lobster element will be high, tight, clean, and centered. But I will match the sunset colors of the shell fins of the tail with similarly colored and fanned peach slices, which will duplicate the appearance of the fins to make you smile just before you dig in.

It is good to have methods that you can fall back on, because they give you confidence, but you want to try to avoid letting them slip into becoming dogma. Having a methodology will allow you to be comfortable enough in any setting to do good work, but leaving yourself open to your own freedom of expression can lead to bigger and better things.

When I worked at Trump, I received a call from my then boss, Walter

Kohlross, who asked me to host some visitors from the Navy. We had an advanced "cook and chill" system that I had installed, which allowed us to cook, bag, and blast-chill food items and then serve them later at a very high level of freshness. This was an important tool when you had to service multiple restaurants, banquets, and room service for a large hotel and casino on a daily basis. As it turns out, it was also a great idea if you had to centrally prepare and distribute food for a fleet of submarines that might be deployed for months at a time.

A gentleman arrived who was introduced to me as the Commander of Naval Supply; he had about a dozen Navy officers in uniform along. I spent the day showing them around, explaining our operations to him, as well as the cook and chill system, and made them lunch and dinner. As they were leaving, the commander expressed his gratitude and offered, "If I can ever do you a favor, just let me know."

In point of fact, I did have something in mind. Not that long before, I had been on a visit to the CIA (the Culinary Institute of America, not the Central Intelligence Agency), and I noticed a couple of chefs who had jackets with White House emblems on them. I asked if I could get my hands on a couple, and he said he would look into it on his return to D.C. We shook hands and they left.

A couple of days later, I got a call from Tony Powell, who was then deputy director for Presidential Food Service for the White House. We had a great conversation. He took down my size, said he would take care of it right away, and gave me the option of coming down to the White House to pick them up, which invitation I accepted.

In my estimation, Tony is one of those guys who only come along rarely in a lifetime. He grew up in the Bronx, New York, is retired from the Navy after twenty-eight years of service, and through hard work has risen to enjoy the confidence of some of the most powerful people in government. He is smart and disciplined, but never rigid and always open to new ideas.

I met him in his office and he graciously showed me around the White House food operation. I have never been shy about offering an opinion, and I started to talk to him about what I saw as inefficiencies in the way they were putting food out of their kitchen. For one thing, they had completely different sets of china for orders from the East Wing and West Wing. That left cooks competing against one another to grab the correct dishes when things got busy. Uniform china would have eliminated this problem in one stroke. Their stations were disorganized and left people crossing into one another's areas to perform the simplest tasks, like getting to the dishwashers. I could see that some people had too many of the wrong kinds of responsibilities, some had too few.

We talked some more, and Tony invited me to come back whenever it was convenient to talk to his cooking staff and share some new ideas with them. I left with my jackets and spent the next sixteen weekends in a row driving back to Washington, talking to and training White House chefs, servers, and staff. They had to put out between one and two hundred lunches a day, and nearly always found themselves in the weeds and behind service when they were busy, because the menus hadn't been well thought through. I helped to revise their menus and organize them according to ingredients and prep times whilst punching up some of their presentations. I helped to reorganize their stations in a more systematic way. I reworked their scheduling. They used to schedule prep for lunch at 4 a.m. and barely get everything finished in time; then everybody would quit for the day. I split their prep between that big chunk of down time in the afternoon and a later call time in the morning and took the pressure off. They had virtually no freezer space, and no dessert space. We drew up a grand plan on a couple of napkins, and with Tony clearing the way, we worked together to solve both of those problems and even had gas laid on in the kitchen to replace all of their inefficient electric cooktops.

All of this effort has led to another unexpected and satisfying twist in my career, cooking as a guest chef in the White House, for both Presidents Bush, the elder and the younger, as well as for President Clinton. Including the time I cooked for President Reagan's birthday on the *Britannia,* I have served my food to four U.S. presidents. I have enjoyed a whole second wave of opportunity to present my food to world leaders. I have had the chance to cook special orders for the commanders in chief and their first ladies. I have made Cowboy-Style Rib Eye Steak paired with truffled mashed potatoes and a twenty-year balsamic demi-glace; I have put peerless Japanese Kobe beef in a shepherd's pie (usually made with ground lamb), to be served to Prime Minister Tony Blair at a gala state dinner; and I have served up giant Wisconsin-prime freedom burgers on brioche rolls with mammoth Idaho freedom fries in recent times of diplomatic stress with our French allies.

Tony Powell and I have become great friends since then; I call him "my brother from another mother." I recently attended a reunion dinner in Washington of all of the chefs who have cooked at the White House since the Nixon administration. I went bowling in the basement of the White House, and there was a lovely speech made about my contributions at a picnic afterward. You never know where grabbing a frying pan and spatula and having a good time is going to lead you.

In the time that has intervened since, I have kept busy spreading the culinary faith. I have variously consulted on food management and service at Resorts Hotel and Casino in Atlantic City, worked on the development of my line of food products and equipment, have plans in the works for a restaurant of my own in St. Petersburg, Florida, and have been given the chance to realize a longtime goal, that of making a mark in the world of television.

Prior to shooting the television pilot for Food Network, which I mentioned in the introduction to this book, my producers and I were obliged to put together a short demo, or "sizzle" reel (appropriate for a chef), that showcased my skills in the kitchen and that proved that I could cook and speak on camera at the same time without accidentally cutting off any important parts of myself or my coworkers.

Through a good friend of mine, we managed to get in touch with the people who run a training facility for both the New York Knicks and the New York Rangers, way out in the New York countryside. I have always been fascinated by the eating habits of athletes, and this was a rare opportunity to put some of my theories into practice. They allowed us to come in and cook a fantastic lunch, without any warning, for the players and coaches of both teams. I literally had a little more than two hours, during which time I was able to come up with eleven hot entrées and ten cold, with the help of George and George, served buffet-style in their cafeteria. The menu included Tastiest Ribs with Three Bean Ragout, Country Chicken–Fried Steak with Corn Bread, Creole-Style Red Snapper with Farmhouse Grits, Seared Tuna, Spicy Flank Steak, Seared Chicken Fontina, Cold Lamb Salad with Beets and Feta, Colossal Crab, Apple, and Fennel Salad, Horseradish-Crusted Salmon, Beef Tenderloin, Nantucket Bay Scallop Ceviche, Shrimp Scampi, and much more, including a chocolate fountain with fresh strawberries.

During the mad scramble to get things done, I had a chance to chat with the nutritionist for both teams, and we talked about the food requirements for athletes of this caliber, in what proportions they need proteins to build and maintain muscle mass, and at other times, usually in the same day, carbohydrates for quick bursts of high-intensity energy. She referred to them as "anaerobic animals" who often look at food as fuel, and that made perfect sense to me. In point of fact, the Rangers actually had a game on for that night, and there was some concern that a few of them might be breaking their food rituals for our buffet.

In the end, the food was a smashing success. We fed Knicks forward Malik Rose; Knicks guard Stephon Marbury; coaches Herb Williams and Mark Aguirre; Rangers defenseman Darius Kasparaitis; Rangers right wing Jaromir Jagr; Knicks general manager, Hall of Famer, and hard-court legend Isiah Thomas . . . and the entire lineups for both teams. They ate like lions, and took all of the leftovers home in carry-out containers. Both teams went on to win their next games, and the Knicks actually broke a losing streak. As he ate plate after plate of my food, Jaromir Jagr insisted on giving me an incredibly detailed description of the Czech dishes his mother makes at home, but finally had to admit that my food was good. Isiah Thomas—in a state of calorie-induced euphoria—equated his experience of the day with what his mother always told him about the importance of marrying a good cook and actually proposed marriage—to me. Of course he's a fine-looking man, and makes a good living, but alas . . . I had to break his heart and tell him I am already married.

All kidding aside, we must have "sold the sizzle," since we got our chance at the pilot.

These are some of the recipes I cooked for the New York superstar athletes and coaches. They are all healthy, and though some are more filling (you should have seen the size of some of those guys) and others provide more energy and fewer calories, they are all well balanced and nutritious. I also served my Tastiest Ribs (page 7)—the Czech hockey players went wild over them.

Spicy Flank Steak with Watermelon and Cherry Tomato Salad, Tossed with a Cilantro Lime Vinaigrette

SERVES 6

FOR THE RUB AND FLANK STEAK

2 teaspoons ground coriander

2 teaspoons ground cumin

2 teaspoons ground thyme

2 teaspoons salt

2 teaspoons black pepper

2 teaspoons garlic powder

3 pounds flank steak, trimmed

FOR THE CILANTRO LIME VINAIGRETTE

2 ounces lime juice (from 3 limes)

⅛ cup chopped cilantro

2 ounces (¼ cup) grapeseed oil

Salt and pepper

FOR THE WATERMELON/ CHERRY TOMATO SALAD

1 cup seeded, medium-diced watermelon

1 cup cherry tomatoes, quartered

½ cup seeded, peeled cucumbers, diced ½ inch

1 small red onion, diced small

⅛ cup scallions, thinly sliced

In a large plastic bag, mix the coriander, cumin, thyme, salt, pepper, and garlic powder. Place the steak in the bag and shake to coat. Refrigerate the rubbed steak for 1 hour.

Combine the lime juice, cilantro, grapeseed oil, and salt and pepper to taste in a cruet or jar and shake to combine well. Refrigerate. (Preheat the oven broiler for the steak.)

Combine the watermelon, cherry tomatoes, cucumbers, red onion, and scallions in a mixing bowl and toss with the vinaigrette.

Place the steak on a lightly greased baking sheet and broil for 5 minutes on each side or to desired doneness. Let the steak sit for 5 minutes before slicing. Slice the steak against the bias or grain, into 1-inch strips.

PRESENTATION

Divide the sliced steak evenly among 6 plates and arrange the slices all in the same direction on each plate. Spoon the salad down the middle of the row of steak slices.

FOR THE CORN BREAD

¾ pound (2¾ cups) cornmeal

1 pound (3¾ cups) all-purpose flour

¾ ounce (1 tablespoon) baking powder

¾ pint (1½ cups) sour cream

¾ cup milk

4 eggs

2 teaspoons salt

1 stick (8 tablespoons) melted butter

FOR THE COUNTRY GRAVY

2 cups half-and-half

1¼ sticks (10 tablespoons) butter

¾ cup flour

2 cups (16 ounces) chicken broth

2 bay leaves

2 teaspoons freshly cracked black pepper

2 teaspoons salt

FOR THE COUNTRY STEAK

Six 5-ounce flat-iron steaks

Salt and pepper

1½ cups milk

1½ cups flour

⅛ cup canola oil

FOR THE SPINACH

2 ounces canola oil

1 large red onion, finely diced

10 bunches of fresh spinach, washed and drained

Juice of 2 fresh lemons

Salt and pepper

EQUIPMENT

A loaf pan, greased

Country Chicken-Fried Steak with Corn Bread and Wilted Spinach

SERVES 6

Preheat the oven to 425 degrees. In a bowl, mix the cornmeal, flour, baking powder, sour cream, milk, eggs, salt, and melted butter. Bake in a greased loaf pan for 20 to 25 minutes until golden brown and a toothpick inserted into the center comes out clean.

Scald the half-and-half in a small saucepan. In a separate saucepan, melt the butter and whisk in the flour. Add the scalded half-and-half, chicken broth, bay leaves, black pepper, and salt, and simmer for 30 minutes, or until the mixture reaches the desired consistency. Remember to remove the bay leaves before serving.

Whilst the gravy is simmering, prepare the steaks and spinach.

Season the steaks with salt and pepper, then pound them flat with a meat mallet. Moisten the steaks in milk, then dip them in flour. Repeat, as this will give you a nice even coating. Heat the oil in a sauté pan. Fry the steaks in the oil until golden brown. Remove to a utility platter and pat off excess oil. Let rest.

Heat a sauté pan. Add the oil and onion. Cook until translucent. Reduce the heat to low. Add the spinach and lightly sauté, enough to break down the spinach, but do not overcook. Add the lemon juice and salt and pepper to taste. Remove from the heat.

A Note on Sandy Spinach Fresh spinach is among the greens with an uncanny ability to retain copious amounts of sand. Remembering that patience is a virtue, soak them repeatedly in successive bowls of clean water until you see that no more sand is falling to the bottom of the bowl. For the Country-Fried Steak with Corn Bread and Wilted Spinach recipe, it is especially helpful to dry the spinach with a salad spinner and/or pat it dry, since you will be sautéing it. Dry greens will be less apt to spatter in the sauté pan.

Colossal Crab, Apple, and Fennel Salad with Chive Oil

SERVES 6

In a large bowl, mix together a dressing of mayonnaise, chives, Old Bay seasoning, Tabasco, red onion, lemon juice, mustard, salt, and pepper.

Place the crabmeat in another bowl and pour on enough dressing to coat. Toss the crabmeat very lightly—try not to break the crabmeat into small pieces. Let sit in the refrigerator.

Prepare the fennel salad by tossing the fennel in a large bowl with the apple along with the lemon juice, olive oil, chives, fennel frond, parsley, and Parmesan cheese. Mix well.

To make the chive oil, start by having a bowl of ice water ready. Then briefly cook the chives for 10 to 15 seconds in a quart of boiling, salted water and strain. Place the chives into the ice bath, then remove and pat dry with paper towels. Cover and turn on the blender and whilst it is running, add the dry blanched chives through the feed tube (so they will get chopped), and then slowly add the oil through the feed tube, blending until all the chives are incorporated with the oil.

PRESENTATION

Place the crabmeat in a 2-inch round mold in the center of a plate. Carefully and gently pull the mold away without knocking down the crabmeat. Place the fennel salad on top of the crabmeat. Place the chopped parsley and microcelery greens on top of the fennel salad. Drizzle the chive oil with a spoon around the crab mixture.

FOR THE CRAB

½ cup (4 ounces) mayonnaise

2 tablespoons chopped chives

⅛ teaspoon Old Bay seasoning

Splash of Tabasco

½ red onion, diced small

Juice of 2 lemons

1 tablespoon whole-grain mustard

Salt and freshly ground black pepper

1½ pounds colossal crabmeat, picked over for shells

½ teaspoon chopped fresh parsley

Microcelery greens

FOR THE FENNEL SALAD

1 fennel bulb, shaved paper thin with a mandoline or a meat slicer

1 Granny Smith apple, cored and julienned

Juice of 1 lemon (squeezed over the apple)

2 tablespoons extra virgin olive oil

⅛ teaspoon chopped chives

⅛ teaspoon chopped fennel frond (top leaves of the fennel)

1 teaspoon chopped fresh Italian parsley

2 tablespoons shaved Parmesan cheese

FOR THE CHIVE OIL

1 bunch chives

1 cup canola oil or grapeseed oil

EQUIPMENT

A 2-inch-diameter circle cutter or ring mold

A blender

Seared Chicken Fontina with Warm Cabbage Slaw

SERVES 6

FOR THE CHICKEN

6 boneless, skinless chicken breasts

Salt and pepper

¼ cup light olive oil

2 plum tomatoes, thinly sliced

3 slices Bel Paese cheese

FOR THE WARM CABBAGE SLAW

½ cup chopped bacon

1 red onion, diced

1 stick (8 tablespoons) unsalted butter

1 head of white cabbage, thinly sliced and core removed

¼ cup rice wine vinegar

Juice of 1 lemon

¼ cup chopped chives

3 ounces Boursin cheese (optional)

Preheat the oven to 325 degrees. Season the chicken breasts with salt and pepper to taste on both sides. In an ovenproof sauté pan, heat the oil until the pan is smoking. Sear each side of the chicken breasts until golden brown. Remove and allow to cool for a couple of minutes.

Place 2 slices of tomato on top of the chicken and then top with a slice of cheese.

Finish the chicken in the oven, 25 to 30 minutes, testing for doneness.

Meanwhile, in a large sauté pan, cook the bacon until all the fat is rendered out and it is crisp. Remove and set aside on paper towels to drain.

In the same pan, cook the diced onion in the bacon fat until translucent. Melt the butter in the pan, add the cabbage, and toss with the onion, cooking until it is wilted but still crisp in texture. Add the rice wine vinegar, lemon juice, crumbled bacon, and chopped chives, and cook together for a couple of minutes.

Note: If you want to make the cabbage salad richer and really creamy, add Boursin cheese into it just before serving.

Adjust the seasoning and serve.

PRESENTATION

Place a little of the cabbage mix into the center of each plate and top with the chicken.

Shrimp Scampi Provençal

SERVES 6

Bring a pot of salted water to a boil for the pasta.

Dredge the shrimp in the seasoned flour. In a sauté pan, heat the oil and sauté the shrimp until light golden. Remove the shrimp from the pan to a utility platter.

To make the scampi sauce, use the same pan and add the wine and cook, reducing by half to intensify the flavor. Then add the tomatoes, tomato juice, lemon juice, garlic, basil, and chicken broth. Let reduce until thickened, then add the butter. (Begin cooking the pasta at this point; cook to al dente.) Simmer the scampi sauce on low heat for 8 to 10 minutes. Place the shrimp back into the sauce.

Drain the pasta.

PRESENTATION

This can be plated individually, or on a single serving platter with a bed of pasta or rice in the center. Arrange the shrimp on top and spoon the sauce over. Garnish with basil sprigs and lemon wedges. (Your guests may enjoy squeezing the juice from the lemon wedges over the top to their liking. I think the lemon juice adds another "layer" of flavor to the scampi.)

> *A Note on Shrimp Sizes* Shrimp (and scallops) are sold by count per pound. The larger the shrimp is, the lower the count per pound. "U" represents the word "under." U/15 shrimp are of such a size as to equal a "count" of fewer than 15 shrimp in a pound.

30 U/15 shrimp (under 15 shrimp per pound), peeled, deveined, tail on

1 cup flour, seasoned with salt and pepper

¼ cup canola oil

½ cup white wine

6 plum tomatoes, medium diced

⅓ cup tomato juice

⅓ cup freshly squeezed lemon juice

4 garlic cloves, chopped

3 tablespoons chopped basil

1 cup chicken broth

1¼ sticks (10 tablespoons) unsalted butter

Pasta (your choice) or rice, over which you will serve scampi

6 basil sprigs

2 fresh lemons, cut into 12 wedges

Leave room for your own personal style to shine through. At the end of the day, I don't ever believe in slavish devotion to a recipe. Generally, if you go to the trouble of memorizing the name of one of my recipes in this book, say, Short Ribs Braised with Mushrooms, Pearl Onions, and Bacon, you are well on your way to figuring out a preparation for this dish of your very own.

We are all a result of the confluence of influences in our lives, and we each communicate those influences in a different way. Personal travels, holiday traditions, the news of the day, friends and family, nature, TV, art, magazines, and for me, especially music and weather, all shape our unique sense of style. I am an Englishman, and my style is influenced by my homeland to a degree, but it is also constantly evolving as I open myself up to new sensory stimulation. It is all reflected on my plates, because that is how I communicate myself to people.

Go forth and communicate. I hope you enjoy these dishes in style.

Maine Lobster Salad

SERVES 6

This is an expressive interpretation of the main element in the dish, featuring a palette of color and taste.

(The dressing benefits from being refrigerated overnight. Don't add the fruits in advance because they will oxidize. Add instead 1 tablespoon orange juice to the dressing so that it can infuse with the other flavors.)

FOR THE POACHING LIQUID

Thyme, about a handful, stripped from the stems and chopped

Tarragon, about a handful, stripped from the stems and chopped

2 to 3 bay leaves

Salt and pepper

Enough water to cover the lobster tails

6 lobster tails

Remains of the segmented orange prepped for salad

½ cup hazelnut oil

¼ cup rice wine vinegar

1 tablespoon finely chopped
fresh chives

1 tablespoon lightly chopped
fresh tarragon

1 tablespoon fresh chopped
thyme

¼ cup diced Bermuda onion

1 tablespoon orange juice, if
preparing dressing in advance

FOR THE SALAD

½ pound white grapes, halved,
and seeds removed

½ pound black grapes, halved,
and seeds removed

½ pound red grapes, halved,
and seeds removed

1 kiwi fruit, roughly chopped

1 English cucumber, peeled,
seeds removed, and diced

1 Bermuda onion, diced

2 peaches, finely sliced with
skin on

1 navel orange, skin and all
white pith peeled off,
segmented

3 avocados, removed from
black skin and roughly
chopped

3 tablespoons white truffle oil

GARNISHES FOR PLATING

1 head of butter lettuce

About 6 radicchio leaves,
thinly sliced

Leaves from 1 or 2 endives

1 or 2 peaches

EQUIPMENT

12 bamboo skewers

Add the thyme, tarragon, bay leaves, salt, and pepper to the water, and heat to the point just before boiling (a "simmer"), when the bubbles are rising to the surface but not breaking the surface. Insert 2 bamboo skewers into each tail to stop the lobsters from curling up. Chop off the ends of the skewers if they are long. Add the lobster tails to the poaching liquid and squeeze the juice from the segmented orange over the tails. Simmer for 8 to 10 minutes. *Do not over-cook*. Shock in ice water when done.

Combine the hazelnut oil, rice wine vinegar, chives, tarragon, thyme, and onion in a bowl and whisk together until combined. (If refrigerating the dress-ing overnight, add 1 tablespoon orange juice for fruitiness.) Put the salad in-gredients (white, black, and red grapes, kiwi, English cucumber, onion, peaches, navel orange, and avocados) into a bowl, pour the dressing on top, and fold together.

PRESENTATION

Put several butter lettuce leaves on a plate as a bed. Place a portion of sliced radicchio in center. Arrange 3 endive leaves, pointed end out, in thirds sticking out of the lettuce bed. Spoon the fruit salad into the center of the lettuce bed. Remove the bamboo skewers from the lobster tails, break off the tail fins (to use later), and peel the whole lobster tail from the shell. Slice the meat at an angle and arrange on top of the salad. Place the tail fins in the center as decora-tion. Slice a piece of peach and "fan" as a decoration with the tail fin. Drizzle with truffle oil and enjoy!

Crispy Potato and Goat Cheese, Chive Oil, and 8-Year Balsamic

SERVES 6

This recipe provides the elements you need to make a wonderful presentation of this most memorable appetizer. I love the feeling of architecture, where the "chips" stand erect. Like a sculptor, feel free to be creative.

6 large Idaho potatoes, peeled and sliced paper thin (use a mandoline)

1 bunch of chives

Two 10-ounce logs goat cheese

6 portobello mushroom caps, cleaned

¼ cup olive oil, or as needed to coat mushrooms and toss greens

Salt and freshly ground black pepper

¾ cup canola oil

1 bunch of baby greens (like frisée or mâche)

½ cup aged balsamic vinegar, as needed to toss into greens

6 yellow teardrop tomatoes, quartered

EQUIPMENT

A mandoline

Parchment paper, oiled

A squeeze bottle, like the ones used for ketchup or mustard

A bowl of ice water standing by

Preheat the oven to 275 degrees. Cover a sheet pan with oiled parchment paper and lay the potato slices out on the paper, making sure that you will have enough for 6 slices per plate (a total of 36 slices for 6 servings). Place a second sheet of oiled parchment paper on top of the potatoes and another sheet pan on top. Bake for 40 minutes.

Take 2 or 3 of the chives and chop them finely. (Keep the rest of the bunch of chives whole to be blanched for the chive oil.) Cut the logs of goat cheese in half lengthwise and roll in the chopped chives to coat. Slice the goat cheese logs into ½-inch-long pieces, giving you a total of 36 cylinders or disks. Set aside.

Preheat the grill. Remove the black gills from the mushrooms. Rub the mushrooms with olive oil, and season with salt and pepper. Grill the mushrooms for 2½ to 3 minutes on each side.

Blanch the bunch of chives in boiled, salted water for 10 seconds. Plunge the chives into ice water to stop cooking. Squeeze the water out of the chives. Place the chives in a blender with the canola oil and salt (to taste). Puree until liquefied. Pour into a squeeze bottle.

Toss the baby greens with a little bit of olive oil and vinegar, and season.

PRESENTATION

Slice the 6 mushrooms into sixths (as you would a pizza), forming a circle of 6 wedges on each plate. Place 6 goat cheese disks around the circle of mushroom wedges on each plate. Then lodge a potato crisp (standing on edge) into each portion of cheese. Place the salad greens in the middle of each circle of wedges. Drizzle the remaining balsamic vinegar and chive oil around the plate, and place 4 of each of the tomato quarters around the plate. Serve.

A Note on the Mandoline Nothing slices perfect vegetable slices for a recipe quite like a mandoline. If you invest in one, buy the best you can afford. (You can also use a meat slicer, but obviously one of those is more expensive.) The slicer disks on food processors do not always cut as thinly as you need, and (depending on the size of the vegetable) may also necessitate cutting the product down to size to fit through the feed tube. For a recipe like Crispy Potato and Goat Cheese, Chive Oil, and 8-Year Balsamic—which is as much about the look of the food as the taste—a piece of specialized equipment such as a mandoline will help you make the impression for which you are hoping.

Black-Peppered Skate with Arugula, Peach, and Wild Rice Pilaf and a Citrus Emulsion

SERVES 6

Skate is a fish that looks fabulous on the plate, like a fan. It also has the distinction of being a rarity in most grocery stores, so if you can get your hands on some, it can be a real eye-opener at an elegant dinner party.

FOR THE RICE PILAF

6 cups chicken stock

Salt and freshly ground black pepper

2 cups wild rice

1 stick (8 tablespoons) unsalted batter

3 ripe peaches, washed, pitted, and diced small

2 shallots, diced small

2 bunches of baby arugula, well washed and stems removed

FOR THE CITRUS EMULSION

2 shallots, diced small

½ stick (4 tablespoons) unsalted butter

1 quart orange juice

¼ cup heavy cream

Salt and freshly ground black pepper

FOR THE FISH

½ to 1 cup Wondra flour, as needed

6 tablespoons freshly ground black pepper

6 skate wings, cleaned

¼ cup canola oil

3 ripe peaches, washed, pitted, and diced small

1 bunch of microcelery

6 lemon wedges

Add the chicken stock to a deep stockpot, season with salt and pepper, and bring to a boil. Add the wild rice, then return to a boil and reduce the heat and simmer. Cook the wild rice for 45 minutes, or until tender, keeping covered at all times. (Whilst the rice is cooking, begin preparing the citrus emulsion as described below. Then complete the rice pilaf.)

To complete the rice pilaf, in a sauté pan, add 4 tablespoons of the butter. Toss in the peaches; slightly caramelize the peaches. Add the shallots and arugula, and toss in the pan. Add the wild rice and the remaining butter. Adjust the seasoning with salt and plenty of ground black pepper, and set aside.

To make the Citrus Emulsion, sauté the shallots in 1 tablespoon of the butter (reserve the other 3 tablespoons). Add the orange juice and reduce by half. Add the heavy cream and reduce again by half, over medium heat, making sure it doesn't burn. Remove from the heat and slowly whisk in the rest of the butter. Season with salt and pepper and set aside. (Complete the rice pilaf as described above.)

To prepare the fish, mix the flour and black pepper together. Dredge the skate wings in the flour mixture. In a sauté pan, heat the canola oil. Cook the fish until it begins to brown on the edges. Be patient for at least 2 minutes before peeking, to allow the flour mixture to adhere to the surface of the fish. When golden brown, flip and brown the other side. Reduce the heat to low and continue to cook until it has cooked through. Depending on the size, this may take 8 to 10 minutes, but . . . it may take a lot less time. Do not overcook the fish or you will lose the delicate flavor. It will continue to cook even after it is removed from the heat, a phenomenon known as carryover cooking. Trust yourself to check the fish for doneness rather than relying on strict times.

PRESENTATION

Place the diced peaches and the rice pilaf in the center of each plate. Top with the skate wings. Drizzle the citrus sauce around the fish. Top with the microcelery and serve with lemon wedges.

A Note on Skate Skate, a fish which looks something like a small ray, may not be available at supermarkets, but you will be able to get it from your fishmonger. This is a good thing because it is challenging to clean, and the fish market will do it for you. It is worth seeking out because it has a very unique taste.

Sautéed Red Snapper and Shrimp with Salad of Fennel, Zucchini, and Roasted Tomatoes

SERVES 6

I used tiny melon ballers of different sizes to cut the zucchini and to create this effect with the grape tomatoes. I think they look like colorful costume pearls surrounding this entrée.

FOR THE SNAPPER MARINADE

4 tablespoons olive oil

2 tablespoons chopped
fresh thyme

4 tablespoons lemon juice
(1 lemon)

Salt and pepper

FOR THE SHRIMP MARINADE

3 tablespoons honey

2 tablespoons lime juice (from
about ½ lime)

2 tablespoons soy sauce

FOR THE SNAPPER AND SHRIMP

Six 6-ounce red snapper fillets

12 extra-large shrimp, peeled
and deveined

FOR THE SALAD DRESSING

8 tablespoons extra virgin
olive oil

4 tablespoons 8-year balsamic
vinegar

Juice of 3 limes

2 tablespoons chopped mint

Salt and pepper

FOR THE ROASTED
VEGETABLE SALAD

1½ pints grape tomatoes
(about 1 pound)

¾ cup fresh corn kernels (from
about 3 ears)

1 large zucchini, balled with a
melon bather

2 fennel bulbs, very thinly sliced
(preferably on a mandoline)

5 tablespoons olive oil

Kosher salt and freshly ground
black pepper

4 tablespoons unsalted butter

PREPARATION AND COOKING TIME (ESTIMATES)

Ingredients prep	*20 to 30 minutes*
Marinade prep	*5 minutes*
Marinating time	*1 hour*
Cooking times:	
Tomato roasting	*5 minutes*
Sauté snapper	*8 minutes*
Sauté shrimp	*4 minutes*
Vegetables	*2 minutes*
Assembly	*10 minutes*
Total time	*about 2 hours*

To make the red snapper marinade, in a bowl, mix the oil, fresh thyme, lemon juice, salt, and pepper. Place the snapper fillets in a suitable container and pour the marinade over.

To make the shrimp marinade, mix the honey, lime juice, and soy sauce. Pour over the shrimp.

Set aside both the snapper and shrimp to marinate for 1 hour.

Preheat the oven to 375 degrees.

Prepare the salad dressing by whisking together the olive oil, balsamic vinegar, lime juice, and mint. Season with salt and pepper to taste.

To roast the vegetables for the salad, toss the tomatoes, corn, zucchini, and fennel with 2 tablespoons of olive oil. Season with salt and pepper to taste. Roast on a baking sheet for 15 to 20 minutes.

To cook the snapper and shrimp, heat 3 tablespoons oil and 4 tablespoons butter in a skillet over medium-high heat. Sauté the snapper 3 to 4 minutes on each side, and remove to a utility platter. Sauté the shrimp 1 to 2 minutes on each side, and transfer to the utility platter. Whilst the pan is still hot add the roasted vegetables and half of the dressing to the pan and combine to make a warm salad.

PRESENTATION

Divide the warm salad among 6 dinner plates. Top with the snapper and shrimp. Drizzle the remaining dressing over the fish and serve.

Mango Barbecued Mahimahi over a Corn-Chipotle Salad

SERVES 6

This dish just seem to knock everybody's socks off whenever I serve it for friends. I know that perfect grill marks have something to do with it.

Peel the mango, cut into slices, and drop into the feed tube of a running blender to puree. Add to a saucepan along with the maple syrup, barbecue sauce, ginger, lime juice, and canola oil. Place on top of the stove over medium-low heat. Cook for 20 minutes without letting the sauce boil, stirring occasionally.

Turn on the grill. Rub the fish fillets with olive oil, salt, and pepper. Place on the hot grill, skin side facing up. Brush on half of the barbecue sauce. Turn the fish over after 3 to 4 minutes. Brush with more barbecue sauce. Cook for another 3 to 4 minutes, or until done. Do not overcook the fish. It is done when the flesh springs back. Remove the fish to a utility platter.

On the same grill, brush the corn with canola oil, salt, and pepper, and grill over moderately high heat until charred in spots, but still slightly crisp, about 7 minutes. Let cool slightly, then cut the kernels from the cobs.

In a medium bowl, mix the sour cream with the lime juice, chopped chipotles, scallions, onions, and chopped cilantro. Season with salt and pepper, and serve immediately.

PRESENTATION

Place the corn-chipotle salad on each plate. Top with the mahimahi. Drizzle some barbecue sauce around the plate and top with chopped scallions.

A Note on Chipotles A chipotle is a jalapeño pepper that has been dried and smoked. Adobo sauce is a dark red sauce consisting of spices and vinegar. Chipotles in adobo sauce can be found in Latino markets if you are unable to locate them in your supermarket.

FOR THE BARBECUE SAUCE

2 or 3 mangoes (enough to make ½ cup when puréed)

¼ cup maple syrup

1 cup bottled barbecue sauce

1 tablespoon ground ginger

Juice of 1 lime

2 tablespoons canola oil

FOR THE FISH

Six 6-ounce mahimahi fillets

¼ cup olive oil

Salt and freshly ground black pepper

FOR THE CORN-CHIPOTLE SALAD

5 ears corn

⅛ cup canola oil

Salt and pepper

4 tablespoons sour cream

Juice of 2 limes

2 chipotle chiles in adobo sauce, seeded and finely chopped

2 scallions, thinly sliced

½ onion, diced small

2 tablespoons finely chopped cilantro

Salt and pepper

Scallions, chopped, for garnish

Mango Barbecued Mahimahi over a Corn-Chipotle Salad

CODA:
IS THIS DINNER . . .
IMPOSSIBLE?

W HEN LAST WE LEFT OUR HERO . . ." (I GUESS THAT'S ME.)

I arose that beautiful morning in May out of a comfortable bed in a hotel room in Princeton. I wish I could tell you that I blinked awake out of a deep, restful slumber, filled with dreams of pretty pictures of food and messages of peace from the universe, but in point of fact I didn't get a blasted wink of sleep. If there is ever any kind of stressful event in my life waiting for me on the other side of a night's sleep, especially if it involves cooking and planning, I inevitably, without fail, do not get any.

This night was worse than most. If I have a big banquet or a high-profile event on for the next day, as I lie awake counting the cracks in the ceiling and listening to my own breathing, I can usually at least comfort myself with an obsessive review of the plans I have laid in advance, the menu, the ingredients, the timetable, the assignments for my kitchen staff, the layout of the room, the deployment of servers, the audience for whom I will be cooking, their likes and dislikes; I can use that time in the dark waiting for and seizing upon sudden inspiration for the courses I am about to create, and I have risen out of this nervous but trancelike state reasonably refreshed and armed quite often with good, new, and unexpected ideas.

Not tonight. Tonight was as pure a state of simple, blank, tortuous worrying as I have ever achieved. There was no menu to chew over, no dishes to prepare again and again in my imagination until they had penetrated into my central nervous system, no scheme for delegating tasks to my staff to review, no nothing. Tomorrow crept over the horizon and into the room through the parted curtains to reveal itself as the day we were about to shoot the pilot for my new Food Network show, now called *Dinner: Impossible!* To reiterate, the "hook" in this show, the cute little twist, is that the chef (me again) must have no advance warning whatsoever as to the circumstances in which he will be asked to cook. All I get to know is that I will be cooking and that said circumstances will be as close to . . . wait for it . . . *impossible* as the producers can make it.

One of the core values in my life is to be prepared. I will cook for you anytime, anywhere, and you can bring as many people as you like. I'll whip up a party for eight hundred without batting an eye. I was making lunches for two thousand people at a go when I was fifteen. I've cooked at military installations for six thousand at a sitting. But, for pity's sake, I always knew who was coming and when, had a sense of what they liked to eat, and always had the opportunity to inventory, lay in ingredients, and put together a plan to make sure that they got to enjoy the very best food I could deliver. As the pressure built behind my eyeballs and sinister rays of daylight insinuated themselves into my room, I could only think what a terrible, foolish trap I had blundered into: I had handed the reins of my culinary fate over to television producers.

To their credit, the producers, whom I count as good friends when I'm not lying awake in the middle of the night cursing and fearing them, had done an admirable job of keeping the secret of my ultimate destination from me. I hadn't a clue. Whenever I hinted around, they either clammed up or evilly misdirected me: "Maybe you'll be at the circus . . . Have you ever cooked giraffe? . . . How do you look in a clown suit? . . . Heh, heh, heh . . ."

Ah, to hell with it. I climbed out of bed, tired already, shaved, showered, dressed in the cool black T-shirt they designed for me (which I really like, by the way), checked out, grabbed a very large, very hot coffee, climbed into the car, and opened the envelope. Inside was a piece of paper, an address at which I was to arrive to receive my assignment for the day. I programmed it into my onboard GPS navigator and drove away.

I shortly found myself in an attractive suburban neighborhood and pulled up behind a van that held some of the production team for the day's shooting. Greetings all around, a bit of running about, lots of walkie-talkie cross chatter, then there they were in front of me, reading. "Good morning, Robert. Today, Fred and Paula are getting married . . ."

A wedding. At last I was on solid ground. I knew how to cook for a wedding. Maybe I could nip back to the hotel for a quick nap. I started to relax, just before the cold, cruel reality starting to creep up, first at the knees, then as a cold shiver up the old spine. I said a bad word in my head. The wedding's *today*.

I have cooked at a lot of weddings. As you know, I even did my bit for the wedding of Charles and Diana. Their *cake* alone took what felt like half of my teenage years to complete. Weddings are not only logistically difficult to accomplish, from the standpoints of quality, quantity and, most critically, timing, but you are simultaneously taking responsibility for one of the most emotionally charged events in the life of the marrying couple, especially in the life of the bride. My initial involvement in the planning for the food for a wedding can start a year ahead of time; the active prep time for a wedding is typically three to five days out, longer for the cake. Usually the bride has been seriously planning for well over a year. She has also typically been imagining this day since the first time she was read *Cinderella* at the age of three.

I heard the rest of the details. This was to be a wedding reception for more than two hundred people. I was also to be responsible for creating more than one thousand hors d'oeuvres, both hot and cold. I was not in charge of the cake, thank you, God, but I needed to make dessert as well as an original signature cocktail for the groomsman's toast. The bridal party would arrive at the venue at six; dinner would be served at eight. The bride and groom were awaiting me at the bride's parents' house down the block. The countdown clock started ticking right then.

They rushed me back to my car for the 200-yard trip, so that I could dramatically pull into the drive and stride purposefully into the house. Time was wasting. It was nearing eight-thirty already, and I still didn't know how far away my kitchen for the day was, or if I even *had* a kitchen. I did know at this point that George and George would be waiting for me. The number of things I didn't know so far outweighed the pittance I did, it was more than a bit overwhelming. I made the drive in one take and even managed the walk up to the house without falling on my face. Paula and Fred, the bride and groom, greeted me at the door and we went inside and sat at the kitchen table.

I got a read on them both pretty quickly. Fred was a genial guy who loved food and had probably begged his fiancée, Paula, to let me come in and do this on their wedding day. Paula was being as game as she could possibly be, appearing on camera for national broadcast in curlers early in the morning on the most important day of her life. He was giddy with excitement; she was potentially a nervous wreck.

We reviewed the menu items they had indeed planned well over a year ago. I could see immediately where I could add some style and flair to a good menu that looked like it would offer me lots of material to work with. I would stick with the mahimahi because Paula loved fish. Fred asked if I could possibly come up with a beef dish. I got the sense that this was the one item he had lost out on in the negotiations. Chicken was on the menu and I proposed a roulade, a rolled and deep-fried preparation that I would stuff with spinach, sundried tomatoes, and prosciutto, if I could get my hands on them. I promised them a vegetarian option as well, and swore a blood oath that this would be the best food they could possibly imagine for their reception. I shook hands, left, and hoped that my confidence was warranted.

On my way to the car, I was handed the location for the reception, a place called Knowlton Mansion on the northeastern outskirts of Philadelphia. This put me nearly another hour's travel time away. I sped off with a cameraman in tow and a knotted stomach.

En route, I phoned Little George and told him what I had learned so far. I shaved many more minutes than I legally should have off of my travel time. I arrived at a beautiful, picturesque historic stone mansion, the cameras took their positions, and I grabbed my knives kit and went inside.

In a line at one end of a spacious, majestic, wood-carved party room stood my guys, George, George, and Ruben; a lineup of skinny, gray-T-shirted kids I called "the Knowlton Boys," and in front, a rather stern-looking young Scotswoman who introduced herself as Christina. She was the events manager for the mansion and made it clear that it was her job to keep me on point and to make sure that I didn't louse up dinner for her precious clients that evening.

I shook her hand, greeted my men, and assessed the lads who would comprise my cooking crew for the day. They were five in number and looked as if they'd been pulled out of their bunks and ordered to assemble for firing squad duty, and were wondering which end of the rifles they'd be on. They reminded me of myself when I first started cooking in the Navy. I took a moment to reassure them as best I could and hurried everyone into the kitchen.

Christina gave me the nickel tour. It was a good-sized kitchen with space for prep, cooking, and staging. It looked as if they had enough ovens and burners—I would have to find out how well they worked as I went. I gathered my team around me and went through a quick checklist of what was on hand and what we needed to buy. I had a few thousand dollars to spend, given me by the show, and was determined to maximize the value of every penny. I picked out one of the Knowlton Boys and grilled him for ingredients: "Have you got English cucumber? Thyme? Duck? Parmesan cheese, risotto, onions, skewers, stone-ground mustard? . . ." —in all a list of about twenty items. He did well under fire and gave me the answers I desperately needed.

Ruben, one of my personally trained chefs, had been given me as a runner for shopping. I barked out a list for him that included sun-dried tomatoes, cannellini beans, strawberries, potatoes, and sweet corn, among many items, and kicked him out the door. I started on a menu with George and George.

These guys have been with me for a long time; they know what I need, and I think I know their strengths and weaknesses even better than they do themselves. This challenge was tailor-made for them. I assigned them to start work immediately on a killer selection of hot and cold appetizers. Little George would do a Sesame Chicken Saté with Peanut Sauce, Goat Cheese Tartlets, Shrimp and Crab Cakes, and a Beef Tenderloin with Red Onion Marmalade; Big George would put together Brie with Strawberries, Roasted Duck with White Bean Ragout, Sea Scallops with Guacamole, and Tuna Tartare in a Cucumber Boat Topped with Black Caviar.

I pounded out the entrées: Seared Mahimahi would be paired with Saffron Risotto and Mango Sauce; I would do the chicken roulade; the vegetarian dish would be Roasted Vegetable Crepes with Roasted Red Pepper Sauce; for dessert, we'd serve Tahitian Vanilla Crème Brûlée; and for the toast I would do a variation on a Kir Royale, a champagne, orange juice, and cassis cocktail layered to look like a sunset in champagne flutes.

I figured I would just lay Fred and forty-nine of his closest friends flat out with Center-Cut Dry Aged Prime Filets with a Blue Cheese Crust, served with a Sweet Corn and Potato Hash and a Merlot Reduction. I got on my cell phone to Esposito's in the Italian Market in Philly and ordered fifty of the best (and most expensive) steaks they had, to be delivered asap.

Then we went to it. When I'm working, I take very little direction from the TV people. Our camera and sound guys are brilliant, and they somehow manage to stay out of the way without missing a single moment. Wrapped in a cocoon of concentrated effort, I started to feel for the first time that we were going to be able to get this done.

The first real curveball I had to manage was having a cadre of basically untrained kids trying to follow my directions. I had all of about fifteen minutes to figure out how to deploy them, what their relative skill levels were, and how to whip them into a team. Their first assignment was to peel six hundred pieces of asparagus. I have a very specific way I like to do that. I showed them that I wanted them to peel until the "white" showed on the stalk, and to take that up to the tip. That leaves a beautiful white spear with a bright green tip after cooking and makes a very nice presentation on the plate. They had done nearly the whole six hundred when I checked in on them . . . and they had only taken the peel halfway up the stalk. I took a couple and cut off the bottom halves, which had the effect of completely eliminating the peeling they had accomplished thus far. Their faces fell as they realized I was making them start from scratch. When I saw the wind come out of their sails, I yelled: "Do it right or go and be a cabdriver . . . don't give me *garbage* or you're gonna get it back!" I didn't talk to them that way because I'm a mean guy or because I was upset—I said it to give them a shot of adrenaline, to challenge them, to make them mad enough at me for the moment to take it out on the asparagus and get the job done even faster this time around.

More minor catastrophes occurred: the ovens never quite worked properly, the exhaust fans only worked intermittently, so it got hotter and hotter; we triggered what we thought was a fire alarm and nearly abandoned the kitchen—turned out that the timer on the braiser had been turned on accidentally and no on knew how to turn it off. When she wasn't breathing down my neck at every turn, Christina had to burn the phone lines all over town to find someone who would deliver black caviar. Ruben came back from the shopping without any fresh corn for the potato hash, which really burned me. We scrounged up some canned corn, which I perked up by dicing in some sweet, fresh rhubarb and caramelized onion. My beautiful steaks got delivered only in the nick of time and nearly got overcooked whilst finishing in the unruly ovens. And somebody burnt the beef stock.

If you really want to get me wound up, try seeing if you can slip a burnt stock past me before service. Stocks are foundational. Start with a bad stock and you can have the best piece of meat in the world and the meal is ruined. I popped my cork for a couple of minutes, but never really found out what had happened to it. With the invectives of Taffy Jones and Michel Roux ringing in my head, I shouted for new ingredients and had Little George reassemble the stock I was going to use for my reduction sauce. Happily, everything got done and everyone pulled together as a team, and we made it through to the cocktail hour.

The guests began to arrive. Platter after platter, dish after dish of hors d'oeuvres took off from the stainless-steel front prep tables, like F-18s off an aircraft carrier. In the meantime, I had to design separate platings of every dish we were making for the cameras to photograph for beauty shots in the back of the kitchen. The bridal party arrived and seemed to really enjoy our opening salvo. Paula looked radiant. Her parents were beaming. Fred even managed a few minutes to see us in the kitchens and reveled in the proceedings. He left to rejoin his bride, and we returned to incinerating the sugary tops of the crème brûlées with our blowtorches.

Then the real dance began. Though Knowlton Mansion is a very successful catering venue, they have no hot boxes on the premises. In a hotel, all of the dishes could have been plated and stored at the perfect temperature well before being required at the tables. This allows me to plate the dinners when *I* am ready. Here, every plate needed to built individually at the moment it was called for, when the *servers* were ready. So, if a table of eight calls for three chickens, two fish, two steaks, and a veggie, then and only then could you plate them and send them out the door.

I assembled every Knowlton Boy, the dishwasher, George, and Ruben and formed an assembly line, with me at the front barking orders. Christina expedited, calling out dishes as they came up. George would pipe hot potatoes out of a pastry bag, the other George would give it a drizzle of white truffle oil, I would lay on a fan of sliced chicken roulade, then it would move down the table, get a sauce, get a garnish, and fly out the door. The beef would start on a ring of potato hash, I'd top it with the crusted fillet, slide down the line, sauce, garnish, on to the next, over two hundred times in a little over twenty minutes.

Then the moment of truth arrived. It was time to serve the bride and groom. Just earlier I had donned my chef's whites, the jacket I wear when I serve the president. I built their dishes, fish and beef, both high, tight, clean, and centered, and carried them out into the ballroom. To a thunderous ovation, I laid down the plates before them, wished them well, and strode away. I have seen their reactions since when I watched a rough cut of the show. I hope that Fred always gazes at Paula with the look of pure love that lit up his face when he bit into that steak.

Back in the kitchen, as cleanup began, I assembled the Boys. I was truly moved by how well they had performed that day. Here I had come thundering into their kitchen with a full production crew, my men and my demands, and they took everything I had to dish out and triumphed. I gave a little speech of thanks and it was from the heart. To my surprise, I turned around and saw that the unyielding Christina had burst into tears. She had not only personally done a terrific job that day, but had seen "her boys" grow through the experience right before her eyes. I went over and gave her a hug and we all broke into a round of spontaneous applause. Dinner: *Accomplished*.

And that's our show for now. Variations on some of the recipes for the entrées prepared for the pilot appear elsewhere in this book. Here are recipes for four of the hors d'oeuvres for *your* next party (or wedding!).

Brie with Strawberries on Brioche Crostini

SERVES 6

6 slices brioche bread, sliced 1/4 inch thick

3 ounces whipped cream cheese, at room temperature

½ teaspoon chopped chives

1 large strawberry

½ small (about 2-inch diameter) Brie wheel

6 sprigs of parsley

EQUIPMENT

A 1½-inch-diameter circle cutter/biscuit cutter

A pastry bag with star tip

Preheat the oven to 325 degrees. Using your 1½-inch-diameter cutter, cut the sliced bread into 6 circles and put on a baking sheet. Toast the brioche circles in the oven for 3 to 5 minutes until golden brown.

With a rubber spatula, fold together the cream cheese and chopped chives, and place in a small pastry bag with a star tip.

Pipe out about ½ ounce cream cheese and chive mixture onto each toasted brioche circle. Cut off the top of the strawberry, slice in half lengthwise, then cut each half into 3 wedges. Cut the ½ wheel of Brie into 6 triangle wedges. Place 1 wedge of strawberry and 1 wedge of Brie standing up on the cream cheese. Place 1 parsley sprig on top of each.

Sea Scallops with Guacamole

SERVES 6

FOR THE SCALLOPS

1 tablespoon olive oil

Six diver or jumbo sea scallops (10 to 20 count per pound), muscle pulled off

Salt and freshly ground black pepper

2 pieces white toast

FOR THE GUACAMOLE

1 California avocado, seeded and peeled

½ tablespoons lime juice

¼ teaspoon crushed garlic

1 tablespoon finely chopped onion

1 teaspoon chopped cilantro

Splash of Tabasco

Salt

Heat the olive oil in a nonstick pan over moderately high heat. Season the scallops with salt and pepper, and cook for 1½ minutes on each side, or until golden brown.

Using a fork, coarsely mash the avocado with the lime juice and garlic. Stir in the onion, cilantro, and Tabasco to blend. Season with salt to taste.

Trim the crusts off the toasted bread and cut the bread into 4 triangles. Spoon 1 tablespoon of guacamole on top of each toast triangle. Place a scallop on top of the guacamole.

Tuna Tartare in a Cucumber Boat Topped with Caviar

SERVES 6

With a heavy, sharp knife, chop the tuna into very small pieces. In a mixing bowl, combine the tuna, chives, capers, shallots, lemon juice, oil, salt and pepper, and chill for 1 hour.

Whilst the tuna is chilling, prepare the cucumber boats. Peel the cucumber and cut into 2-inch-long disks. With a teaspoon, scoop out the seeds from inside the cucumber without touching the very bottom of the cucumber. (In other words, leave a "bottom" in the hollowed-out center of the cucumber.)

PRESENTATION

Season the cucumber with salt and pepper. Fill with 1 teaspoon of tuna tartare. Top with ⅛ teaspoon of caviar. Garnish with a sprig of parsley.

6 ounces sushi tuna

1 tablespoon chopped chives

½ tablespoon chopped capers

1 tablespoon chopped shallots

Juice of 1 lemon

1 tablespoon extra virgin olive oil

Salt and freshly ground black pepper

3 to 6 cucumbers (to make 6 cucumber boats)

1 ounce black caviar

6 sprigs of parsley

Sesame Chicken Saté with Peanut Sauce

SERVES 6

FOR THE CHICKEN

6 pieces boneless chicken breast, cut into strips

¼ cup white sesame seeds

¼ cup black sesame seeds

2 tablespoons chili powder

2 tablespoons salt

1 tablespoon garlic powder

FOR THE PEANUT DIPPING SAUCE

½ cup peanut butter

½ cup Coco Lopez coconut cream

⅛ cup soy sauce (low salt)

4 tablespoons honey

¼ cup chicken broth

EQUIPMENT

Bamboo skewers, 6 or 8 inches long

Preheat the oven to 325 degrees.

"Weave" a bamboo skewer through the length of each chicken strip (as you would run a straight pin through fabric). Mix the sesame seeds, chili powder, salt, and garlic powder in a shallow bowl. Dip the chicken into warm water and roll in the seed mixture. Bake on a lightly greased sheet pan until done, about 20 minutes.

To make the dipping sauce, in a mixing bowl, combine the peanut butter, Coco Lopez, soy sauce, and honey, and mix well. It will be thick. Slowly mix the chicken broth into the peanut butter mixture. It should be of medium consistency for dipping. Serve with the sesame chicken.

AFTERWORD

BY NOW, WE ARE WELL INTO PRODUCTION ON OUR NEW SERIES FOR FOOD Network, starring your humble correspondent. It's all very hush-hush at this moment, but if and when everything goes to plan, it should be coming to a television screen near you, and then we will all hope for the best.

This is a goal I have had for a long time, and I have pushed for it in a number of different ways over the past eleven years or so. There have been many twists, turns, and stumbles and, I have to admit, I despaired of the idea more than once.

I'm your chef . . .

Then I decided simply to focus on the food. Come what may, I went about my business, leaving myself open to fate and opportunity, and I tried to make every menu, every dish, every plate, and every bite just the tiniest, most incrementally smallest bit better than the one before.

So far, so good.

You have and will have big challenges in your life, so here's a last bit of culinary advice. It has to do with a classical recipe for serving a whole elephant. The recipe is simple. First, you catch the elephant, then you cook it.

But if you ever want to finish it, you have to eat it one bite at a time.

Bon appétit!

ACKNOWLEDGMENTS

THE AUTHORS WISH TO THANK EVERYONE WHO HELPED TO MAKE THIS volume possible. Brian Murray is at the top of the heap, as Admiral of the Fleet. Virginia O'Reilly headed up the home test cooking, edited the recipes to help make them accessible to the home cook, did research, reviewed the manuscript, performed art direction, and pulled every loose oar without hesitation. Without her hard work and focus, we might still be working on it to this day. Gavin provided invaluable help with home recipe testing, sorting photographs, organizing recipes, and wrangling props. George Galati, George Kralle, and Ruben Espinal—the three men of steel—are worth their collective weight in gold (which, as you will realize when you see photos of their muscular physiques, is about the sum total of the stores at Fort Knox, with a little loose change left over). Tom Briglia (*PhotoGRAPHICS*, Linwood, New Jersey) did a magnificent job on the photographs, which have drawn oohs and aahs from everyone who has seen them. Matt Rodin and David Brandt more than pulled their weight in the kitchens of the Atlantic County Vocational and Technical Institute, the institution that donated its facilities for three intense days of cooking and shooting pictures. Guy Dunagan, the gifted pastry instructor at the school, unflinchingly met all of our crazed demands over the days of that shoot. Elise Dunn handcrafted many of the ceramics as well as the handmade paper used as props in the photographs accompanying the recipes. Frank May provided a record for posterity of candid photos documenting the home test cooking process. Gerry Agnew, Maryfrances Strey, and Chris Gordon braved some pretty cryptic handwriting to do the typing of the recipes. Joe Anderson, of Fortessa, Inc., loaned us his beautiful plates and silverware. Thanks to Randy and Kathy Bobe and Randy, Jr., who have not only lent their unwavering support in every endeavor but also donated the proteins for the pictures in this book. Thanks to good friends Bill and Wendy LaTorre, Kevin and Crystal Harrington, Laura Olsen, and to Randall Williams, for his stalwart belief and his guidance. And thanks to the guy we affectionately refer to as "Television's" Marc Summers, our associate and friend.

Robert would especially like to express his love and appreciation to his wonderful family, whose undying support has allowed him to excel in the pursuit of culinary happiness.

INDEX

Note: *Italicized* page references indicate recipe photographs.

Zucchini, and Roasted Tomatoes, Salad
of, Sautéed Red Snapper and Shrimp
with, *273,* 273–74
Fertoukh, Marc, 13
Field Gun competition, 162–65
Fish
Black-Peppered Skate with Arugula,
Peach, and Wild Rice Pilaf and a
Citrus Emulsion, *271,* 271–72
Creole-Style Red Snapper with
Farmhouse Grits and Red Pepper
Coulis, *26,* 26–27
Crisp Sea Bass with Stuffed Leeks, *41,*
41–43
Horseradish-Crusted Salmon with
Braised Endive and a Beet Reduction,
46, 46–47
Mango Barbecued Mahimahi over a
Corn-Chipotle Salad, 275, *276*
Marinated Black Cod with Acacia
Honey, 137
Pan-Roasted Black Bass with Prawns
over Cauliflower Risotto, 243–44
Pan-Roasted Wild Striped Bass with
Roasted Tomato and Broccoli Rabe
Medley, 125
Pan-Seared Salmon, Haricot Vert Salad,
and Herbed Mustard Dressing, 169–70
Pan-Seared Salmon with Bok Choy
Cashew Salad and Orange Soy Glaze,
151, *151*
salmon, raw, note about, 287
Sautéed Red Snapper and Shrimp with
Salad of Fennel, Zucchini, and
Roasted Tomatoes, *273,* 273–74
Sautéed Sea Bass with Crisp Potato
Crust, *134,* 134–35
Sesame-Crusted Tuna with Asian
Mushroom Salad and Ponzu Sauce, 131
skate, note about, 272

stock (fumet), note about, 244
tuna, raw, notes about, 131, 287
Tuna Poached in Olive Oil over Shrimp
and Yukon Gold Mashed Potatoes,
158
Tuna Tartare in a Cucumber Boat
Topped with Caviar, *286,* 286–87
Fisherton Arms, 96–97
Flan, Warm Rock Shrimp and Lobster,
Baby Arugula Salad, and Champagne
Sabayon, 21–25, *23*
Flan pans, note about, 213
Fleur de sel, note about, 158
Flour, cake, note about, 39
Food
aromatic impact of, 142
bitter flavors, 124
dietary fats, 140
flavors and taste, 44–45, 120–21, 124,
130, 132, 136, 149–50
for healthy diet, 162–68, 185
high-quality ingredients, 48, 113–15
leftovers, 62–63
marinades for, 136
passion for, 37
philosophy about, 33–34
physiological impact, 44
pleasure gained from, 106–7
portion sizes, 166
presenting, 254–55
salty flavors, 124
sour flavors, 124
spices, 126–27
sweet flavors, 124
temperatures, mixing, 132
textures, 132–33
umami flavors, 130
Food Network, 258, 278–83, 289–90
Foxx, Jamie, 18
Frittata, Asparagus Parmesan, 206